reminder of your visit to this valley.

Fondest Best Wishes

Adrian & Jane.

REFLECTIONS
THE BREAMISH VALLEY AND INGRAM

Sarah Wilson

Photographic Acknowledgements:
Front Cover: Joyce Tully
Design: Ian Scott Design.
Text and photographs © Northern Heritage 2005

ISBN No.0-9544777-6-6

Printed and bound by Compass Press Limited.

British Library Cataloguing in Publishing Data
A catalogue record for this book is available from the British Library.

Northern Heritage, Units 7&8 New Kennels, Blagdon Estate, Seaton Burn,
Newcastle upon Tyne NE13 6DB
Telephone: 01670 789 940
www.northern-heritage.co.uk

Grant aided by the
Northumberland National Park Authority

Introduction and Acknowledgements

I came to live in the Breamish Valley in 1977 when I married Johnny Wilson of Ingram. Although a city girl from Newcastle-upon-Tyne, I spent much of my childhood at Ilderton Moor, a farm not far from Ingram. Mum and Dad rented a cottage there from 1964 until 1976.

Walter Brown, the farmer, had worked in the valley as a young man. It was he who first kindled my interest in days past, with stories of shepherds, snowstorms and wartime plane crashes. Fascinated by his memories, it became apparent that a way of life that had sustained countless generations was ebbing away as the advancing 20th century brought irrevocable change. Unless someone recorded these memories and recollections they would be lost forever with the passing of a generation.

Whilst the valley has featured in many guidebooks over the years as a place to walk and explore, several merely re-phrasing what W.W. Tomlinson wrote in 1889 in his fascinating and well-researched "Guide to Northumberland", few have touched upon the everyday lives of its people.

Samuel Donkin is one exception. Born and bred at Ingram, where his father farmed for 65 years, his book "Reminiscences" published in 1886, gives us a brief glimpse of life in the valley in the early 19th century. However, most of its pages are filled with dull treatises on agriculture and politics of the day.

My research began in 1984 with a working brief entitled 'in living memory', the past 100 years as recalled by men and women who had lived and worked in the valley. As I discovered, several contributors had family associations with the valley going back three or more generations. Many were getting on in years then but their memories of childhood, day-to-day life, people and places were quite clear. What was especially rewarding was to see the obvious pleasure it gave them to talk about the 'old days' even though not all memories were happy ones. One contributor would put me in touch with another and, from the 30 or so lengthy interviews I did, I always learnt something new.

Whilst recording oral history was my main priority I was keen to set it against a factual background of contemporary events and happenings over the century. As a reporter with the Northumberland Gazette in the 1980s I spent considerable time scanning the pages of the bound file copies in the archives. I always remember the Alnwick Mercury of 1877 - and my delight at finding an advert for the Donkin farm sale at Ingram! The old papers yielded a wealth of information, from court stories and inquests to the social scene in the district, all invaluable reference material.

The archives - and the staff - at the Northumberland County Record Office have been most helpful, enabling me to verify and compliment personal recollections of events and occasions where, by admission, the contributors were too young at the time to remember much detail.

Over the lifetime of "Reflections" I have amassed a treasured collection of photographs and postcards. I would like to say a big thank you to Richard Westmacott for sourcing cards from fairs all over the country, to Peter Carne for providing me with copies of old maps and to Ian Davison for his delightful pen and ink sketch map of the valley. Sincere thanks to Joyce Tully, of Wooler, for her lovely watercolour painting of Peggy Bell's Bridge which features on the cover, to Tony Hopkins for his photograph of the Breamish and to Mandy Brown for her assistance with illustrations.

Without the encouragement, help and enthusiasm of many people this book would never have been written. After the death of my parents in the early 1990s it was put on the 'back burner' for several years. My horse riding companion Clare Scott gave me the push I needed to get going again.

In 2001, Foot and Mouth year, Lord James Percy kindly let me stay in his cottage at High Linhope. Not far to go for a holiday! It was there that the framework of "Reflections" first came together. I was most pleased therefore when he kindly agreed to write the Foreword, for which I thank him, and also for his contribution to the Linhope chapter.

A special thanks are due to my family, Johnny, Ross and Emma, for their enduring support and incredible patience. I know they often wondered whether "the book" would ever be finished. Behind the scenes I am indebted to Paul Frodsham, Anne Hunter and Adrian Levien for chivvying me on and for their help with the text. Their advice and constructive criticism was much appreciated. Thank you all.

I have been particularly taken by the willingness of everyone I have spoken to, to help in whatever way they could. Through "Reflections" I met strangers who became friends. All were either pleased to share their memories, answer questions or lend precious photographs. Often it was a combination of all three. My great regret is that since I first started research, twenty one years ago, many contributors have died. This book is in their memory.

Compiling a list of people who I would like to thank is somewhat risky for fear of missing someone out. Fingers crossed I have not, but if so, my apologies. Similarly I know there will be mistakes, but hopefully not many.

Alec Adams, George Anderson, Betty Anderson, Ambrose and Joan Anderson, Belle Armstrong, Sylvia Armstrong, Ken Armstrong, Betty Ashworth, Florence Baker, George and Mame Bell, Colin Beveridge, Bobbie Blain, Lillie Brown, Margaret Brown, Walter Brown (Ilderton Moor), Walter Brown (Langleeford), Valerie Burrell, Canon Bob Burston, Susan Cable, Robbie and Peggy Chisholm, Mrs Naomi Church, Johnny Clark, Dr. Colin Clark, Bill and Ethel Cook, Valerie and Gio Corno, Robbie and June Cowens, Auntie Nellie Crerar, Ian and Keith Davison, George Dodds, Malcolm Elliott, Anne Ferguson, Rupert Gibson, Jimmy and Jean Givens, Rosemary Glen-Davison, Canon Charles Hay, Jack Hope, Sandy and Wilma Hunter, Hannah Hutton, Bob Jackson, Ina Keen, Peter Kellett, Rev. Rob Kelsey, John McCann, Paul Lemeunier, George Lillie, Ramon and Winnie Little, Mary Macklon, Jo Mills, Tibbie Murray, Edwin and Mary Nelson, Stuart and Sarah Nelson, Basil Oliver, Rev. Hugh Priestner, Margaret Purvis, Mark and Janet Purvis, Sue Ruskin, Andrew and Jessie Scott, Stephen and Dorothy Shell, Stephen Shell, junior, James Shell, Jackson Shell, Adam Sisterson, Ken Smart, John and Robert Smith, Graham Stephenson, Gordon Storey (15th Whitley Bay Scout Troop), Ian and Dorothy Swanston, Nancy Taylor, David Taylor, Opie Telford, Anne Timlin, Ralph Thompson (Museum Assistant (Regiment), Discovery Museum, Newcastle-upon-Tyne), Stephen Tully, Winnie and Sarah Thompson, David Whitehead, Frank Wilson, Jim and Pat Wilson, Judith Wilson, Jake Wright.

FOREWORD

The Breamish Valley holds a fascination for those that know and love it that is like no other that I have experienced. Perhaps it is the very nature of the Cheviot Hills that inspires such emotion. Soft foothills rising up through grass and glitters, cleughs and pastures to black, mist covered moors and hidden valleys. Then again perhaps it is the romance of history, of border strife, smugglers and the grisly end on the Hanging Stone of some murderous vagabond, bloodied and swinging in the wind at the head of the River Breamish. It was no accident that in the ghost story, The Shadow on the Moor, written by my grandfather, Black Tom met his fate in the River Breamish at the foot of the Ingram Glitters. What ever it is that triggers the mood, no one can fail to be touched in some way by the Breamish Valley.

This book by Sarah Wilson explores the last 100 years of the lives and times of the people and places that make up this remote corner of England. Her research has revealed the colourful characters that have and still make up the human element of the valley - shepherds, gamekeepers, farmers, fencers, mothers, daughters, lairds and all. Each have played their part in valley life and shaped its fortunes over the years. It shows how the chill wind of major events such as war, epidemic and extreme weather touches the lives of people in far places as well as towns and cities. The book, at face value a wonderful narrative of a magical place, is also a fascinating insight into how rural life over the whole country has changed.

My family has owned land up the Breamish Valley for hundreds of years and when I came to live at Linhope I was and am proud to be part of such a magnificent place. Of course valley life is not Utopia, it would be naïve to expect as much - the tragedies and set backs of farming life, of family life, the harsh economics of upland agriculture, making ends meet and investing in the future. How to secure long term jobs and create a viable economy that everyone can benefit from? How to stop the school closing or the local shop? But on the good days, and there are plenty - the sights, sounds, resplendent nature, the awe-inspiring views, and the smiling faces. A walk to the Big Cheviot, the meet of the hounds, the shoot days on the grouse moor, a fat brown trout from the River Breamish for breakfast. Warm April sun on the backs of newborn lambs, sweet grass after summer rain, young trees stretching towards the light, old trees fighting the wind, the smell of heather burning on your clothes. These are the essences of valley life today, as they were a century ago.

Enjoy this book as I have - written by a lady who, by confession, came from the "Town", but who quite evidently has a fierce love for life in Ingram and the whole Breamish Valley and who has taken the time and trouble to listen and remember, and to put in writing a fascinating and colourful piece of history from the quiet but proud valley of the River Breamish.

Lord James Percy

CONTENTS

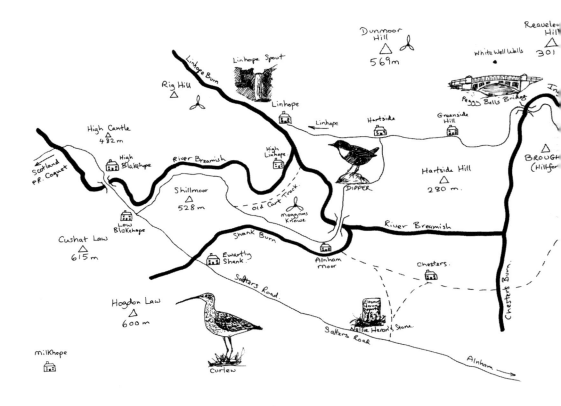

1
The Breamish

"There foaming white o' rock and linn,
Loud, loud let thy waters roar,
While echoes wild in yonder glen
And distant hills rehearse the din,
Along thy rugged shore."

On a November night in 1890 Annie Grey, a domestic servant, was swept to her death when a wooden footbridge near Brandon collapsed into the rolling floodwaters of the Breamish.

No one missed her for several days. Her parents had not expected her home. When she failed to return to work at Great Ryle farm, a groom was sent to her parents' cottage at Brandon "to ascertain the cause". A hat belonging to her was found close to where the bridge had stood but Annie's body was not found until four months later, in March 1891, entwined in the branches of a willow tree, several miles downstream in the River Till.

On its journey to join the River Tweed, the Breamish changes its name to the Till.

"The foot of Breamish and the head of Till
Meet together at Bewick Mill."

The name Breamish is derived from ancient Celtic, "breme" meaning furious, swelling or raging

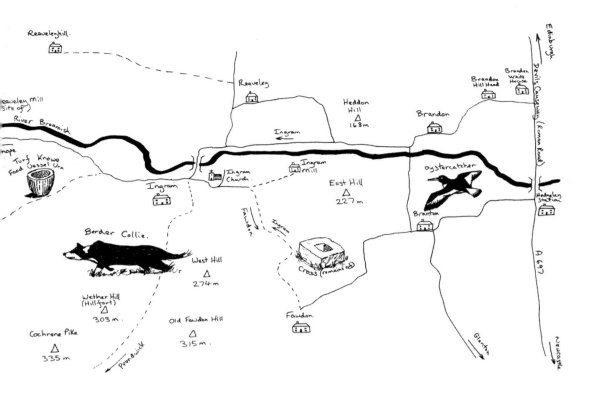

and "uishg" or "uisge" meaning water. Over the past half century an irritating misnomer 'the Ingram Valley' has crept into everyday use. Hopefully this book will make some amends, for a valley is **always** named after its river.

The river has inspired poets, musicians and landscape painters. The opening verse, above, is from a poem dedicated to the Breamish. It is to be found in a little book, published in 1908, entitled "Breamish and other Poems" by P. Hall. His father was a gamekeeper on the Beanley Estate [now part of the Hedgeley Estates]. The poem is couched in romantic, flowery prose. What is of more interest, I think, is the prelude. It captures the spirit of the valley.

"It is hardly possible for imagination to conceive a picture nearly so grand as that which the Vale of the Breamish displays. More especially in early summer morning; far away westward, rising through the grey mist, we have Reaveley Hill, Ingram Glitters, Greenside, Hedgehope, Cheviot and others; wild, historic and grand; abounding with the remains of the camps of the ancient Romans, and relics of by-gone ages; rugged, rocky glens where the tumbling waters, roaring, dash down the linn, then glide away like a silver streak by Ingram, Brandon and Hedgeley."

A tune entitled "The Breamish" is played today by fiddlers, Northumbrian pipers and accordionists. It is styled 'traditional' because no one is exactly sure who wrote it.

From humble beginnings as a spring on Scotsman's Knowe, a shoulder of Cheviot, the river increases in strength, fed by sikes and small streams that tumble over waterfalls and gush down steep-sided cleughs.

It is from these small burns that 'walls of water' are born. They come with ferocity and suddenness after heavy rains, thunderstorms or melting snow. In such conditions the Breamish is no respecter of roads or bridges, land or trees. It shifts its course as it pleases, rolling giant boulders and stones along its bed with an accompanying roar. During a dry summer the opposite is true. The river becomes little more than a trickle, its flow benign.

A newspaper report of 1888 paints a picture of the river below Ingram: **"Through this long tract of land, which is composed of gravel banks, coarse vegetation, and which seems to have been the bed of a vast mountain stream of bygone ages, the Breamish water runs along in many channels, which it appears to cut afresh for itself whenever floods quicken its life and strengthen its powers.**

"For about two miles the roadway, such as it is, intersects these streams, there being at these points the rudest of footway bridges for man, whilst vehicles and horses must wade when the state of the waters from off the hills permits of a passage, or otherwise go miles round."

In the new millenium the Breamish is little changed. On a dark November morning in 2000, in heavy spate, it washed out the road below Ingram Bridge and carried away an electricity pole.

Farmer Edwin Nelson was commuting to Low Blakehope, as he did early every morning, thinking about the day ahead. The Land Rover headlights did not pick up the hanging electricity wires until they hit the cab, nor the gaping drop into the river where the road should have been. In a sixth sense reaction Edwin spun the steering wheel sending the Land Rover onto the grass. The loss of the electricity pole resulted in power cuts as far away as Wooler, and the road was closed for three months, with all traffic diverted via Reaveley.

On some days serenely calm, on others destructive and raging, the River Breamish was aptly named by the Celts.

2
In Cheviot's Shadow

In the upper reaches of Breamish Water the two farms of High and Low Blakehope lie at either end of a broad, glaciated valley. Two more remote places would be hard to imagine. The Cheviot summit is about three miles distant, yet the main Morpeth to Coldstream road is ten miles away.

The name Blakehope, or Bleakhope to use the modern day spelling, is derived from old English, "blaec" meaning black or dark coloured, rather than bleak, and "hope", a small enclosed valley, a valley within the Breamish valley which is exactly what it is.

The spelling of the word is puzzling. It would appear to depend on who wrote it down. Local people did and still do pronounce it 'Blake' even though the modern spelling is 'Bleak'. Strangers however invariably pronounce it 'Bleakhope'. On Armstrong's map of 1769 it is spelt 'Blackhope' but the Enclosure map of 1776 uses 'Blakehope' as do wills and documents written in the 1800s. In the early 20th century both versions 'Bleak' and 'Blake' appeared in local newspapers, but to the guidebook writers of the 1930s onwards it was always 'Bleakhope'.

Personally I like the old spelling, it is true to the land, and to the generations of Armstrongs who lived there, with its connotations of black, from the heather, rather than bleak (dreary, bare, chilly). On some days the Blakehopes are undoubtedly that but on others the little valley is truly beautiful. Seeing it for the first time is to discover a secret.

The two farms are about half-a-mile apart, within sight of each other, overlooked by the hills of High and Low Cantle, Shill Moor, Cushat Law and Bloodybush Edge.

For centuries two tracks were the main links with the wider world. One came through Linhope, lower down the Breamish and wound its way uphill to the Snout End, a high exposed shoulder on Shill Moor, with sheer drops to the river below. When snow fell it quickly became impassable and

'Seeking the Groceries' - the cart track to Blakehope near the Snout End.

it was not uncommon for the Blakehopes to be blocked in for weeks. The same still happens today. The other track is the Salters Road, an ancient highway between England and Scotland. From the south it crosses Shill Moor and descends into the valley at Low Blakehope. It continues through the meadow, past the door at High Blakehope, and follows the Breamish for a short distance before turning west towards the Scottish border. Its formal origins date back to 1775-76 when, under the Alnham Moor Enclosure Award, "Common and In Field Grounds" in the vicinity of Alnham were allotted to various 'proprietors'. They included the Duke and Duchess of Northumberland, Alexander Collingwood Esquire and the Vicar of Alnham.

In addition the Enclosure Award laid out a network of new highways, roads and ways over the hills between Alnham and the Breamish Valley. They varied in width according to importance. Some were sixty feet wide, others thirty feet and the narrowest six feet. When the Salters Road was staked out and appointed as a public highway it was sixty feet wide and known as the Alnham West Road.

An extract from the Award reads: **"Beginning at the said east end of the said Town of Alnham and going through the said town of Alnham and to the west end of the said Town, and there turning northward and going in a direct line to a place called Northfield Head and from thence north-westward in different directions, a little to the east of Ewart Law Shank House, and crossing Shank Burn to a place called Low Blakehope and from thence up the north side of the River Breamish to a ford across the said River a little below a place called High Blakehope crossing the said River into a Public Highway ..... which goes to another ford across the said River Breamish into that part of the said Moor or Common intended to be divided and lying (near?) Black Cleugh and *Austie Burn and from thence to Austie Burn Foot and there turning west and leading to a place called The Foulstep and from thence into a certain Highway or Road leading through certain Lands and Grounds called Kidland Lordship to a Town or Village of Cocklaw Foot in Scotland."** * Now the Ainsey Burn

The surveyors who assigned the road added a rider about the use of the new Highways:
"It shall and may be lawful to and for all Persons whomsoever at all times hereafter to pass and re pass in through and along all and every of the said respective Public Highways on foot and on horseback and with horses, coaches, carts and with all manner of Carriages.
"And also to lead and drive all manner of Cattle and other things along the same and for all other purposes whatsoever at their free wills and pleasures."

The Award stipulated that all the roads and ways were to be completed within two years and the 'proprietors', with the exception of the Vicar of Alnham, were to contribute towards the cost of construction and maintenance according to the value of their land.

Smugglers traded illicit whisky along the cross border thoroughfare, and salt was carried by packhorses into Scotland, which is how it acquired the name of Salters Road.

High Blakehope

Against this backcloth of isolation, six generations of the Armstrong family lived and farmed at the head of the Breamish Valley. At the top of the family tree is James Armstrong. He moved to High Blakehope sometime between 1771 and 1775 from the parish of Arthuret near Longtown in Cumbria. Little is known about him except that he was a shepherd and had 11 children who were all born before the move to Northumberland.

In his book "Reminiscences" Samuel Donkin recalls a much talked about occasion at High

Blakehope when, during the winter of 1775, a coffined corpse was kept buried in a snow wreath in the garden for weeks, owing to the impossibility of having it 'lifted' to Alnham churchyard.

James died in 1804 and was buried at Alwinton. The family tree charts his descendants who lived at High Blakehope. We read of *George (1762-1835), Andrew (1801-1861), **George (1840-1891), James (1871-1914) and finally his two sons, ***George and James.

In December 1834, declaring himself "in sound mind and judgement", *George wrote his last Will and Testament:

"His son Andrew to have of his effects twenty pounds sterling more than George and John and house furniture, except the press, and he to have the cart and all other utensils also, and James has got all that he is

Two views of High Blakehope circa 1914.

The Armstrong family tree (Design: Gio Corno).

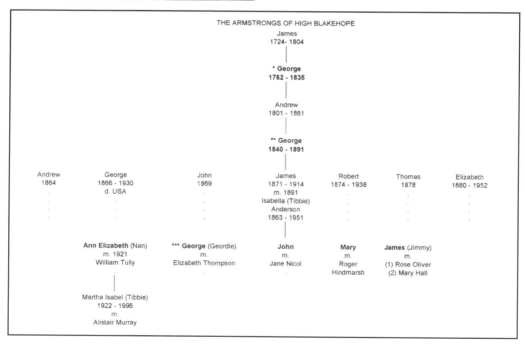

THE ARMSTRONGS OF HIGH BLAKEHOPE

James
1724- 1804

* George
1762 - 1835

Andrew
1801 - 1861

** George
1840 - 1891

Andrew 1864	George 1866 - 1930 d. USA	John 1869	James 1871 - 1914 m. 1891 Isabella (Tibbie) Anderson 1863 - 1951	Robert 1874 - 1938	Thomas 1878	Elizabeth 1880 - 1952

	Ann Elizabeth (Nan) m. 1921 William Tully	*** George (Geordie) m. Elizabeth Thompson	John m. Jane Nicol	Mary m. Roger Hindmarsh	James (Jimmy) m. (1) Rose Oliver (2) Mary Hall

Martha Isabel (Tibbie)
1922 - 1996
m.
Alistair Murray

to get, and Alison has got all that she is to get, and Thomas is to have fifty pounds sterling and that is to be under Andrew's care, until he sees him in need of it.

"And Mary is to have fifty pounds sterling, and the press, and ten pairs of blankets, and four woolen twills and two cotton ones, four pillows, three bed ticks, and three bolsters, and four pairs of pillowslips, and two pairs of sheets, but her money she is not to have until she is married, it is to be under Andrew's care also, and after all the above legacies is paid, Andrew, George and John is to have an equal share; and my prayer is that God would bless you all and be a guard about your souls and bodies and present with you in all your dealings and bring you to that inheritance that fadeth not away, where God is all in all."

The press - a large piece of furniture usually with drawers underneath and a cupboard on top.
Twill - "A woven fabric characterised by parallel diagonal ridges or ribs, produced by causing the weft threads to pass over one and under two or more threads of the warp, instead of over and under in regular succession, as in plain weaving. 1779." (The Shorter Oxford English Dictionary on Historic Principles. 1933)
Bed ticks - cases that feathers were put into.
Bolsters - long cylindrical pillows used on double beds, rather than the smaller individual pillows we know today.

Andrew Armstrong died in 1861 at the Besom Inn near Framlington, now Longframlington. He bequeathed household possessions to his wife Elizabeth and "the sum of two pounds, ten shillings to be paid annually, so long as she remains my widow."

At the time of the 1881 census **George Armstrong and his wife Mary were both aged 41. They had eight children ranging in age from 17 years old to Elizabeth, the only girl, who was 11 months. Two of the boys are described as "farmer's son" and four as "scholars".
On census day, in addition to the large family who lived in the two-bedroomed house at High Blakehope, we read of Agnes Turnbull, 19, a general domestic servant and two visitors: a joiner from Longhorsley, and a "saw sharper" from Ireland who was described as a "lodger".

In the late 1880s, by which time the family had the tenancy of a second farm, Haughters Law, on the moors above Chillingham, one of the sons, George, went to America as had relations before him. Many people were emigrating then, looking for a better way of life in a new country. Eventually he found work as a shepherd in Montana. A few years later, unsettled, George returned to his native Northumberland only to emigrate again, this time with his wife and family. Later he became an American citizen.

With few social opportunities, marriages between neighbouring families were common. The Armstrongs of High Blakehope, and the Andersons of Milkhope, were great friends. They lived just a few miles apart, the two farms 'marching' each other. The house at Milkhope still stands in what is now the Kidland Forest, land once grazed by sheep now planted with trees.

In the early 1890s **George and Mary's fifth son, James, married Isabella Anderson. The census of 1891 tells us that she was employed at High Blakehope as a "general servant, farm and domestic".

Isabella was always known as 'Tibbie'. One of ten children (eight girls and two boys) she had grown up at Milkhope where her father was shepherd. Large families were an accepted part of life then. For five years Tibbie's mother had a baby every year, all born at home. By the time she had her tenth and last child in 1869, the oldest was eighteen.

Tibbie and James set up home at High Blakehope and were to have five children: Ann Elizabeth

'Nan', ***George 'Geordie', John, Mary and James 'Jimmy'.

Only Nan and Geordie received any formal education. They boarded with relations who lived just off the Salters Road near Alnham. From there they could attend the village school that had opened in 1871. The younger children never went to school but were described as "great scholars", taught at home by their elder brother and sister.

With no modern communications and few people to talk to, passing travellers on the Salters Road were a welcome sight. They provided company for a 'crack' in this remote part of the valley. The house at High Blakehope and the hospitality of the Armstrong family became well known.

An article in a local newspaper of 1906 provides an interesting contemporary account of a visit to High Blakehope. It is entitled "A Mounted Trip to the Cheviots".

"A few days ago, a party of excursionists from Rothbury, Thropton and Snitter, consisting of publicans, butchers, tailors, farriers, carriers, millers, coal merchants, etc. left in the early morning determined to reach the top of Cheviot, and behold the oft talked of view from the summit. A packhorse was requisitioned to carry the panniery, well loaded with every requisite for the appetite and toilet...

"The route taken was by way of Netherton,

The Armstrong family pose in Sunday best for this photograph which dates from about 1897. James and Tibbie are pictured with their children Mary, in arms, and (l-r) George, John and Ann Elizabeth 'Nan'. Jimmy was not yet born.

Milkhope, the Anderson's family home.

Scrainwood and then over the hills with little or no track to follow…

"Blakehope, nestling at the foot of the Cheviots, was eventually reached, and the good lady at the farm, Mrs Armstrong, engaging to cook the lamb, new potatoes, etc., for the return of the party, horses being made safe, and a stalwart shepherd guide engaged to conduct and lead up the easiest way, the lot set out for the summit with a good supply of sandwiches, field-glasses, "Scotch", etc.

"The track to the foot of the hill was reached without any apparent sign of fatigue, and a little spring water, slightly diluted, was enjoyed here. Scotsman's Knowe was then to face, which taxed the endurance of the heavy weights…but some purer springs having been discovered and sampled, the party struggled on till they got to that famous spring known as White Burn Head. Here a welcome halt was enjoyed and the scenery around much admired…

"The summit was gained at last. What a view! Right into Scotland, Farne Islands, Bamburgh Castle and places too numerous to mention were easily seen. A Scotch mist came driving over the brow of the hill and obscured the view, but whether it was the Scotch mist or the now missed Scotch which mostly affected the party, all felt ready to descend.

Blakehope was reached without mishap, a splendidly cooked dinner awaited the party, who will never forget the kindness of those hill people, especially the good lady at Blakehope.

"Homewardbound past Linhope, Alnham Moor, Alnham and Netherton, no mishap occurred to mar this pleasant outing. So much was the trip enjoyed, that all agreed to make this an annual mounted excursion."

In December 1914 James Armstrong died after a short illness. He was 43. An obituary, in the County Gazette and Guardian, described him as a "well known and much esteemed Border yeoman".

"Lying right upon the Breamish towards the Cheviots, his house was a convenient halting place for those going to or coming from our Northumbrian highlands and many a weary, belated or storm caught traveller has enjoyed the hearty hospitality of Mr. Armstrong and his kindly spouse. The Border country is poorer by the loss of one who was known to and loved by all around and who will be greatly missed in Cheviotdale."

James was buried in Ingram churchyard, his headstone made from two almost-rounded granite boulders taken from the river at High Blakehope. A similar headstone in Eglingham churchyard marks the grave of his sister-in-law, Elizabeth.

Stephen and Florence Stothard.

At this time the farm belonged to Mr. Thomas Taylor, who lived in London. He wrote a letter of sympathy to Tibbie and thanked her for a box of heather which she had sent. "Mr. Armstrong seemed so well when I visited High Blakehope that it came as a shock to me to hear he had passed away. If there is anything I can do for you in this time of great trouble I would be glad if you would let me know."

Tibbie declined the tenancy of the farm and it passed to her late husband's unmarried brother and sister. They employed Jimmy and Geordie, Tibbie's two sons, as shepherds. To help make ends meet Tibbie took in paying guests, especially fishermen. It was through this that a lasting friendship was formed with a couple from Sunderland. Stephen and Florence Stothard came year after year to fish the Breamish and Usway burns. They journeyed by train to Hedgeley Station, and walked the 11 miles to High Blakehope.

Stephen was a keen photographer and took numerous photographs of the Armstrong family and surrounding places. He made many into postcards which he wrote back to them on. They provide a fascinating insight into day-to-day life at High Blakehope around the turn of the 1920s - Nan washing clothes at the spring, Jimmy and Geordie stacking peats, loading wool packs onto the cart, sheep shearing days, and so on.

Jimmy and Geordie stacking peats.

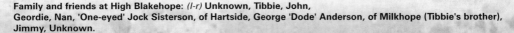

Family and friends at High Blakehope: (l-r) Unknown, Tibbie, John, Geordie, Nan, 'One-eyed' Jock Sisterson, of Hartside, George 'Dode' Anderson, of Milkhope (Tibbie's brother), Jimmy, Unknown.

Top-
Sheep shearing at High Blakehope.

Middle-
Loading wool packs onto the cart. Pressure was applied to the shafts to prevent the cart tipping backwards, until the load was balanced.

Bottom-
Tibbie, in later years, riding Tommy.

Left-
Nan washing clothes at the spring. The wooden posser, laid across the tub, was used to 'beat' the washing clean.

The Pipers - Tommy Clough and his son, Tommy.

The Armstrongs were great lovers of traditional music, as were Tibbie's family, the Andersons. It brought people together and many an evening was lightened by music making, to the glow of paraffin lamps. Among the regular visitors were Tommy Clough and his son from Blyth. They played the Northumbrian small pipes and were well known in their day.

Geordie Armstrong was a very talented fiddler often sharing his repertoire of tunes with others. One was a fellow hill shepherd, Willie Taylor, who lodged at Low Blakehope. In later life Willie played to folk festival audiences throughout the country, and his playing has had "tremendous influence" on a younger generation of musicians including Kathryn Tickell. Willie always attributed his style of playing to the many hours he and Geordie spent "whiling away the long winter nights learning new tunes and going over old favourites until they achieved just the 'lift' they wanted."

The words belong to Alastair Anderson, a leading exponent of traditional music, who lives near Whittingham. When Willie died in November 2000, aged 84, Alistair spoke at his service and wrote a moving tribute for "The Guardian" newspaper. Willie is remembered with fondness.

In 1921 when Nan Armstrong was thirty years old she married William Tully, a shepherd from Alnham. The wedding was at Branton Presbyterian Church. Afterwards the guests came back to Linhope and walked to High Blakehope for tea. Their wedding presents included two pigs!

The Armstrong family's long association with High Blakehope ended in 1939. Tibbie was living with relations and Jimmy had moved to Linhope. His brother Geordie was the last Armstrong to live at the farm. In 1939 he married his cousin, Elizabeth Thompson of Greenside Hill and moved away. The Armstrong line subsequently died out.

Building the new road in the mid 1950s.

During the 1940s "carding nights" were popular winter entertainment, and High Blakehope was a convenient halfway house. Shepherds walked from Uswayford in the Coquet while others came from Alnham and Prendwick, walking the Salters Road and meeting up with others on the way. The card schools were mostly men-only occasions held in the colder months, after the pigs were killed in the autumn and before lambing came around in the spring. Nap was the most popular game. Money was gambled on cards until well into the early hours - it was often daylight when the company walked home.

As the tide of innovation and change rippled into the valley in the early 1950s, a major project was being engineered that would change the way of life at the Blakehopes forever. A new road had been built between Hartside and Alnham Moor. Over the course of three years it was slowly extended westwards, to the head of the valley, by Mr. Harold Rutherford, who owned High Blakehope farm. He lived at Wall, near Hexham, and ran a contracting business. His lorries led in stone from Ingram Glitters and most of the levelling work was done by hand, which is why it took so long to complete. Before the

In front of the old house: *(l-r)* **Winnie Thompson, Tibbie Murray and Valerie Corno.**

final section was made between High and Low Blakehope, the river was moved into a new, straighter channel, which required only a single road bridge. The three old ford crossings disappeared. Shortly afterwards, following heavy rain, the river reverted to its original course and the newly dug channel had to be deepened.

A new house was built in 1956. With three bedrooms, living room, sitting room and a bathroom it was far superior to the old house next door. In 1972, after Mr. Rutherford's death, the 1200-acre farm was put up for sale. The particulars noted a very comfortable farm house, with garden at the front and the old stone built cottage which required repair. In addition we read: "The upkeep of the road from Hartside to Low Bleakhope Farm is shared with the Duke of Northumberland's Estates, half of the cost of any repairs being payable by the purchasers."

At a public auction in October the farm was sold to Hugh, 10th Duke of Northumberland (1940-1988) for £42,000, £35 an acre.

At about this time Tibbie Murray returned to High Blakehope to see the house that held so many happy memories of childhood. As a little girl she had stayed with her granny, Tibbie Armstrong, during the school holidays. It was a sentimental journey. She remembered the long walks from Hedgeley Station with her mother, Nan, and staying a night or two with the Thompsons at Greenside Hill. The next day, the draughty ride to the farm, in Uncle Jimmy's cart, with the wind howling around the Snout End.

This day she was in a car and there was a proper road all the way from Hartside. Tibbie was accompanied by two great friends; one was Winnie Thompson, and the other, Valerie Corno, a distant cousin with whom she shared the same great, great, great grandfather, old *George Armstrong, who wrote his will in 1834.

The saddest sight was the empty house, its windows partially boarded, the peat hearth long since cold. Visitors to High Blakehope always remembered the hearth, with those slender white-painted bars around the fire. At bedtime red-hot peat was buried in the ashes, in the well beneath the grate. Next morning it was lifted out and dry peat placed on top. The fire burned straight away. The three ladies posed for a photograph outside the old house and all agreed: the new house looked quite out of place in the valley.

By the late 1970s walkers were appearing in ever growing numbers in the Cheviot Hills. They were often poorly equipped, with no map or compass, and lost their way. Instead of coming down into the Harthope or Usway valleys, they found themselves at High Blakehope. The nearest telephone was a mile away at Low Blakehope, the Nelson's home. Jimmy Givens, the National Park warden, was well used to their calls, usually on a Saturday evening. He drove from his home at Brandon to the head of the valley, collected the hikers and took them back to their cars. If they had parked at Langleeford in the Harthope it was a round trip of more than 40 miles.

In 1991 a telephone was installed at High Blakehope, Graham Nelson's wedding present to his new wife, Ruth. Planning regulations stipulated that the cable went underground, so Graham and his brother Stuart dug the 1,000-metre trench by hand. The National Park Authority paid half of the £640 bill; the phone would be useful in emergencies when lost walkers knocked at the door.

The Salters Road is still a popular walkers' route but sadly its designation as an "ancient immemorial road" has been to its detriment. Motor vehicles are legally entitled to use it, and trail bikes have caused considerable damage along part of its course. In wet conditions the fragile surface is no match for powerful engines and spinning wheels. Parts of the old road now resemble a scene from the Somme.

Since the mid 1990s a gamekeeper has lived at High Blakehope. The land is managed for shooting as part of the Linhope Estate and farmed in conjunction with Low Blakehope.

Walkers on the Salters Road near Low Blakehope.

3
The Cloudburst

In July 1893, at the end of a very hot week, swirling storm clouds met over Bloodybush Edge, one of the high hills in the upper valley that forms a watershed of the Breamish. Distant thunder was heard and two hours later the clouds broke, covering the hill with "a sheet of water". The thunderstorm had devastating and far-reaching consequences.

Acres of peat were gouged out, down to the bedrock, by the sheer force of the rain, and torrents of black water surged into the Breamish. The resulting flood came down like a wall with a

"suddenness and power for which neither the memory of the oldest inhabitant nor the rumour of past tradition could find any parallel."

In the space of an hour and a half on Sunday afternoon, July 2nd, bridges were swept away, roads destroyed and hundreds of trout washed up on the haughs. It was a similar story in the Coquet valley where the Alwin and Usway burns overflowed their banks. For several weeks afterwards a black tidemark lay along the banks of the River Coquet, far below Rothbury, a distance of some 25 miles from the scene of the storm.

The aftermath of the cloudburst.

It is thanks to the Reverend Jevon Muschamp Perry, the vicar of St Paul's at Alnwick that detailed descriptions of the flood, and its aftermath exist. An amateur meteorologist, his account of 'the cloudburst' was published in "British Rainfall", the journal of the Royal Meteorological Society, and also in the country magazine "The Field".

After the storm the Reverend walked up to Bloodybush Edge which he described as "torn to rags and tatters". He took photographs and a local shepherd helped him plot a scaled map.

"For a space of at least 30 acres or 40 acres the upper layer of peat has been ploughed up to the depth of some five feet, and the moor bed beneath laid bare. Enormous masses of this dark peaty soil have been hurled right and left, piled one on the top of another, and a vast quantity of blocks of earth have been carried hundreds of yards down the hill, so as to present the appearance of a broad stream of blocks.

"As we did not know of any rain gauge at Low Blakehope, we made enquiries and were informed that a previously empty bucket, exposed to the rain, was found to contain 15 inches of water. Making full allowance for the shelving sides, this could hardly represent less than 8 inches, and that enormous amount is reported to have fallen one and a half miles from the focus of the mischief.

"It is simply appalling to contemplate what would have been the result if the waterspout,

instead of falling in the wilds of the Cheviots, had descended upon the hill side of some thickly populated town."

The phenomenon was widely reported in local newspapers. In the Alnwick and County Gazette of July 8th 1893 we read: "A heavy thunderstorm on the western hills caused the Breamish to rise **40 feet** on Sunday afternoon in half-an-hour. Two bridges at Ingram were carried away, while serious damage has been done to the banks and road. Mr Armstrong, Brandon White House, lost several sheep."

The aftermath of the flood was more fully described by the correspondent to the Alnwick Guardian on 29th July.

"Having heard of the enormous flood on the Breamish and the destruction caused by it, I took a trip up that river the other day to see the landslip caused, as supposed, by a waterspout. Starting from Hedgeley Station, and crossing the very beautiful and substantial iron bridge, taking the footpath to Brandon and right on to Ingram, I found unmistakeable traces of a monster flood, as the haughs are all covered with moss, trees, and fragments of bridges.

"Arriving at Ingram, I found a staff of workmen busy erecting a handsome iron bridge with stone bearings at the ends and iron pillars in the middle instead of the wood bridge that has done such good service in the past, and was wrecked by the flood. Leaving Ingram, and wending my way towards Greenside Hill, I came to Peggy Bell's Bridge, which also is wrecked, and a much higher one would have received the same fate.

"Passing on towards Linhope, the summer seat of Major Joicey, and crossing the water near the keeper's house, I noticed much damage to the wire fences and stone walls, which in many places had been carried away. Towards Blakehope the scenery becomes very wild; indeed, before reaching Blakehope I found the road completely washed away in different places, stopping all traffic with carts; it is scarcely passable even for a pedestrian; I had almost to creep along the hillside.

"On reaching Low Blakehope, I found the field above the house in utter desolation. A great deal of the stone wall is taken away by the flood, which has swept the space at the foot of the hills, carrying everything before it. I was told that two sheep came sailing down the middle of the field; one managed to escape, but the other was carried away by the current. It must have been rather alarming to those few dwellers in this isolated part. It may seem strange, but nearly all the water that caused such destruction, I was informed, fell mostly in a small space.

"Having got instructions, I passed on to the centre of attraction - the landslip. Leaving High Blakehope a little to my right, and going in a southerly direction, I soon came in sight of what proved to be the landslip. It had rather a strange appearance at a distance. On approaching it from below you first come to a great space covered with moss to a considerable height, and large lumps of unbroken moss are lying in all directions. Passing up towards the top the lumps get very large. Some of them are several tons in weight, and the force of water must have been very great. My opinion is, that if the cloud had not got exhausted when it did, a great deal more of the hill side would have been shot away, as there are a great many very large cracks above it. Some of them are about seven-and-a-half feet in depth, about 1 yard wide, and 40 or 50 yards long.

"I find it impossible to describe it, but people will find it well worth seeing, although there is a good deal of hard labour before you can reach it. This rare spectacle is on the Bloodybush Edge on His Grace the Duke of Northumberland's land, and on Low Blakehope farm."

The events of that July day in 1893, when according to one report the Breamish rose "40 feet", passed into history; filed away in newspaper archives, recalled only when browsing through Dippie Dixon's book "Upper Coquetdale".

In the summer of 2003, 110 years after the great flood, Dr Colin Clark made the long drive from Somerset to the Breamish Valley to find out more about "the waterspout".

Colin's work is in the field of hydrology and meteorology which when combined make hydrometeorology, in layman's terms, the study of water going up, evaporation, and water coming down, rainfall. His aim was to discover exactly how much rain had fallen on Bloodybush Edge that July day. This type of information is vital for the safe design of flood alleviation schemes but in particular for the design of dam spillways. Colin says that at long last the powers-that-be are beginning to realise that some dams in the United Kingdom have been 'under designed'.

Walking friends Anne Hunter and Ian Davison pictured in one of the many erosion gullies that still scar the hillside today.

Several days were spent surveying and measuring the upper valley, and gathering scientific data from the soil, and boulders that had been moved by the flood. Today, apart from boulder evidence, the main legacy of the 1893 storm is a series of erosion gullies on the hillside. Colin walked to Bloodybush Edge to take photographs and read, for the first time, the account of the storm in David Dippie Dixon's book. A search of several rural life museums for a bucket, similar to the one that filled with rainwater at Low Blakehope, drew a blank. None seemed to slope enough to convert 15 inches of water to eight as described by Rev. Muschamp Perry.

By November 2003, after a second trip to the valley, Colin was pleased. The extrapolated data added up to a peak discharge over Bloodybush Edge of 400 tons of water a second, a rise in river levels of between 14 and 15 feet, and rainfall over the 12km (about 8 miles) catchment area of about 170mm, nearly 7 inches, in an hour-and-a-half.

The rise of 40 feet was, Colin said, not credible. It was probably a slip of the tongue, or the pen, forty instead of fourteen.

In 2004 the evidence from the 1893 flood, amongst others, was featured at a conference in London entitled "Hydrology: science and practice for the 21st century". Earlier this year Colin's report of "The Cloudburst of 2 July 1893 over the Cheviot Hills, England" was published in the Royal Meteorological Society journal "Weather".

It is a blend of history and mathematical equations far beyond my understanding. By comparison with other storms Colin has demonstrated that the events of 1893 stand out 'head and shoulders' above others, a fine example of a 'flash flood'.
He says: *"Of all the rainstorms that have occurred in England perhaps the greatest of all took place over*

the Cheviot Hills in northern England. The assessment of the 1893 event in this paper, albeit imperfect, strongly suggests that much safer design standards need to be adopted. At the time of writing, the use of historic flood data to propose substantial improvements to one dam in England, are being considered. The wider adoption of a higher standard of design may only be a question of time."

As a result of his work, the Centre for Ecology and Hydrology in Oxfordshire has asked Colin to help in their national revision of extreme floods. So we must remember the name of Reverend Muschamp Perry still lives on today.

The old house at Low Blakehope with the byre and stable adjoining. Washing is hung out on the line and nearby a stack of peats is sheeted to turn the rain.

4

Low Blakehope

Half a mile downstream from High Blakehope, at the point where the Salters Road leaves the Breamish Valley and begins its ascent of Shill Moor, stood another old house, Low Blakehope.

Historically its farming links were never, as one would expect, with High Blakehope but with the farm of Alnham Moor, just over two miles away along a cart track. The two farms were owned by the Duke of Northumberland and formed part of the extensive Northumberland Estates. They were let to a tenant farmer who managed them both but lived elsewhere.

In 1904 when Mr Ralph Storey of Beanley retired after a tenancy of 25 years, a farm sale was held at Low Blakehope and Alnham Moor. The assembled company walked between the two farms. His 3,000 sheep were auctioned by the father and son partnership, Robert Donkin, senior and junior, of Rothbury. The Low Blakehope blackfaces were sold in the morning, the chief buyer being the new incoming tenant, Mr. William Elliot, of Hindhope. It was the start of a long family association with the valley that was to last until 1975.

After a substantial lunch, served in a specially erected tent by Mr. Edward Brown, proprietor of the Tankerville Arms at Eglingham, the Cheviot sheep at Alnham Moor came under the hammer. The prices paid reflected their decline. Many hill farmers were moving over to the more prolific blackfaces.

The Elliot family employed shepherds to look after the day-to-day work and seldom visited the farms. The shepherd in turn took on 'hired lads' to help with the work. Single men, of varying ages, they were employed on an annual basis. The younger ones were climbing the ladder, getting experience, moving from place to place, living as lodgers, until they married and looked for their own place. A job that offered better pay, and more secure prospects.

Andrew Scott was 22 when he was hired at Hawick by Charles Beattie, who was moving to Low Blakehope with his wife Meg and their four children. The previous shepherd Tommy Armstrong and his family (no connection to the High Blakehope Armstrongs) were moving to Alnham Moor.

It was May 1932. Andrew arrived at Low Blakehope wearing a pair of specially made "Highland Shepherd" boots that cost 27s 6d - more than his weekly wage. His work depended on the season. Every day, no matter what the weather, he had a hill to 'look' or 'herd'; it was considered a crime if you didn't. The sheep were moved up and down the hills to ensure the ground was evenly grazed and a watching eye kept on their welfare. There were no routine vaccinations to protect them from the fatal soil-born diseases of blackleg or pulpy kidney, and many died. When a tremendous scourge of dysentery affected the Low Blakehope lambs they were dosed with a potion of gin mixed with a white powder. Whether it was effective was a matter for speculation!

Braxy was another killer, usually striking the ewe hoggs between October and March, outbreaks coinciding with the onset of frosts. Strangely it affected sheep that were doing well or 'thriving'. Several usually died at once, but if a braxy hogg was spotted alive, it would be standing away from the rest of the flock, looking dull and refusing to eat. Lawrence Goodfellow, one time shepherd at Low Blakehope, concocted his own 'remedy'. He put the pigs onto grass pasture for a while (they were usually kept in pigsties), collected the droppings and mixed them with water. The braxy patient was given a dose of this horrible medicine and, whilst it was never clear whether it had any useful effect, it probably stopped the animal thriving and apparently did prevent some losses.

Veterinary surgeons were rare visitors to farms then but on one occasion a vet was called to Low Blakehope when a house cow went down with milk fever (calcium deficiency), a condition that often proved fatal. Andrew walked to Linhope to telephone for the vet and returned with a bicycle pump, the old fashioned remedy. The theory was that if air was blown into the teats the milk would be forced backwards and calcium reabsorbed into the blood. What the outcome was and what the vet prescribed is not known. Nowadays the condition is treated by an injection of calcium solution into the vein or under the skin.

Andrew was paid twice yearly, £24 every six months. It was the only time that Charles and Meg Beattie went to Wooler, to draw the wages and pay the bills. The grocery order was posted to the Glendale Stores in Wooler and delivered to Hartside, once a month, on a yellow and green striped, flat-backed lorry. The huge 16 stone bags of meal were split into smaller sacks to get them onto the cart.

A travelling draper supplied most of the men's working clothes, the children's too. Willie Robson, or "Stocking Willie" as he was known, came from Leitholm, north of the Border. He drove a car but used a pushbike to get to the out-bye farms. His visits were every three months or so and he worked in arrears. What you got the last time you paid for this time and if he didn't have what you wanted he would send it on.

Since 1930 Andrew had courted Jessie Henderson, a shepherd's daughter from Skirlie in the Harthope Valley. Every Sunday evening, weather and work permitting, he walked to Linhope and then cycled to West Street Church in Wooler where Jessie sang in the choir. They rarely met during the week.

Their wedding day was arranged for February 25th 1933, at West Street Church, but neither had reckoned with snowstorms. Jessie's home was blocked in, the banks full with snow, quite impassable for the wedding car. The local roadman, Andrew Whittle, walked out from Wooler to see what he could do. Cajoled by Jessie's mother, and sustained by a glass of whisky, he began 'casting' the road with a shovel. It took five men from eight o'clock in the morning until two o'clock in the afternoon to open the road.

After the wedding there was no honeymoon, quite the reverse in fact. Andrew and Jessie separated until May when his job at Low Blakehope came to an end. They saw each other only rarely during those first three months: there was the winter to contend with and then the lambing. Finding a new job was difficult. The dark clouds of the agricultural depression hung over the countryside. Often twenty or thirty men would apply for one post. Eventually Andrew and Jessie got 'their own place' at Sprouston, near Kelso, and they did get a honeymoon, many years after.

At the end of May the sheep were gathered for 'cutting', castration of the young lambs, but the busiest time of the year was the clipping, done in July when the new wool was starting to 'rise'. With no clipping machines, it was labour intensive work requiring a sharp set of shears and a strong back. In the 1940s a reciprocal arrangement existed between the two farms whereby the shepherds at Alnham Moor helped at Low Blakehope and vice versa. In addition 'tramp' clippers were employed. They moved from place to place in much the same way as contract shearers do today.

It took three days to clip all the sheep. Whilst it was best to have them dry on many occasions they were clipped wet, the fleeces hung over fences to dry out. Nowadays sheep are often housed overnight. Electric machines cannot handle a wet fleece.

The first day's clipping was at Low Blakehope when the out-bye sheep were done. The next two days were at Alnham Moor with a mix of sheep from both farms. Mr. Elliot, the farmer, always came to help. It was a busy time for the shepherd's wife, who had all the men to feed: breakfast, lunch, tea and supper. Mr. Elliot provided the meat, home-killed mutton, and nobody took a packed lunch.

The 1952 Clipping.
Back row (l-r): **Philip Athey, Low Blakehope; Robbie Elliot 'the boss', Chatto and Sunlaw Mains; Robert Smith, Alnham Moor; George Taylor, Linhope; John Smith, Alnham Moor; Jimmy White; Willie Scott, Brandon.**
Front row (l-r): **Stan Humphries, Low Blakehope; Ninian Glendinning, Reaveley; Jack Smith, Alnham Moor.**

Carting the woolpacks in the 1940s. Alwyn Bland *(left)* hired man at Low Blakehope and Robert Smith, Alnham Moor.

Usually there were 12 or more men hand shearing. Between them they could clip 40 or 50 score of sheep (800-1000) in a day, with one man averaging 60 to 80 sheep. Now, with machines, a skilled man can clip 300 in a day.

The fleeces were rolled and tied (with the neck wool) into bundles and stacked until the clipping was finished. Later they were packed into big hessian sacks, known locally as 'packs' or 'sheets'. Each sack was hung up between two gates, or suspended from the rafters, with the top left open. Once full they were stitched up and taken away, two at a time, by a horse and cart to Hartside. There they were stacked and covered to await collection by a lorry.

The summer dipping was done at the beginning of August. Each sheep was individually dunked in a solution of water and Dieldrin, a very toxic but effective dip that killed parasites and prevented 'fly strike' with the consequent hatching of maggots. An organo-chlorine, Dieldrin was banned several years ago because of the disastrous consequences when it seeped into watercourses. Fish stocks and wildlife were wiped out. However, many shepherds will say there has never been such an effective dip since.

At the end of August the lambs were weaned or 'speaned' from the ewes. The ewe lambs were retained for breeding, but the castrated male lambs, the wethers, were sold because there was not enough 'keep' to last them over the winter. The wethers from both Mr. Elliot's farms went away in one day, four shepherds driving up to 800 lambs down the road to Ingram where they were held overnight in the stack-yard. The next morning they were walked to Hedgeley Station and loaded onto railway wagons bound for Scotland.

In October the oldest ewes in the flock, 'the drafts', were sold to make way for younger ones coming on. The annual draft ewe sale at Rothbury was a Red Letter day on the shepherd's calendar, an important social occasion, and a rare chance to have two nights away. It was always held on a Thursday and Friday; Cheviot ewes were sold on the first day and blackfaces on the second.

The sheep were walked the 15 miles to Rothbury, the journey split into three stages with overnight stops. On the Wednesday Mr. Elliot's shepherds left the two farms, Walter Beatty driving the Low

Blakehope ewes along the Salters Road. The Alnham Moor sheep went via Cobden Dene to Alnham and on to Scrainwood, a journey of about eight miles. The sheep were rested overnight and then walked on to fields at Thropton. That evening the shepherds and their dogs stayed at the Turk's Head Hotel in Rothbury dinner, bed and breakfast paid for by Mr. Elliot. The final leg of the journey was early on Friday morning, a two-mile walk to Rothbury, the road full of sheep, droves nose to tail, all heading for the mart.

The appearance of livestock wagons, in particular the development of floors or 'decks' that enabled many sheep to be transported at once, brought an end to the age old task of driving animals to markets. During the 1940s Mr. Elliot began hiring a wagon from Tommy Mossman of Glanton. After that there were no more walks to Rothbury or Hedgeley Station.

In 1949 Jake Wright arrived at his new home with his parents and sister, Nell, their possessions stacked on the back of a tractor and trailer. At one point it looked as though the family might not get to Low Blakehope at all. Half way up the hill out of Linhope Jake's mother Violet wanted to turn back. She was horrified at the prospect of living so far out in the hills, and even more dismayed when she set foot in her new home.

The family had moved from Eagles Nest, near Peebles. There was a road to the house and it had electricity, a bathroom with inside toilet and a pleasant fireplace. The two-storey house at Low Blakehope had none of these things. Dilapidated and very damp, the worst sight was the old range in the living room. Jake, who was six years old at the time, remembers thinking 'not alot' of his new home.

The only door into the house opened into a lean-to back kitchen. The sitting room was used as a bedroom, and the two hired men slept upstairs. From a small window at the top of the staircase there was a fine view up the river to High Blakehope.

Jake's father kept two house cows, their grazing was part of his wage. Every year they were blood tested for tuberculosis. Raw milk was a source of glandular TB, particularly in children, and at that time there were no effective drugs. The testing was done by a veterinary surgeon from Alnwick, Mr. D.J. MacPherson. He was always known as "Mr. Mac". With several cows to test at different farms, most of them inaccessible by car, he walked. It was about ten miles and took a whole day but "Mr. Mac" enjoyed walking. With equipment in his coat pockets, his first call was at Alwinton then to Milkhope and around the lower slopes of Cushat Law to Ewartly Shank. Here he picked up the Salters Road to Low Blakehope and from there to High Blakehope before finishing at Linhope. Three days later "Mr. Mac" re-traced his steps when he returned to 'read' the test.

Tuberculosis or 'consumption' is no longer a major health problem thanks to rigorous testing, the culling of 'reactors' (cows that test positive for TB), and the introduction of pasteurised milk.

In the mid 1950s the new road brought welcome changes for the Wright family. Jake's father bought a Morris Standard pick-up and groceries were delivered to the door. When Dr Jaboor came from Wooler he borrowed a jeep and no longer had to walk from Linhope.

As shepherds' homes in the valley were gradually modernised, a decision had to be made about the old house. The Northumberland Estates decided not to spend money on it thereby sealing its fate. Building work started on a new bungalow. The bricks were led in by a succession of lorries whose drivers, with the exception of one, all refused to make a return journey because of the frightening sheer drops off the new road.

With four bedrooms, a living room, bathroom and kitchen the new house was finished in 1956.

A stone plaque inscribed with the date and the Percy "crescent" was set into the wall. The old house became a hay store and later housed the Lister engine that brought electricity to Low Blakehope for the first time. Its distinctive noise, a regular 'putt', 'putt', 'putt', was to become a familiar sound in the evenings when lights were switched on in the house. The new television however was not a success: there was interference from the engine and the screen 'flashed' with sparks.

During the winter of 1962-63 the family was snowed in for three months. A Hercules transport plane dropped bales of hay for the sheep. They were tied with wire and every one broke on impact. Groceries and provisions were brought in by helicopter and on several occasions it took hay out to the sheep. Jake walked out to meet it and got a ride home! It was a far cry from the winter of 1947 when the shepherds walked from Alnham Moor to Low Blakehope, through deep snow, carrying hay on their backs for the house cows.

When Jake left secondary school at Wooler he came home to help his father and stayed until 1965 when he left the valley to get married.

In 1975 Mr. Elliot's widow gave up the tenancies of Alnham Moor and Low Blakehope because their son was not interested in farming. It marked the end of a long association with the valley that had begun in 1904. R.W. 'Bob' Telford of Fawdon took both farms, going into partnership with Edwin Nelson at Low Blakehope.

Edwin and his wife Mary had lived all their married life as joint tenants of an out-bye farm in Upper Coquetdale. Away from mainstream services, they had learnt to adapt or do without. Their sons Graham, aged 11, and Stuart, 8, had known nothing else. When the family moved to Low Blakehope Mary's elderly parents came too. They could no longer manage on their own. Her mother was disabled and caring for her was a full time job, with little supportive care from the community health services. The farm was too remote for regular visits.

A new diesel generator supplied limited electricity, at night times only. It was not on during the day. The family could watch television however, if Mary wanted to use the washing machine she had to juggle other appliances. She had no fridge and the two freezers ran on 'maximum' to stay cold during the hours there was no power. Edwin could not have a gang of men at shearing time because the generator could only run one clipping machine.

For several years the family had no telephone, the nearest was at Linhope. When a line was installed in 1979, part of the cost was met by the Northumberland National Park Committee. The telephone was to be a valuable lifeline in emergency situations when walkers got lost in the hills.

The boys' education was a problem. Although a taxi took other children in the valley to Branton School - Ingram having long since closed - it would not make the six-mile detour to Low Blakehope. Edwin could not undertake the daily journey because of work commitments and Mary did not drive. Graham and Stuart became weekly boarders at Rothbury attending firstly the middle school there and at the age of 13 moving on to the high school in Morpeth. During one bad winter they were at school for only a week between January and April. The farm road was either blocked with snow or hazardous with ice.

Mary kept a weather station at Low Blakehope and sent in regular reports to the Meteorological Office. Mindful of winter weather, she shopped in bulk if snow threatened. After the house cow went there were always cartons of long life UHT milk in the store cupboard. In the late 1980s she took driving lessons and passed her test first time. A new car meant she was no longer dependent on Edwin and the boys.

By then Graham was living at High Blakehope and the family were sole tenants of both farms, the 4,000 acres stocked with 2,000 Swaledale sheep. When Stuart announced plans to get married, Edwin and Mary decided to move to Glanton, to a house they had built a few years previously. Edwin then began the daily commute to Low Blakehope, a round trip of 30 miles.

Before Stuart and Sarah's wedding, in 1994, the bungalow was extensively modernised, oil-fired central heating installed and the kitchen transformed into a light airy room with double doors opening onto a patio. Sarah's mother gave them a fridge. It cost £1000 and ran on Calor gas or electricity. Sarah's greatest dislike is UHT milk. The fridge meant she could buy it fresh. More recently a wind turbine and solar panels have greatly improved the electricity supply. They feed into a battery bank that is boosted by the generator if the power is low. Now they have a computer, on a separate circuit because the uneven supply can cause power surges, and a huge electric fridge in the kitchen.

Everyday life takes on different dimensions living at Low Blakehope. Collecting the daily paper is a 24-mile round trip, but you never go just for the paper, often you do without. Sarah does the supermarket shop in Alnwick, combining it with the nursery school run, a 50-mile round trip. Their youngest son Charles, who is four, goes to nursery two days a week. That allows Sarah some time on her own, to work. She drops him off in the morning and collects him later in the day. In just one day 100 miles is added to the Freelander 'clock'.

When Charles was diagnosed with diabetes in 2002 it meant extra journeys to hospital in Newcastle. Sarah is well prepared for emergencies and keeps stocks of insulin and needles at home.

Their eldest son William attends Branton Community First School about 13 miles away. He is collected and delivered to the door, snow and ice permitting, by the school taxi. Both Sarah and Stuart know they will spend even more time on the road when the boys are older and want to do activities after school.

The road near Low Blakehope in February 2001. *(Photo: Sarah Nelson)*

Adjusting to life at Low Blakehope was a challenge and a big change for Sarah. A farmer's daughter from near Amble she is a qualified rural practice chartered surveyor. For the first three years of married life - until William was born - she commuted every day to Co. Durham, a round trip of 132 miles, often leaving and coming home in the dark. The time it takes to travel anywhere from Low Blakehope was an influential factor in her ultimate decision to work from home; the other was the problem of trying to juggle nursery opening hours with a full day at an office.

In 1999 Sarah was appointed secretary of Glendale Agricultural Show working alongside Stuart who is the show director. August is a quiet month on the farm but a busy one for them both in the run up to the show. Sarah particularly enjoys the social side, meeting new people in the locality because, apart from visiting friends for supper or going to the West Percy and Border hunt balls, they rarely go out.

The Nelson boys William *(left)* **and Charles on the Ski-doo.** *(Photo: Sarah Nelson)*

Stuart's working days are mostly spent with his father, the herding done on quad bikes. Edwin's help has been vital since Graham was seriously injured in a road accident and had to give up work on the farm. Sheep numbers were reduced to 1300 when both High and Low Blakehope entered Countryside Stewardship schemes. In return the Nelsons are paid to preserve the landscape. They work long hours, often in isolation, but the presence of gamekeepers, now that the shooting is managed, has made a difference. They have other people to talk to apart from each other. Stuart takes on casual work, night lambing duties and clipping, to help pay for a family holiday. It has high priority being one of the few occasions when they are together for any length of time.

In March 2001 the farm was snowed in for three weeks. It was bad snow for the sheep, falling suddenly and quickly, whipped into drifts by a strong wind. The sheep were out on the hills, scattered. There had been no time to gather them into shelter. The day after the first snowfall Stuart walked to High Blakehope, hoping to get out to the sheep. Up to his waist in snow, it took him an hour and a half to cover half a mile. The conditions were so bad that he turned around and followed his footsteps home. It was three days before Edwin got into the farm on the Ski-doo, a specialist snowmobile which runs on skis and a rubber track. The family's supply line with the outside world, he brought basic groceries and of course, fresh milk. A rugged, powerful machine, the Ski-doo is purpose-made for deep snow. During those three weeks Stuart took the family over the hills, to places undreamed of in the bad winters of years ago.

Someone once remarked to Sarah that she should be on "Hearts of Gold" for living at such an isolated place. Journalists, writers and television crews drive the roller-coaster road to find out how, in the 21st century, the family leads a modern lifestyle in the totally un-modern surroundings of Low Blakehope.

The answer rests partly with the Freelander that celebrated its first birthday with 27,000 miles on the clock.

5
Alnham Moor

It was wartime, May 1940, when John Smith moved to Alnham Moor with his mother and father, Jack and Jemima, and his two sisters, Cicely and Annie. He was 14 years old and had lived all his life at Chatton Sandyfords, an isolated shepherd's house on Chatton Moor, where he was born. His elder brother, Robert, had worked as 'hired lad' at Alnham Moor since 1938. When the householder moved to Uswayford in the upper Coquet, John's father got his job.

Moving house was complicated by the rough tracks at either end. A horse and cart took the furniture to Quarry House where it was loaded onto a wagon. At Hartside it was off-loaded again, onto a cart. There was no lift for the two house cows. They walked the four miles to Beanley and rested overnight. The next day John, and several collie dogs, drove them the final seven miles to Alnham Moor.

The farm steading at Alnham Moor, early 1970s. *(© Sky Views and General Ltd.)*

The farm steading was traditional in style, the buildings surrounding a yard at the back of the house. It is little changed today. There was no electricity, no bathroom or inside toilet. The netty was across the yard. Bath time was either a wash in the Breamish or a tub in front of the fire. The open range was the only source of heat in the house. Lit every day, meals were cooked in the oven and water boiled in the set-pot, a large deep metal pot, built into the side of the fireplace.

The nearest telephone was at Linhope Lodge. If needed, but only in an emergency, Cicely walked over the hill and across the footbridge, known locally as Postie's bridge, a handy short cut that saved the postman going round by the road.

Dances were held in the local village halls. Powburn and Ingram were within cycling distance, but often a crowd, a dozen or so, walked over the hills to Netherton or Alnham and back again.

Mrs Smith *(left)* **and her sister-in-law, Bella Keen, pictured on Postie's Bridge, near Linhope.**

The farthest away was the Askew Hall at Windyhaugh in the Coquet Valley. If you'd been to a dance there you didn't get home until breakfast-time.

The range fire was fuelled by peat. Readily available, it cost nothing and was cut by hand from the hag or 'dubb' on top of Shill Moor Hill. Most places in the upper valley burnt peat but the quality varied from place to place. The Alnham Moor peats were amongst the best, black and slow burning, whereas on Low Blakehope they were light in colour, almost grey, and quickly burnt away.

The peats were cut once a year after lambing time, a spell of fine weather being essential to help them dry out. It was a laborious job. In ideal conditions the whole operation took three weeks, John, Robert and their father combining it with 'looking' the sheep.

The turf was removed with a horizontal cut by a long-handled, angled spade. A different 'winged' spade cut the peats into rectangular shapes. They were lifted individually out of the 'dubb', which was about three feet deep, and laid out flat in rows. When a water-repellant 'skin' had formed, the peats were put into 'fittings', two parallel with another two parallel on top, herringbone-style. Finally, they were built into 'rickles' or piles, about five-feet high, wide at the base and narrower at the top, allowing the air to circulate which helped them to dry. The peats were led home on the cart and stacked ready for use the following autumn. The draught horse, Jean, had the hardest job of all. It was a round trip of three miles, up and down the hill, with a maximum of four journeys a day. In hot weather she was lathered. The working horse played an important role on the farm. There were no tractors or quad bikes to do the humping and hauling.

In the summer the grass in the meadow was cut for hay. The field was shut off in late spring and not grazed. This allowed the grass to grow and every year a myriad of wild flowers appeared.

The hay was cut with a single horse drawn reaper, a machine with sharp blades that cut the grass with an action similar to a barber's shaver. The steep banks or 'braes' at the edge of the meadow were cut by hand with a scythe. The hay was left to wilt for a few days then shaken out by hand.

A horse drawn rake gathered the hay into arch-shaped 'wind rows', the wind, and hopefully the sun, helping it to dry. When it was 'fit' or ready, ideally crisp to touch and crackly to sound, it was gathered up into 'kyles' or small heaps, by another horse drawn machine, a "tumbling tam".

A wooden framed implement it had a beam across the back with two handles that the horseman hung onto. Three spikes projected down from the underside and dragged the hay into heaps as the horse walked down the 'wind row'. At the place where the pike was to be built the handles were released and the frame "tumbled" over towards the horse, dropping the hay and then righting itself.

Several 'kyles' were dropped together and built up into a conical pike, or stack, six to seven feet in height. The pikes were left for two or three weeks then led in to the hayshed on a bogey, a low, flat cart. When the shed was full any remaining pikes were built into haystacks in the meadow and on the hill. They were thatched with rushes to repel the rain and secured with hemp ropes, although some farms used a stack net instead.

The hay was fed in wintertime to the horses and house cows. The sheep got a bite only in heavy snow. Then the hay was cut from the stack with a hay knife, a triangular-shaped, sharp metal tool and the 'desses' or chunks loaded onto a horse drawn sledge.

Nowadays hay is baled by machine. A baler ties it into big round or rectangular bales (so heavy that a tractor is needed to lift them) or smaller square bales that can be lifted by hand. The bales are stacked in a shed and haystacks are now but a memory.

When the horses needed new shoes they were ridden to the blacksmith's forge at Powburn next to the Plough Inn. Sometimes there was a queue and you had to wait your turn, the horses standing on the road (there wasn't much traffic on the A697 then) or behind the forge. On occasions, if no shoes were 'made up', ready, the blacksmith started from scratch. Huge bellows pumped air into the fire to make it roar. A straight bar of iron was heated up until it glowed red, and could be hammered into shape on the anvil.

The Lillie family had been blacksmiths for generations, since 1840 when George Lillie had the smithy at Reaveley, in a croft opposite the farm. He moved the business to Powburn in the mid 19th century. His son Robert travelled the countryside with a horse and cart, shoeing the draught horses on local farms. Some had a forge on site. In the immediate locality there were blacksmiths'

Jack Smith with Jean harnessed to a bogey. The cut rushes 'thak' were used to thatch the haystacks.

shops at Branton, Fawdon, Ingram Mill and Brandon. The latter is still used today as the farm workshop.

Robert Lillie's son George took over the business in 1904 - a blacksmith almost until the day he died, in his eighties. The war and the coming of tractors brought inevitable change. The draught horses that came to the forge gradually disappeared and the 'mend and make do' of wartime gave way to spare parts. There was little repair work.

In 1975 George Lillie, the fourth generation of the family, shut up the blacksmith's shop to join the county council's bridges department He had never wanted to be a smith but felt obliged to help his father. His interest was welding, and he is remembered as one of the best. The parapet railings on the County Bridge at Powburn, and Weldon Bridge, near Longframlington, are testimony to his work.

Nowadays blacksmiths travel to customers and horses are rarely taken to a forge. Most shoes are factory made and either put on 'cold' or heated in a gas-fired oven in the back of the smith's van. Hence the term 'hot shod'.

Almost a year after the Smiths moved to Alnham Moor a tragic air crash occurred that served to heighten the growing hostilities between Britain and Germany.

It was lambing time, April 24th 1941. John and Robert had done their first round of the day, checking the ewes in the fields and on the hill. After breakfast they were outside again when the morning quiet was shattered by the sound of an aircraft engine. John glanced the plane coming from Linhope, too low; in split seconds it went over the house and down the meadow as if looking for somewhere to land. Seeing a steep hillside at the end of the field, the pilot turned and flew back. Losing height and with engines screaming the plane just cleared the chimney pot then nose-dived and somersaulted into the bracken on Meggrims, an undulating tract of ground between Alnham Moor and Linhope. It burst into flames and, as John and Robert walked towards it, bullets exploded all ways. There was no hope of saving the pilot.

Blacksmiths *(l-r)* **Billy Prosser, George Lillie, senior, and his brother Jack Lillie outside the forge at Powburn.**

Pilot Officer Martin Rivers had gained his 'wings' in March, a month before his ill-fated flight. He had taken off from the recently opened RAF training airfield at Ouston, near Stamfordham, now the site of the Albermarle army barracks.

The local police constable then was Jack Inchmore from Powburn. He walked out from Hartside and waited most of the day at the scene of the crash until RAF personnel arrived. The wreckage of the Hawker Hurricane was loaded onto two farm carts and taken to Hartside to await collection by special transport. The bracken has since been ploughed out and the land fenced but John remembers finding pieces of metal for many years afterwards.

At some time during the war he came across a machine gun on Shill Moor. Bullets were scattered about and one theory was that it had been dumped by a fighter aircraft to lighten its load. Again PC Inchmore was called and the gun trailed down the hill to Linhope.

The Smith family was largely unaffected by wartime. Whilst some commodities such as sugar and flour were rationed, there was plenty of home produced food and no reason to travel far. Robert joined the Home Guard at Ingram.

In wintertime, when the nights drew in early, John and Robert spent many hours in the byre 'dressing' sticks, shepherds' crooks. Hazel was most commonly used but if you were lucky enough to get a blackthorn it polished up nicely, after the knots in the wood were dressed and varnished. The wooden shanks had to be straight. They were cut and dried out for at least a year, in the old bothy above the byre.

The brothers mostly made everyday working sticks strong enough to hook round a sheep's neck. The head or top of the stick was made from horn, preferably from a tup because it was stronger than a ewe's horn, although occasionally a piece of curved beech or thorn was used. The horn was roasted over a paraffin flame until it was soft enough to 'turn' into the required shape. The head was spliced onto the shank, the stick rubbed smooth with sandpaper and finally varnished.

Shepherds often took an ornamental stick, a Sunday best, when going to shows or sales. The horn head was more elaborately carved with a thistle, a fish, or whatever took their fancy.
Nowadays stick dressing is not just the prerogative of shepherds: it is a popular leisure pastime with enthusiasts learning the skills at evening classes and exhibiting plain and fancy sticks at local shows.

Another job for the winter nights was rug making. There was no wall-to-wall carpeting, the cold cement floors were covered with mats, made from old clothes. Worn out trousers and jackets were cut up into 'clippings': precise short lengths for "stobby" or "proggy" mats and longer lengths for "hooky" mats. The 'clippings' were poked through tiny holes in a mat-shaped piece of hessian stretched over a wooden frame to keep it taut. When the mat was finished a sack was hand stitched to the underneath to form a backing.

The end of January 1947 heralded the start of what was to become one of the worst snowstorms this century. Along with the winter of 1962-1963 it is indelibly printed on peoples' minds and generally acknowledged to be the worst of the two, coming as it did when the hill ewes were heavy in lamb. There was not only the sheer depth of snow and heavy drifting to contend with, but the fact that it lasted until the end of March.

The Smiths were snowed in for eight weeks, no one particularly minded. Families were well prepared for bad winters, buying in provisions in the autumn. John's abiding memory is of 'casting' snow, every day, until it became impossible to clear it. During the winter the draught horse from Low Blakehope was kept at Alnham Moor together with Jean, the Smith's horse, and Ginger, a pony that Mr. Elliot rode when he went to Low Blakehope. They were stuck in their stalls for more than a week, the drift outside the stable so high that John cut steps down into it to get to the door.

Gangs of roadmen worked to open the road between Greenside Hill and Hartside. The drifting was particularly bad, as it can be today, because the road lies in a cutting. With their jackets hung on top of the telegraph poles, one gang shovelled off the top layer of snow as another moved in to take off the next. And so it went on.

Many sheep died, buried under drifts, but worse was still to come: in early April the weather turned to wet, cold sleet that persisted for a month. Newborn lambs stood no chance and hundreds perished. There were several 'fresh starts' whereby entire batches of lambs were wiped-out, only to be followed by another lot. It was a lambing John would rather forget.

The early 1950s heralded a time of great change at Alnham Moor. Paraffin lamps gave way to Calor gas lighting; the range

Harold Rutherford levelling the riverbed under the new road bridge at Alnham Moor. The old footbridge can be seen in the background.

was taken out, replaced by a modern fireplace and Mrs Smith got a Calor gas cooker. The back porch was converted into a bathroom with an inside toilet. It was always the coldest room in the house.

Electricity came sooner than anticipated thanks to Mr. Houseman of Linhope. He installed a supply to the Lodge but did not want unsightly electric poles along his private drive. Instead, the line was routed towards Alnham Moor with a 'dog's leg' to Linhope. It was now relatively easy to take electricity to Alnham Moor, the cost to Mr. Elliot much less than expected.

For John the most exciting change was the construction of a proper road from Hartside to the farm. The contractors, the Alston Lime Company, used local stone from Hartside Hill. It was hand 'penned' or hewn and rolled down the hillside to the field below. A new Bailey bridge was built over the river, just downstream from the footbridge. Groceries could now be delivered to the door with certainty. Sometimes the ford had been so deep that a horse and cart could not get through.

It was 1952. Robert bought a motorbike and John bought a car, a black Morris Minor registration number FTY 943. He had never driven before. After buying the car in Morpeth his brother-in-law, Annie's husband, took him for a 'spin' around Tranwell aerodrome.

John practiced driving at home to save the cost of lessons at Alnwick. On the day of his driving test he caught an early bus to Alnwick, drank two 'drams' to steady his nerves and passed first time!

The car made life much easier. The weekly shop in Wooler no longer depended on bicycles and buses, and visiting friends or going to funerals took much less time than it used to. There was no more walking to dances.

Farm mechanisation came in the mid 1950s when Robbie Elliot sent a tractor to Alnham Moor and a man to explain how it worked. The family was the last in the valley to use a working horse. Gradually the old implements were adapted for the tractor or simply abandoned as obsolete.

The Smiths were great supporters of the West Percy Hunt and followed the hounds whenever the meets were local. Cicely 'walked' a foxhound puppy every year. It was rather like a gap year for the puppy: an opportunity to experience life, meet people and learn about sheep before joining the pack in the hunt kennels. Cicely won many prizes at the annual puppy show. Then, everyone who walked a hound was given a silver teaspoon, a token of thanks, inscribed with the puppy's name and the year. She had a lovely collection.

Cicely had gradually taken over the shepherding work from her father. In 1975 she tragically collapsed and died whilst looking the sheep on the Hett Hill. She was just 43.

In 1984 John and Robert both received medals from The Royal Agricultural Society for more than 40 years' service in the agricultural industry. Their names were put forward by R.W. 'Bob' Telford who took over the tenancy of Alnham Moor when Mrs Elliot gave it up in 1975. The Duke of Northumberland presented the medals at a special ceremony at Ingram Farm, attended by Society members from all over the country.

In 1987 John and Robert retired and moved to a house near Whittingham. George and Babs Elliott came to Alnham Moor in 1990. As Babs Cowens she had spent her early years at Linhope and met George when he worked at Greenside Hill, as a hired lad. They left the valley on Saturday November 2nd 2002 when George retired.

John's new car - and his nephew Robert Foggon.

6
The River

From Alnham Moor the river flows in an easterly direction around the foot of Hartside Hill, passing the old hay meadow. There are few wild flowers now - artificial fertiliser blamed for their demise. Buzzards glide in the airstreams over the hill; in contrast lapwings, newly arrived from the coast, tumble and turn, as if pleased to be back in the valley.

At a narrow point, hemmed in by three hills, the river makes a northward turn into a particularly beautiful stretch of the valley. Ancient grass-topped anthills cover the valley floor, their occupants providing a tasty treat for badgers that can dig deep enough.

The area is a favourite with oystercatchers that nest close to the river. Grey wagtails, much shyer than their pied cousins, bob and bow to each other at the water's edge. A white-breasted dipper darts up and down the river pausing fleetingly to land on a stone and dip his head into the water in search of a meal.

In 2000 English Nature designated the Breamish a Site of Special Scientific Interest, part of the Till Catchment SSSI that flows into the River Tweed, which is why the Breamish is designated a Scottish river. More recently it has merited inclusion in the European Habitats Directive "Special Areas of Conservation". The Tweed SAC is important not only in a national but a European context.

Its ecological importance lies in the wildlife habitats, the flora, bird life and fish stocks that the river supports. Of interest at European level is the presence of different species of lampreys (a primitive jawless fish resembling an eel), otters and Atlantic salmon. All require unpolluted water to survive.

Also singled out is Ranunculus Fluitans (river water-crowfoot), a very pretty floating buttercup with a liking for swift-flowing water. Whilst it grows in profusion on the Alwin and Bowmont rivers, covering the surface with a carpet of white flowers, it is a very rare sight on the Breamish. Indeed local botanists, with years of experience, have never seen it. The smaller flowered common water-crowfoot, Ranunculus Aquatilis, prefers ponds and ditches. It was flowering in the valley in 2004.

Otters are occasionally sighted on the river. Usually it is the evidence they leave behind, spraint and prints, which provide clues as to the whereabouts of these lovely creatures.

Every three years the Tweed Foundation undertakes a survey of the young fish stocks in the river to ensure that all is well. The most recent was in 2004. A mild electric current is passed into the water with a probe. This attracts the fish which are scooped up in a net. The tiny salmon and trout are individually measured and recorded, then returned to the river.

The eel population has declined in recent years. James Hunt, assistant biologist with the Tweed Foundation, believes over exploitation in parts of Europe is to blame; with fewer eels reaching the spawning grounds in the Sargasso Sea, fewer are coming into the river.

Head gamekeeper
Adam Sisterson below
the Black Lynn water-
fall, early 1900s.

7
Linhope

Tucked away in a cul-de-sac at the foot of Ritto Hill, Linhope takes its name from ancient Celtic, Lin or Lynn meaning a deep pool, particularly below a waterfall, and Op or Hope, a vale without a thoroughfare.

It is quite descriptive of the place. The main valley road ends here and close by, on the Linhope Burn, are two spectacular waterfalls: the seldom seen Black Lynn, hidden away in a narrow tree-hung gorge and further up the burn, The Spout, a fine cascade of water that falls 56-feet down a cleft in the rocks to a deep black pool below. A favourite with photographers, it is also a popular destination for walkers.

Look up to the surrounding hills in August and September and they are ablaze with heather, the staple diet of the shy Red Grouse. These beautiful game birds, and the hardy sheep which graze the hills, have shaped the fortunes of the Linhope Estate over the past century.

In the closing decade of the 1800s Major William James Joicey bought the estate. He was a wealthy gentleman, his money having come from the family's coal mining empire in County Durham. His cousin was the 1st Baron Joicey of Ford, knighted in 1906, who rose from 'hands on' miner to become the richest and largest coal owner in the world.

Major Joicey's main residence, which he had bought in 1891, was

Major William James Joicey, owner of the Linhope Estate.

Sunningdale Park in Berkshire, an imposing white country mansion where he lived with his wife Mary, son James and a full retinue of domestic staff. The family also had a town house in London at 8 Lennox Gardens. But Linhope, with its 3000 acres and wooden shooting lodge or 'box' as it was termed was to be his country retreat, a place to entertain friends and business connections with house parties and shoots at the height of the grouse season in August and September.

His priority was the shooting. He built two new houses, one at High Linhope overlooking the River Breamish, for his head gamekeeper Adam Sisterson and, in 1899, a substantial detached house near the lodge for Adam's eldest son, Jack, who was following in his father's footsteps. The Sisterson family's association with the Estate was to span three generations.

On August 3rd 1902, the year after the death of Queen Victoria, Adam's son William and his wife Elizabeth had their first child, a boy. Named after his paternal grandfather Adam, he too was to become a gamekeeper.

Young Adam grew up in the days when horses and carriages were hired from Alnwick to bring house party guests from Hedgeley Station to Linhope. The arrival of the Joicey family in time for the Glorious Twelfth was the highlight of the valley calendar.

On one particularly windy night a lady was collected from the train. When the coachman stopped just past Greenside Hill to open one of the many gates on the road, she offered to do it for him. Thinking he heard the door shut and the lady safe inside he drove on to Linhope. A footman came out to open the door only to find the lady's luggage but no lady. The howling wind had

Major Joicey's gamekeepers *(l-r)* **Adam Sisterson, his sons William and Jack, and Bob Reay, gamekeeper at Ilderton Moor.**

The Gamekeeper's House built 1899.

played tricks with the coachman's ears. He turned round and collected her near Hartside. Adam could hardly tell the story for laughing!

In 1903 the wooden shooting box was badly damaged by fire. Little is known about the incident, but over the following two years the house was completely rebuilt, one half one year, the other the next, using stone from the field walls.

The reconstruction was completed by 1905, the date set in stone over the front door. Major Joicey insisted on heavy fireproofing, all the walls and ceilings were lined with asbestos and rock wool. A grander version of its predecessor, the lodge was nicknamed "The Capital H" because of its shape. With 13

The stone built shooting Lodge.

bedrooms, a smoke room, bathrooms, inside water closets, and servants' quarters it was the first house in the valley to be lit by 'new' acetylene gas lighting. Outside were larders for game, meat and fruit, an ice house, a gas house and a gun room.

In those halcyon Edwardian days, William James spent his money lavishly. In 1906 he bought the adjoining estate of Greensidehill, Grieve's Ash, Ingram Haugh and Hartside. He also owned Ilderton Dod, the Dod Moor (now known as Ilderton Moor) and fields at Glanton. A gamekeeper's house was built at Hartside and a private drive made from Hartside to Linhope. It is still "private" today. Travelling on the unmade valley road in a horse and carriage was a bumpy experience. There were numerous small streams to cross in addition to the Breamish itself at Hunter's Ford, just below Ingram Glitters.

In 1907, when Major Joicey was in residence at Linhope, a telegram was delivered from Glanton informing him about an important meeting in Newcastle. He set off but was forced to turn back at the ford because the river was in flood. He was apparently so angry about the whole affair that he gave orders for a new road bridge to be built before he returned the following year. The single span concrete bridge was erected about 200 yards upstream from Peggy Bell's footbridge, the builders being Tully Brothers of Wooler. A photograph records the formal opening in 1908 with the Joiceys crossing their personal bridge in a horse drawn carriage.

In those days there were gates at either end that were closed when the family was away. Over the years they disappeared, and eventually responsibility for the bridge was passed to the county council. Strangely it was never named after Major Joicey but acquired the name of the old footbridge.

Every summer, before the Joiceys arrived, an advance party of domestic staff was sent north from Sunningdale to get the shooting lodge cleaned and aired.

Major and Mrs Joicey, accompanied by liveried coachmen, cross the bridge in an open topped carriage drawn by two horses. Scaffolding is still in situ.

Gasman William Storey was seconded from the Beamish Pit in County Durham to maintain the acetylene supply. The gas was made in the gashouse, a tomb-like place, partly underground with steps down into it. Carbide was put into a miniature gasometer and mixed with water. It was a very messy procedure.

Tully's, the same family building firm, got the place ship-shape and painted. Coal and coke were collected from the coal staithes at Hedgeley Station and delivered daily by Jim Potts with his horse and cart. The local butcher Sam Dodds, of Glanton, had a regular order for the house parties: sixty lambs' kidneys for breakfast, prime joints of beef and lamb and rounds of pickled beef, 40-50 lbs in weight, the fare for casual callers.

The Joiceys had a leisurely journey to Linhope. Getting off the train at Hedgeley, they usually spent one night with their great friends Rev. Roland Allgood and his wife Edith at Ingram Rectory before going to Linhope, the next day.

House party guests - and dogs - at the front door of Linhope Lodge. Major Joicey is pictured (*back right*) holding a dog, with his wife Mary seated in front of him. Their son James is sitting cross-legged on the ground.

When the shooting season was in full swing the lodge resembled a country house hotel, the guests, except those who lived near, staying for several days. With no cars, travelling with horses was a much slower affair.

On shooting days local shepherds were employed as "beaters". They took instructions from the gamekeepers and had to make the birds fly over the guns. The extra money in their pockets was welcome, and the local lads benefited too. They played truant from school and earned four shillings a day, much to the teacher's annoyance. Their absence was noted in the Ingram School logbook as "bush beating".

The shoots were great social occasions, not only for the Joiceys and their houseguests, but also for the staff and locals. There were dances in the hayshed, a dinner for the men and, in later years, after the houseguests had departed, a party and dance in the newly converted garages.

Inevitably romance followed. Carrie Hopkins had worked for the Joicey family at Sunningdale for many years and had risen to the position of head housemaid when she met Tom Anderson. He had lived at Linhope for much of his life, firstly as a child and then returning in 1887 as a young man of 20. He was in charge of the day-to-day farming, which didn't greatly interest Major Joicey, and eventually became the manager. Their courtship, apart from yearly meetings, was sustained with greetings on local postcards. That was how people kept in touch then.

The Linhope Staff circa 1910. Tom Anderson is pictured back row, second right. His future wife, Carrie, is seated middle row, second right. The three boys in the front are grandsons of Adam Sisterson, head gamekeeper, back right.

The Spout. A close look reveals eight men seated amongst the rocks to the left of the waterfall.

In 1907, on a postcard of Linhope Spout with men sitting beside the waterfall he wrote: *"Here is a place you ought to know also some of the faces you will know and some you don't. My hearty congratulations to you once more. We have had some lovely weather. Mrs A. Sisterson is poorly. Clarks leave Hartside in May.*
Best wishes to you and others. TA."

On an unstamped card of the Black Lynn he wrote: *"Dear Miss Hopkins, I thought you might like this card for your collection. I expect Jemmie will have had many a good catch here. With best wishes to all and same to yourself. I am, yours truly TA."*

In 1911, when Tom was 43, they were married at Sunningdale. Among their wedding presents was a desk given by members of the Glendale and Border Shepherds Cow Club of which Tom at various times was treasurer, secretary or chairman, or a combination thereof. A shepherd's house cow was a valuable asset. If it suddenly died it was a financial disaster. By paying an annual premium to the club, rather like an insurance policy, the shepherd was guaranteed a sum of money to help buy a replacement. Whilst it did not fully cover the loss it was a great help.

Tom and Carrie set up home at Linhope. Their son George was born in 1912 and their daughter Elizabeth, 'Betty', in 1916.

Major Joicey was the first person in the valley to have a car, not surprisingly it was a Rolls Royce. A Daimler van carried the guests on shooting days. The partnership of Charles Stewart Rolls and Henry Royce, formed in 1906, subsequently became one of the most prestigious car manufacturers worldwide.

It is most probable that Major Joicey's Rolls was one of the early Silver Ghost models. It was brought from Sunningdale for the holiday and was the chauffeur's pride and joy. Adam remembers it being polished every day until it shone like a 'new shilling'. Woe betide any youngster who touched it.

With typical generosity the Joiceys took some of the Linhope staff to Sunningdale for their annual holiday. On one occasion Adam's grandfather had his pocket picked. The Major thought it very funny but made it up to him.

During their visits the family regularly attended Ingram church. They were generous benefactors. Between 1910 and 1911 Major Joicey paid for the installation of acetylene lighting into the church and the Rectory, and new church furniture, oak pews in the nave, the pulpit and the vestry screen, all still in use today.

A memorial tablet on the wall in the nave reads: *"To the glory of God and in memory of Major W.J. Joicey of Linhope by whose generosity the oakwork in the nave of this church was erected. The parishioners of Ingram placed this tablet in grateful remembrance."*

His wife gave a small organ made by Harrison & Harrison, the famous Durham organ builders. Until the advent of electricity it was driven by waterpower. It worked successfully for some years off a spring supply that also fed the Rectory, but as the pipes silted up the pressure to the house and church got weaker and weaker.

Mrs Naomi Church, the Rector's daughter, vividly recalls the chaotic situation that ensued.
Her mother was the organist. If there had been plenty of rain on the Saturday she could pull out all the stops and the music was magnificent. On the other hand if there was a drought the organ was very weak. If any water was run off in the Rectory during the service it just faded out!

In January 1912 Major Joicey died aged 74. The East window in Ingram Church, made up of three beautiful stained glass windows, is dedicated to him. The inscription entitled "Charity" is his epitaph.

"I was hungry and ye gave me meat. I was sick and ye visited me. Jesus went about doing good and healing all that were oppressed. Go thy way thy faith hath made thee whole.

"I was thirsty and ye gave me a drink. I was prisoner and ye come unto me.

To the Glory of God and in Loving Memory of William James

Joicey. Born June 20th 1837. Died January 23rd 1912."

A re-opening and dedication service was held in the church in September 1912 to mark not only the Joiceys' generosity but also that of the Allgood family. They gave the altar and communion rails as a memorial to James Allgood III, Rector for 35 years until his resignation in 1887 when he inherited Nunwick, the family seat near Hexham. He died in 1910 aged 83.

Mrs Joicey retained the estate for James, the only son and heir. With a reputation as an extravagant spender, his interests lay elsewhere. He amassed a world famous collection of butterflies, and had a passion for orchids that he grew in sphagnum moss, gathered off the hills by local children, for a small fee.

Early in 1914 there was little indication in the local "Gazette and Guardian" that war was looming. Tom Anderson attended a dinner for hill shepherds at Netherton, the Glendale Cinema Company was to stage an exhibition of "moving pictures" in the Jubilee Hall at Hedgeley and Mrs Joicey gave a prize for the clay pigeon shoot at Powburn, which local gamekeepers organised.

By August the news had changed. Local men were leaving for the War, Lord Kitchener was appealing for recruits and Miss Robson of Low Hedgeley wanted help with knitting "body belts" (two purle stitches and two plain alternately), mufflers and helmets for the Tyneside Scottish Battalions. As part of the War effort Mrs Joicey donated sheepskins to be made into coats for men of the "Fighting 5th", the Northumberland Fusiliers, who faced tremendous hardship in the trenches during the winter months ahead.

In October as happened every year - war or no war - blackfaced ewes from Linhope were among the 9,000 sold at Rothbury Ewe Sale. Soon afterwards Mrs Joicey sold ram lambs and rams off Ilderton Moor (formerly known as the Dod Moor) at the Wooler store sheep sale. The highest price she got was £4.10s.

In 1916 Adam Sisterson left Ingram School. He was 13, the minimum leaving age, and could help out on shooting days in place of his father who had joined up. Adam got the job of taking the old men out to the "butts" on the moors. He knew the lie of the land exactly. There were places where people, not knowing the hills, would have disappeared into a bog, absolutely disappeared, pony and all.

Old Baron Joicey of Ford was often invited to Linhope. His great delight was shooting 'bagged' duck, especially reared for the sport, if it could be called sport. It was quite legal in those days. The ducks were caught up off the pond at Hartside and taken some distance away in hampers, hence the term 'bagged'. Three or four were let out at a time. Baron Joicey would stand behind a wall and shoot them as they flew back to the pond.

Despite the War there was still the occasional visitor in the Valley. Writing in the local paper in December 1916 "Rambler" recalls: *"The delightful glen, wood, hill and waterfall in a spot named Linhope, are open to any who have a pair of good lungs and decent boots of leather. You'll bless the treat that Mrs Joicey has provided."*

Early in 1919 the flu pandemic hit Linhope. It had already claimed thousands of lives countrywide. The Joicey's housekeeper, Miss Agnes Inkster, whose home was on Rousay in the Orkneys, had helped nurse the Sisterson family who were all poorly. She caught the flu and died without seeing a doctor. She is buried in the churchyard at Ingram.

That August, George Anderson, Tom and Carrie's son, started school at Ingram. He was seven years old. It was a long day and a long walk, almost four miles each way. If it was very wet or a bad snowstorm he didn't go. Any child who got wet on the way to school was dried out in front of the fire and Mrs Stuart, the teacher, lent them dry clothes. The chance of hitching a lift home was not to be missed. The hill children watched out the window for traffic coming up the Haugh. If any carts were going up the valley, past Ingram, Mrs Stuart let them out early. They ran to the wood corner, where the signpost is now, and got a ride home.

At about the same time as George started school Adam's father was de-mobbed and shipped back to Alnwick Station. After missing a Hedgeley train, and with no bus or taxi to bring him home, he walked the 17 miles to Linhope. The new de-mob boots had skinned his heel, but William returned to his old job as a gamekeeper and was soon out on the moors again.

The Joiceys were at Linhope at the time when his heel became poisoned. With no antibiotics the infection moved up his leg and killed him. It was a sad time for the family. William had gone through the War in horse transport, had two horses shot from underneath him, only to fall victim to septacaemia. Need he have walked all that way home? In those days you just did, without any fuss. His name is one of five on the church memorial to the men who gave their lives in the Great War.

In 1920 Tom Anderson retired as treasurer of the Cow Club, a job he had done for 14 years. He had an exemplary record of never having missed a meeting despite the seven-mile cross country walk from Linhope to Wooler. It had been part of the job. When Tom retired, 400 cows were insured through the Club. During the year twelve had died resulting in an expenditure of £284.

By the early 1920s Mrs Joicey was ageing and could not walk very far. One of her great joys was sitting in an armchair at the top of the front door steps and chatting to the shepherds and passers by. A public right of way went straight past the door. On fine days she went out in the donkey cart, pushed by several staff along the footpath around Ritto Hill. There were seats at certain places where she sat and admired the views. The gamekeepers were under strict instructions not to burn the heather nearby because Mrs Joicey liked it in full bloom when she arrived every August.

During her visits to Northumberland Mrs Joicey supported local events and causes. In 1921 her name featured in the weekly paper amongst the list of prizewinners in the industrial classes at Whittingham Games.

In 1924 the entire estate, which extended to more than 7,600 acres, was put up for auction. Mrs Joicey was getting too old to make the long journey from Sunningdale and money was getting scarce.

The sale particulars for "The Linhope, Hartside, Greenside Hill and Ilderton Dod Estates" ran to eight pages and included photographs and maps. Of interest to prospective buyers was that the shepherds had all been re-engaged until May Day 1925. Tithes were paid to the Rector of Ingram and, for the Dovecote Fields at Glanton, to the vicar of Whittingham.
"The grouse moors on Linhope and Ilderton Dod are noted as yielding heavy bags in any season. Hartside and Greenside Hill yield good bags of Black Game, Pheasants, Partridge and Hares." Black Game or black grouse are rarely seen in the valley now. At Threestoneburn, traditionally a "lek" or

Colonel John George Adamson, owner of Linden Hall and Linhope. *(Photograph by courtesy of Linden Hall Hotel).*

display arena, parts of the wood have been clear felled in an effort to attract the birds back to their old territory.

The shooting lodge was described as centrally heated with "electric" bells and acetylene gas lighting throughout. The sanitary arrangements would definitely not be approved of today. "This is efficient and disposed of by discharge into the River Breamish, on the boundary of the Estate, at a considerable distance from the lodge."

The auction was held on Tuesday March 11th, 1924 at the County Hotel, Newcastle-upon-Tyne at 2 p.m. Auctioneer Mr. Robert Donkin sold the estate in four lots.

John George Adamson, a retired army colonel bought Linhope and 3111 acres for £15,500. William Robinson, a farmer, from Rugley, near Alnwick, bought Hartside and Greenside Hill farms for £13,600, considerably less than the £17,000 that Major Joicey had paid in 1906. Mr. Farquar Deuchar, a brewing magnate, bought Ilderton Dod with its 2478 acres for £25,000. The 50 acres of land at Glanton was knocked down to William Rutherford for £2,600.

It was the end of an era at Linhope. The legacy left to the Valley by the Joiceys has been unsurpassed since. People who knew them remember them as an incredibly generous and very caring couple. They cared deeply about the Valley and their staff and looked after all their employees as family. They felt responsible for them. When the young ones were leaving school if they could give them a job they did.

The new owner Colonel Adamson lived at Linden Hall, near Longhorsley, with his wife Lina and two spinster daughters Miss Eve and Miss Muriel. Their home is now a luxury country house hotel.

Colonel Adamson was a good shot and a keen fisherman. He particularly enjoyed taking his rod up the burns around Linhope and casting for trout. Adam's Uncle Jack stayed on as head keeper until 1927. When he left John Proudlock got his job and Adam was employed as under keeper. The shooting parties continued but not on the same scale as in the Joiceys' day.

During the summer Adam's spare time was taken up with wrestling and sport: it was born and bred into the Sisterson men. From May onwards he travelled the countryside, firstly on a bicycle and later a motorbike bought from his winnings, competing at events as far away as Jedburgh and Hawick and the Highland Games in Scotland. Adam's passion for wrestling and running almost led to a fall out with Colonel Adamson. One Saturday morning he refused to accompany the Colonel fishing because he had a good handicap at a sports meeting at Choppington. He went but spent the day worrying about getting the sack, and where he and his new wife Mary would live because the house was tied to the job. In the event nothing did happen. The Colonel politely enquired how he had done and the matter was closed.

The waterfall at the Spout was a popular destination for visitors who walked along the private drive from Hartside to Linhope. After the Colonel failed to persuade Glendale Council to adopt the road, and with it the upkeep, he put a collector on the gate at Hartside at weekends and charged 6d for "admission to the fall", the proceeds going to charity.

In the mid 1920s Tom Anderson asked the Colonel if he would approve of him getting a car. The Colonel had no objections whatsoever and said he would do better than that: he was changing his car and would give Tom his old one, a Model T Ford. It was a great thrill for George and Betty because few valley children had parents who owned a car.

The Andersons left Linhope in 1929. Tom was 62 and had always fancied farming for himself so the Colonel gave him the tenancy of a farm on the Linden Estate near Longhorsley. After his wife's death Colonel Adamson was rarely at Linden Hall preferring to spend his time at Linhope where a housekeeper, parlour maid and cook looked after him. When he entertained everything was brought from Linden Hall: the food, the butler and extra staff.

The Colonel died in 1932 and the estate passed to his daughters. Adam stayed on as the gamekeeper and the shooting was let, firstly to the Collingwoods of Lilburn and then to Colonel Trench.

Farming was at a very low ebb; Ted Cowens, the Linhope shepherd had sold blackfaced wether lambs at Rothbury for 9s 6d each yet a brace of young grouse sold for 12s 6d to the Savoy Hotel in London.

A manager looked after the farm. In 1936 Walter Brown was hired for six months as 'the summer laddie'. He ended up staying two years. Most farms took on a boy to help with the extra work in summertime. Walter's jobs were varied. He looked after two horses and Dolly, the grey bob-tailed pony, who pulled the trap. He ploughed land for potatoes and turnips, took the pony and trap to the hill to collect grouse from the lunch hut on shooting days and in winter kept the drive open with the horse drawn snow plough.

In about 1940 the Estate was sold again, reputedly for £11,000, to Gerald Sylvester Houseman, a businessman from Alnmouth who had made his money inventing a cleaning 'agent' for ships' boilers. He moved to the lodge with his wife Irene, his spinster sister Mildred, always known as 'Miss Mindy', and their widowed mother. In June 1941 Irene died very suddenly so Miss Mindy assumed responsibility for running the house.

A staff of four girls and a cook looked after the family. Hannah Robson was 14 years old when she started work as an under housemaid. At Miss Mindy's insistence she was known as 'Ann', to avoid confusion with her cousin, also called Hannah Robson, who was the parlour maid.

'Ann's' daily duties included scrubbing the front door step every morning, polishing the brass doorbell, filling and cleaning the paraffin lamps and turning down the beds at night. She learnt to 'wait on' at the table, if the Houseman's were entertaining, but that was only occasionally.

During the night of March 24th 1943 a German bomber crashed on Rig Hill above Linhope, killing the crew. Walter Brown, the 'summer laddie' who now worked at Greenside Hill walked to the scene. He noticed two unusual things: the plane was fitted with Dunlop tyres and the swastika on the tail fin had been painted out. To this day he still has an unopened packet of German cigarettes that he took from the wreckage.

Adam was retained as the gamekeeper but Mr. Houseman was never considered in the same league, shooting wise, as Major Joicey or Colonel Adamson. He had never owned an estate. On one occasion he asked Adam how he knew the difference between old and young grouse forgetting that the gamekeeper had handled hundreds and hundreds of birds during his years at Linhope.

In 1956 Adam and Mr. Houseman had sharp words over wages and Adam handed in his notice. He got a new job as gamekeeper at Lemmington Hall, near Alnwick, and through this was asked to help on shooting days at Alnwick Parks. There he met Lord James Percy, the third son of Hugh, the 10th Duke of Northumberland. Just a young boy then, he was to eventually inherit the Linhope Estate.

The same year, 1956, Robbie Cowens left Ingram School aged 15. He was taken on as a shepherd at Linhope working alongside his father and brother. The family had moved to Linhope in 1950 and lived in the Anderson's old house. By now it had electric lights powered by a big generator at

Robbie and June Cowens pictured at Linhope with their daughters Rosemary (left) and Elizabeth.

the lodge. Mr. Houseman controlled the switch. At 10p.m. every night the lights went out. The Cowens family always lit their paraffin lamps at five to ten!

Long time friends June Redpath and June Turnbull were engaged as housemaids at the lodge. That presented the Housemans with another dilemma over names, as had happened with the 'two Hannahs'. It was decided that June Redpath would be known as 'Jenny'. Some people knew her by that for years afterwards.

Robbie and June (Redpath) were married in 1962. After a year at Ingram they moved out to High Blakehope. The Cow Club was still going and Robbie became a collector, calling on local shepherds to collect the £1.10s annual premium. By then, if a cow died, the Club paid out £40.

In 1968 the family, which now included daughters Rosemary and Elizabeth, moved back to Linhope to Robbie's boyhood home. June's great friend June Turnbull had married Ronnie Oliver of Hartside. Their twin daughters were about the same age as Robbie and June's girls. When the children were old enough to go to school the 'two Junes' went back to work for Mr. Houseman. His business was in Newcastle and he commuted two days a week, driven by his chauffeur Harry Gibson.

As Major Joicey left his mark on Linhope so too did Mr. Houseman. He made the garden around the lodge by fencing in part of the Flagstaff field and planted the Bog Wood between Hartside and Linhope because the ground was too wet for cropping. The private drive was laid with tarmac for the first time, but a dispute arose with the council over a short stretch of road around the house and buildings at Hartside. It was christened 'No Man's Land' and left un-surfaced because both parties insisted it was not their responsibility. Eventually Mr. Houseman won the day.

In the early 1970s, after the Forestry Commission offered him money to sell land for tree planting, Mr. Houseman sold his three farms, Linhope, Hartside and Greenside Hill, to the Duke of Northumberland. Local farmer R.W. 'Bob' Telford of Fawdon was granted the tenancies.

Mr. Houseman died in 1977. He was buried at Ingram with his wife and sister and left legacies to the 'two Junes' who had worked for the family for so many years.

In the late 1980s Lord James Percy succeeded to Linhope with ambitious plans to restore it as a sporting estate. The land was heavily stocked with sheep, the moors barren of wildlife and the shooting run down. The lodge was let out as an old peoples' home.

Lord James went to see Adam, the old gamekeeper, who by then was retired and living in Alnwick. He took him back to Linhope onto the moors he had known so well. Together they went almost to the top of Hedgehope in a Land Rover. Adam lost his bearings. The ground he had walked for years looked so different from a vehicle. Large areas of heather had disappeared, the result of overgrazing, and bracken had taken its place. He helped Lord James plant some heather at the back of Ritto hill but told him he'd never find it again. He was absolutely right - the sheep ate it.

Since then sheep numbers have been reduced, land fenced and the moors managed by gamekeepers. One of their tasks is to kill vermin - foxes, stoats, weasels and carrion crows - that prey on nesting birds. Other predators however, the birds of prey that were not tolerated in Adam's day, are now protected by law. Buzzards, hen harriers, goshawks and sparrow hawks are regularly seen on the moors. The grouse and the many other birds that have returned, curlews, ring ouzels, pipits and skylarks, must take their chance.

In August Linhope stands out from the surrounding countryside the hills once again purple with heather. The gamekeepers burn it on a rotational basis to encourage the growth of tender young shoots on which the grouse feed. Tracks criss-cross the landscape to enable access by four-wheel drive vehicles or quad bikes. Most of the shooting is now 'let' days when wealthy sportsmen, including Americans, pay large sums of money to shoot grouse, partridge or pheasants on a renowned Northumberland estate. Some arrive by helicopter, others by road. They stay at the lodge, or the former gamekeeper's cottage at High Linhope.

Lord James, with son Thomas on his knee, and Lady Lucy, holding Eliza, are pictured with the Linhope staff in 2005.
Back row *(l-r)*: The gamekeepers Ewan Cameron, Richard Liddle and Gary Taylor.
Middle *(l-r)*: Nanny Jacqueline Rudd, household help Linda Lowes and housekeeper Heather Wilkinson.

Both properties have been extensively renovated. The lodge at the time was encased in a plastic 'bubble' to allow the removal of asbestos and rock wool from the ceilings and walls - Major Joicey's legacy following the fire of 1903. When the paying guests have gone, Lord James, his wife Lucy and their children return to Linhope for some family shoots.

All revenue from the let days is ploughed back into the estate. In recent years 75,000 trees, mostly native species, have been planted, 1500 acres of bracken destroyed and 1700 acres of heather improved. In many ways the clock has been turned back and the Linhope Estate restored to its former glory, but there is a great difference between then and now. In Major Joicey's day it was a private, social shoot, purely for sport and personal pleasure financed from his own pocket.

Now it is run as a business, the different elements of farming, sporting, forestry and holiday lets

A bridge that Robbie built over the upper Breamish. *(Photo: Keith Davison)*

held up as an example of integrated management of an upland estate, providing five full time jobs and many part time on shooting days; a successful example of rural diversification at a time when farm incomes face an uncertain future. Lord James is proud to be Linhope's custodian.

In the new millennium the Glendale Cow Club is still in existence and celebrated its centenary in 2001. It was almost wound up because membership had dwindled to a handful with only six or seven cows insured but with enough money in the bank to cover all the cows, if they died, it was decided to carry on. Robbie is still a collector and there are two rates of premiums now, £16 or £12 with payments of £400 or £300 respectively. To buy a good cow costs about £700 and most of those insured through the Club are kept to rear a calf rather than provide milk for the fridge.

Although the Cow Club has survived into the 21st century, the draft ewe sale at Rothbury, for so many years the highlight of the hill shepherds year has not. It was held for the final time in 2000. Following the disastrous Foot and Mouth epidemic the following year, when there were no sheep sales at all, it was never reinstated in the mart sales list. Entries had fallen as sheep numbers generally were being reduced to accommodate Countryside Stewardship and moorland schemes, tree planting and grouse shooting. All livestock sales in the mart premises have since ceased.

By the time Robbie retired in the summer of 2000 he was the only shepherd at Linhope where once there had been three. Apart from a year at Langleeford he had lived and worked in the valley for 50 years.

Since then a hidden talent has been revealed, one he didn't know existed: a flair for building bridges. Initially Lord James asked Robbie if he could build a footbridge for the guns and beaters to use on shooting days. He had never built a bridge before but over the years had learnt to turn his hand to most jobs given a hammer and nails. Without consulting books or designs he set off with a tractor and front-end loader, telegraph poles and timber and built his first one. It was such a success that Lord James commissioned more. None took longer than a week to build, the time taken just depended on the river crossing and how much measuring up and sawing there was to do.

Now there are a series of lovely footbridges across the Breamish and two of its tributary burns, all slightly different in design and all beautifully made. One is wide enough to take the estate Argocat, an eight-wheeled, all terrain vehicle that can travel up steep rough hillsides or move across water. Underneath the wooden deck Robbie added a new nest box - right on the dippers' flight-path.

8
Hartside and Greenside Hill

The snow was drifting and still more falling when Nellie Heron, against all better advice, set out to walk home to Hartside on a bleak December afternoon. The year was 1863 and the middle-aged woman had been treating an elderly shepherd at Alnham with her apothecary skills.

Her way home crossed rough fell land, remote and bleak, with "bogs and morasses" underfoot. It was heavy walking whatever the weather but this day the drifting snow had blanked out familiar landmarks.

The five-mile journey took her firstly on the Salters Road, an uphill climb from the pele tower at Alnham, then onto the old bridleway over Leafield Edge to Cobden Dene. After that it was downhill to Alnham Moor, across the Breamish and home to Hartside. Nellie was about half way home, almost within sight of the shepherd's house at The Chesters, when she sat down for a rest. This was to cost her, her life.

The next day she was found dead, by a shepherd, still in a sitting position, her basket beside her and a walking stick across her knees. She was 50 years old.

Hypothermia, a condition when the body temperature falls below normal, was the most likely cause of her death. The symptoms are varied depending on the severity: it can cause shivering, lethargy, failing consciousness and at worst, a heart attack. In Nellie's case it was severe.

A contemporary source described how Mrs Davidson of Alnham "almost on her knees" had besought Nellie not to set out on her ill-fated journey, and the elderly vicar, Selby Thompson tried to dissuade her, offering a bed for the night at the vicarage. But it was to no avail.
In his beautiful book "Whittingham Vale" David Dippie Dixon describes Nellie as "a person well known and much respected throughout the valleys of the Breamish and the Aln."

The exact spot where she perished in "Shiel Bog" is marked by a stone, not unlike a boundary or 'march' stone. The simple inscription says "Eleanor Heron, Departed Dec. 3rd 1863". It is now quite difficult to find, camouflaged by vegetation and some distance off the hard track that goes to The Chesters.

Nellie is buried in Whittingham Churchyard with others of her family. The headstone stands opposite the south west corner of the tower where the two paths join. Alec Adams, a great-grandson of Nellie's, lives in Powburn today.

Nellie's stone.

In November 1962, almost a century after her death, two shepherds William Middlemiss and Jock Scott perished in deep snow only a mile or two from the spot where Nellie had died. They had been at a sheep sale at Rothbury and were attempting to walk home to Ewartly Shank after abandoning their tractor in a snowdrift.

At the time of his wife's death John Heron was employed as the "husbandman" at Hartside. He worked for John Wealleans whose family had owned Hartside and Greenside Hill since at least the 1820s. John and his brother Christopher lived at Flotterton near Rothbury, and were renowned breeders of Cheviot sheep.

Together with others they were instrumental in the formation, in 1891, of the Cheviot Sheep Society. Both are mentioned in the first Flock Book (volumes I and II, 1893), a beautiful publication, bound in red leather. It was established to provide a reliable record of the pedigrees of Cheviot sheep, their qualities being "hardihood, utility and beauty".

When John died his brother Christopher took over the two farms and employed Tom and Jane Clark to look after his interests at Hartside.

Two letters written in 1904 provide a fascinating contemporary account of the daily comings and goings in the valley a century ago.

They were written by Tom and Jane's grand-daughter Jeanie, to her mother Maria. Jeanie and her younger sister Annie lived at Milkhope but boarded with their grandparents at Hartside so they could attend Ingram School. Jeanie's formal education spanned only four years, from the age of 9 to 13. The letters were written when she was 12.

That they have survived is thanks to Jeanie's daughter Hannah Hutton, who lives in Rothbury. When her mother died in 1975 she came across them in a box destined for the bonfire. They had been kept in a dressing table drawer; Hannah had never seen them before.

Painstakingly written in pen, on ruled pencil lines, they are remarkable for their detail and use of words, some no longer in everyday use. The punctuation is sparse, some words are missing. The letters are copied from the originals, still in Hannah's care, the lay out, spelling and grammar as Jeanie wrote. (The girls always used their pet names: Jeanie was christened Jane and Annie, Agnes.)

Hartside 24th 1904

Dear Mother
I got your card and glad you are
well as we are all well here
and at school every day and getting
on fine now our cows both calved
together yesterday morning the gray
cow has a hard udder but the
quey has not she gives what
serves the calf as yet is so Granda
is not going to Whittingham mart
tomorrow but is going to take her
to Wooler next mart
as we have the calves it is next
Monday the 2nd. Dot says she will
be out soon some Sunday they
have got the corn all in the cattle
is not going away till may. Jim Redpeth was
here with cake and Meggie went to Flotterton with
him, Kitty sent word twice for
her to go she is coming back
tomorrow we are going to a meeting at Ingram this
afternoon
at three o' clock how are they getting
on with lambing it is grand
weather for it George will be pleased with the lambs.
They have got a daughter at
Castle Hill I am going to get
emulsion from the store but
I am quite better no cough
at all Etty Drummond has been at Blakehope a few days
so no more at present with kissies
xxxxxxxxfor you and Dad + bab +
Nettle. we had Mowitt he is
coming your way in a fortnight
he said. much love from Annie.

Sunday night
Dear Mother. We have not
gone to the meeting as it is to windy and stormy
we have got two pigs home last night. Taylor is giving
7 pence for eggs. How is little
Jack getting on with the
lambing. Is the quey doing well I will send a P.P. Card some
day soon. So look out.
Annie is very idle. So with love to all. From Jeanie.

She added a postscript in pencil:
I know the clock now
The school Mrs is coming up to tea tomorrow night
Grandfather has got the
Front gardon set a heavy rain 5 oclock.

An extract from Jeanie's letter dated 24th 1904.

Glossary.

Whittingham Mart was adjacent to the Bridge of Aln hotel (on the A697) and close to Whittingham Station on the Alnwick to Cornhill railway line. The mart closed many years ago.

Quey - a Scottish word for a heifer, a young cow.

A hard udder is a symptom of mastitis. It can compromise the cow's ability to rear a calf, depending how many 'quarters' of the udder are affected.

Cake - cattle food.

George was Jeanie's younger brother. Having just recovered from measles he got soaked walking home one night and died very suddenly, in his sleep, aged 17.

Emulsion - an old word for cough medicine.

The store - The Hedgeley Co-Operative Society shop. It is now part of the Breamish Hall at Powburn.

John Mowitt - the travelling tailor from Rothbury. He came to the valley twice a year and measured the men for suits. He generally stayed for a week spending two or three nights with different families.

School Mrs - Miss Emily M. Crawley, teacher at Ingram School from 1900-1905.

PP card - picture post card.

Meggie - most probably Jeanie's cousin.

Castle Hill - a shepherd's cottage near Alnham.

The staff circa 1910. The young boy in the front is Andrew Chisholm, father of Robbie Chisholm, who was later the postman and then postmaster at Powburn.

Hedgeley Co-operative Store from a postcard franked 1904.

Hartside July 19. 7. 1904

Dear Mother

Just this to let you know Granny got your letter today + Annie and I got each a Pictorial today and Maggie got
two so our collection
is getting up. We spent
a lovely week end at Miss Crawley's, On
Saturday, after having
a picnic at Peggy's bridge we went to the
top of Ingram Hill and
had a nice view down
the country and after
we went and gathered
heather bells, we went to church twice on
Sunday and came
home on Monday night
we went to the (top) of Fawdon
Hill at (night) we saw the price of the cow in
the Daily paper and think it was a good one
Pollie coming in the 13th
of August so we will
be at (home) for our holidays so we wont see her how
is georgie getting on wanting his cowie.
Grandfather has
been out for a load
of peats. What fine weather we (have) just now.
I had a letter from Susan she is getting on
fine. When is the men
going to start the hay
Annie + I has 97 Pictorial now + Maggie has 177 now.
Mrs Buglass is at Linhope and her
five children
and they have all had the hooping cough
but Doctor says it won't
smit now they have
had it 2 months but
we are all never near them.
I must close as it is bed
time so with love
from Jeanie + Annie
We will write before
we have to come home.

Pictorials and Peggy's bridge feature in Jeanie's letter of July 19th 1904 to her mother.

Glossary.

Smit - an old-fashioned word for 'spread' as in catching a cough or an infection.

Susan was a friend who used to live at Alnham Moor. Her parents John and Mary Douglass had 13 children. After John's death in 1901 Susan moved with some of her family to West Harle, near Cambo.

Pictorials - Were they collectable cards similar to those that came in packets of tea or cigarettes, if you had two the same you swopped one for another you hadn't got, or perhaps they were similar to a comic? If only Jeanie had explained.

By May 1906 Christopher Wealleans had died. His Cheviot sheep flock that numbered 2,200, was handed over at valuation to the new tenants, Messrs Ross of Berwick-upon-Tweed. Their values were fixed on an average of the previous 10 years market prices, the owner or his trustees undertaking to buy back the stock at the end of the tenancy. Auctioneer Mr. Robert Donkin, junior, did the valuation and settled the sum of 59s 6d on the ewes and lambs at Greenside Hill, and 57s 6d on those at Hartside.

It was an accepted practice for hill sheep to remain on a farm, even if it changed hands. The sheep were "hefted" to their grazing areas, having been born and bred there. They knew where they belonged and rarely strayed. If unfamiliar sheep were turned out onto an open hill they would be quite lost.

In August 1906 the Wealleans family's long connection with the Breamish Valley came to an end. Hartside and Greenside Hill farms were put up for auction and sold to Major Joicey, of Linhope, for £17,000.

The Clarks left Hartside the following May. Jane was almost 80. Her grand daughter Annie was still at Ingram School just before then. An entry in the logbook dated February 22nd noted that "Agnes Anderson outside the 3 mile limit had not returned since Christmas". Her name was taken off the register but two weeks later she was back at school. Jane Clark died at Fawdon in 1920 in her 94th year. She and Tom are buried at Alnham.

Major Joicey soon made his mark on Hartside. On the opposite side of the road to Tom and Jane Clark's house he built a big detached house on the site of old farm buildings.

Modelled on a hacienda, it had long overhanging wooden eaves which the swallows nested under. He added a plaque on the gable end wall. It depicted a miner, from his waist upwards, with a pick in his right hand and a lamp in his left. Underneath was a fancy scroll.

A rare postcard of Hartside franked 1905 shows how the farm had looked in the Clark's day, their old house with the earth closet down the garden. Exactly when the house was demolished is not known, but it had gone by the mid 1920s. Only the earth closet remained.

The forgotten view of Hartside showing the Clark's house, the netty down the garden and the row of old buildings where the farmhouse now stands. The barn, the tall building on the right, housed a threshing machine driven by water from the pond.

It was used for various things over the years, a shed for garden tools and a sheep shelter, until it was knocked down in the late 1990s. Present day shepherd Malcolm Elliott said that he - and others too - were mystified as to why the netty was so far from the house and across the road.

When the postcard surfaced at a fair in Leeds in 2002 it solved a mystery that had puzzled some folks for years.

In 1921 Samuel and Sarah Thompson returned to Greenside Hill where they had first met and courted some 30 years earlier. At that time Samuel was one of the hired lads who lived in with Michael Nichol, a respected shepherd and "a very successful breeder and exhibitor" of Christopher Wealleans' Cheviot sheep. Sarah helped in the house. She was one of the Anderson girls from Milkhope.

By the time they returned to the valley Samuel and Sarah had a big family, five girls and four boys. Some were married, others working or helping relations but the youngest children Sam, Lizzie, Mary, Sarah and Winnie came to Greenside Hill. Samuel worked for Mrs Joicey, of Linhope. As the householder he looked after the two farms of Greenside Hill and Hartside, helped by of three or four hired men and later his son, Sam.

Sarah was 12 and Winnie, eight, when they started at Ingram School. The worst part was the hour-long walk in all weathers. They liked to get away quickly in the mornings to get round the Knock End, out of sight of the other children who walked from Linhope and Hartside. They always shouted and waved and wanted the girls to wait. That made them late for school and they didn't have a good excuse because they didn't live so far away.

The school day started at 9 o' clock with prayers and scripture followed by arithmetic. All the children took their own lunch, carried in a bag on their back, and a tin bottle filled with cocoa.

Greenside Hill circa 1920s. A horse is working in the hay field behind the house. Pikes of hay can be seen dotted across the top of the field

GREENSIDE HILL

Ingram School pupils circa 1921. Winnie *(middle row)* **and Sarah** (*back row*) **are circled.**

At half past eleven the bottles were put on the hob beside the fire to warm up ready for lunchtime. Nobody's bottles got mixed up because your initials were scratched on the tin.

When Winnie and Sarah left school they stayed at home to help their mother, it was quite the accepted thing to do.

The first job of the day was the milking, at 7.30 in the morning. The four house cows were milked by hand in the byre next door to the house. It took about 10 to 15 minutes to do each one, sitting on a small low milking stool, squirting the milk into an enamel pail. Everything was kept scrupulously clean. The utensils and milk cans washed and scalded every morning and again at night after evening milking. Before separating machines were invented, the milk and cream were separated by hand using a slotted ladle. The separator did the job more efficiently.

The girls looked after the hens and chickens and, for part of the year, the three pigs; they were fattened on a diet of mashed boiled potatoes and meal, mixed with the left over separated milk.

For three years water for the house and animals too was carried in pails from the spring on Hartside Hill across the road. When Mr. Robinson bought the farm in 1924 he laid a piped supply to a new tap in the pantry. It was a great novelty.

The weekly routine altered little. Monday was traditionally washing day, whether it was wet or dry. Greenside Hill was one of the few places that had an outside washhouse with a set-pot, heated by a fire below. It saved the palaver of carrying boiling water from the range. Whites were washed first, boiled in the set-pot with soap flakes scraped from a bar of very hard soap. Most clothes were washed in a metal tub and 'beaten' or pummelled with a wooden poss stick to get them clean. The washing was rinsed, turned through the mangle rollers and hung up to dry preferably outside, or on two fixed pulley lines in the sitting room.

Butter was made on Tuesday, 'churning' day. The time it took very much depended on the consistency of the cream, and that varied from cow to cow. The cream was turned in the churn until it massed together. Then it was put into a wooden butter tub for washing to remove any traces of churned milk. This could taint the butter and affect its keeping qualities. To begin with the butter was washed in the spring, later under the coldwater tap. Salt was added and worked in with wooden patts or 'spades' held in each hand. The butter was cut into blocks, shaped and patterned with the patts and weighed if it was to be sold. Finally it was wrapped in greaseproof paper and stored on slates in the pantry to keep cool.

Wednesday was baking day, the range 'fired up' to get the oven really hot. The secret was to get the fire 'to draw', the fiercer the better. Soot was cleaned out from under the oven and bricks at the side of the fire removed. This directed the heat straight to the oven. Metal rods or dampers were pulled backwards and forwards to create a draught. Hopefully, it 'drew' after that! Usually 15 loaves were baked at a time followed by oven scones and cakes. Rock buns were a great stand-by because they were easy to make. At the weekend girdle scones and dropped scones were baked on a griddle over the fire.

On Saturday mornings, more often if needed, the kitchen range, the steel fender and the big fire irons were 'blackened' with polish and rubbed 'til they shone.

With as many as five men living in the house meals were prepared in copious quantities and eaten around a big kitchen table. Most food was home produced but in the 20s and 30s several local trades people travelled the valley, their horses and carts gradually replaced by vans.

Two butchers' delivered: S.J. Dodds from Glanton and Scott from Whittingham. George Ewart travelled for Dixons, the Whittingham grocer, and also bought suitcases full of draperies. Two brothers called once a week with a bakery van and Tully the carrier from Alnham collected surplus butter and eggs. Maughan the fruiter from Rothbury came on a Monday night. His van had a wooden frame on the back covered with sacking which he threw up onto the top so the fruit and vegetables could be seen. Sweeties, and pomegranates when he could get them, were the children's favourites.

Often there were extras to feed because the travellers usually called at mealtimes. They knew they would be fed and the men would be in the house. That meant better business. Old Bessie and Job Angus came from Glanton in a horse and cart. They sold voluminous shirts out of a very big hamper. Stocking Willie's son sold quality menswear - thick woolly vests and long johns - and lengths of Galashiels tweed. To begin with he rode a bicycle, the pack on the front wrapped up in Moroccan leather to turn the rain.

At shearing time there were more men to feed. In the mornings Winnie and Sarah carried refreshments, 'the 10 o' clock', up the road to Hartside, a mile away. The men clipped in an open-fronted shed in the yard which had been used for generations. Over the years different shepherds had carved their initials into the wooden beams. After clipping, the sheep were 'busted' or marked with the initials "JH", standing for "Joicey Hartside". The men walked down to Greenside Hill for dinner and the girls carried tea up the road again in the afternoon.

Mr Thompson was a good father but Victorian in outlook and a strict Presbyterian. On Sundays, provided the river wasn't in flood or the weather too stormy, the family went to church at Branton travelling by horse and trap.
As a young girl Mrs Naomi Church, watched the scene from her home at Ingram Rectory.
"I shall never forget the sight, I can see it today, of the mother and father, they were staunch Presbyterians, going to the meeting at Branton every single Sunday.

"They had a horse, and trap with large wheels, and they used to come down the valley in their Sunday best, immaculate, Mr Thompson in his bowler hat and Mrs Thompson with a fur probably and always usually in black, and gloves. They would sit on this high trap facing the horse and the three daughters would sit with their backs to their parents, facing backwards, and also immaculately turned out in their clothes, gloves, everything.

"They would go down to the meeting and come back, I suppose they wouldn't get back much before 2 o' clock, you could see that from the Rectory because you could see the bridge in those days. They were very Victorian. I should think those girls were brought up with very strictly Victorian manners, as I was."

With so much to do at home Winnie and Sarah were rarely away. They went to Alnwick, and sometimes Newcastle to buy clothes. During the summer they supported the local village shows, often winning prizes in the industrial tent.

Occasionally the older daughters went to dances but Mr. Thompson did not approve. Before the village hall was built, in 1929, dances were held in the schoolroom. It was a tight squeeze, just enough space for three sets of eight, with the violinist sat up on a windowsill. That was the band.

The Girls' Club was also held in the school, run on similar lines to the Womens Institute but without the rules and regulations. Mrs Allgood, the Rector's wife, was in charge. She organised practical demonstrations such as cake icing and chicken trussing which the girls were then expected to try. Sarah vividly remembered making a man's shirt by hand. With an inner lining as well it was a very laborious job.

The greatest pleasure in Winnie's young life was attending the embroidery classes on a Thursday afternoon in the village hall. Mrs Allgood did the organising and arranged for a lady from the

The Thompson girls *(l-r)* **Mary, Agnes, Winnie, Lizzie and Sarah "the Flowers of the Breamish Lasses"**, an accolade accorded them in a light-hearted piece of contemporary poetry which rated the beauty, or otherwise, of 'the lasses' living in the valley then.

Northumberland Handicrafts Guild to take the class. Winnie's finest piece of work was a beautiful tablecloth. It took a winter to make, much of the tiny, intricate stitching, "drawn thread work", done in the evenings, at the kitchen table, by the light of an oil lamp. When it was displayed at an exhibition in Newcastle it was awarded a medal.

Winnie and Sarah had fond memories of Mrs Joicey's last few years at Linhope. There were some happy, social occasions: dances in the garages at the end of the shooting season and tea parties for the schoolchildren in the lodge.

When Sarah was 21 she left home and went to keep house for her brother, Jack, who farmed in partnership with their uncle at Lumbylaw, near Edlingham. In March 1937 Mrs Thompson died aged 67. Mourners walked for miles through the snow to her funeral at Ingram.

Two years later the family left Greenside Hill. Winnie was not especially sad. Her father wanted to retire and the house was not the same without her mother. There was also the dreadful prospect of a quarry opening up on the eastern end of Hartside Hill with associated blasting and noise. Mr. Robinson who owned the two farms had struck a deal with a builder who had quarries at Embleton and Wooler. As it happened the plan never got off the ground. The county council decided that the Ingram and Peggy Bell's bridges were not strong enough to take the heavy traffic.

During the war years Walter Brown (the "summer laddie" at Linhope) worked as a shepherd at Greenside Hill. He lodged with the Goodfellow family, Lawrence and Annie and their sons Willie and Douglas.

Every year the 1,000 or so Cheviot ewes were taken to Lorbottle Hill, 12 miles away, for a two-week summer holiday. They walked there and back. Walter remembers them, three telegraph poles deep, along the Alnham to Netherton road. Usually Willie Goodfellow lodged near Lorbottle and checked the sheep every day, but one summer Walter travelled to and fro daily on a motorbike. There was no routine dosing then and the change of grazing, from grass onto clean heather, helped break the worm cycle. After the long walk home the sheep looked like whippets but their tummies soon came back with the bite of fresh grass on their hill.

In the summer of 1942 Lawrence set off to take salt licks to the hill but never returned. He tragically collapsed and died and was found at night by Walter and Willie. The valley experienced its second wartime air crash on the night of January 9th 1943 when a Wellington bomber came down on the Cunyan Crags, a rocky outcrop on the south east end of Dunmoor. The countryside was white with snow, the burning aircraft lit up the night sky for miles around.

At Langleeford, in the neighbouring Harthope Valley, Nellie Crerar had just finished milking the newly calved house cow for the third time that day. She came out of the byre and saw a glow over the hills. Thinking a plane had crashed, but not wanting to worry her neighbour Jessie, she said nothing. Jessie did exactly the same. With young children in bed, asleep, and all the men away from home, it was an anxious time. If the plane had crashed on the hill above the farm there might be survivors. What would they do if any Germans walked down to the farm? They both went indoors and waited. When one of the men returned from Wooler they were most relieved; he told them the plane had crashed on the Breamish side of the hill.

Only one member of the all-Polish crew survived. He walked to Hartside where the Oliver family had been getting ready for bed but were now preparing to walk up to the crash. There was a loud knocking at the door and, fearing Germans, Alex Oliver picked up his gun. The Pole was a very tall man built like a stag. In broken English, and with great difficulty, he explained that his four fellow crew-members were dead.

Early next morning the two shepherds from Greenside Hill took PC Jack Inchmore to the scene of the crash. He warned the locals to stay well away, which they did, for a while.

The bodies of the aircrew and other sensitive equipment were removed by RAF personnel. However, the snow made it impossible to lift the plane. It lay on the hillside for another fortnight guarded by soldiers from the Scottish Rifles "the Cameronians". They were supposed to camp in tents but an upstairs granary at Hartside offered more shelter in the wintry weather.

For local lads the crash site was a treasure trove. Basil Oliver of Hartside was a teenager then - and paid frequent visits to the wrecked bomber.

"The bullets were in great long strings, you took so many off and took them away and hid them. There was always ammunition lying about even when they were removing the plane.

"You stuck the bullet into a keyhole and bent it until the bullet snapped out the end of the cartridge. We took out the fine yellowy strings of cordite, laid it in lines then we'd get another cartridge and loosen two or three strands of cordite so it stood proud of the top. We'd put this line of cordite to it and light the end. It ran blazing along this trail of cordite to the cartridge."

Similar amusement was derived from an old syrup tin filled with paraffin. A long piece of thick, hairy string was slotted through a hole in the lid and the end set alight.

"I've seen us tie two or three cartridges together and put the tail end into the flame. Then bang. You had to stand well back but it was great fun. We were often up at the crash. The more mementoes you could get the better. We took bits into school, it was all documented."

After the war the two farms changed hands again and were bought by Mr. Houseman of Linhope. Alex Oliver and his family had lived at Hartside since 1924. Mr. Houseman asked him to stay on to look after general maintenance work on his estate, draining, fencing and rebuilding the dilapidated walls.

Several fields around Hartside and Greenside Hill are quite special in appearance, bordered by stonewalls rather than fences or hedges. That they have survived to this day is largely due to the time Alex spent rebuilding and maintaining them all those years ago. Walls were once a common sight in the valley, dating back to the days of 'the enclosures' in the late 1700s. Most tumbled long ago, largely through neglect, to be replaced by fences.

Hardy Belted Galloway cattle, black with a broad band of white around their bellies, were kept on the hill and

Next door neighbours *(l-r)* **Alex Oliver, Hartside, Willie Goodfellow, Greenside Hill and Jack Smith, Alnham Moor.**

Mr. Houseman bought Alex a pair of coloured horses for farm work, one black and white, the other brown and white. They were an eye-catching team because most draught horses then were plainly coloured.

For reasons best known to himself Mr. Houseman removed Major Joicey's plaque of the miner from the gable end wall of the house, much to the dismay of the Oliver family. Alex would have kept it but it broke into pieces and was beyond repair.

When Alex retired and moved to Wooler, his son Ronnie took over doing similar work to his father but with a tractor, not horses. The family's time at Hartside spanned 64 years and ended in the late 1980s when Ronnie and his wife June moved away.
A time of change lay ahead in part connected to the revival of Linhope as a shooting estate and also to the arrival of All Terrain Vehicles or quad bikes as they are usually known. As tractors had revolutionised farming in the 1950s and forced the disappearance of the draft horse so the new four-wheeler bikes were to put shepherds out of work and change forever the traditional ways of shepherding.

Malcolm Elliott was 16 years old, just out of the Duchess High School at Alnwick, when he started work as a shepherd at Hartside, employed by R.W. 'Roland' Telford. The date is one he never forgets: May 4th 1987. Shepherding was in his blood. His father, grandfathers and uncles had all herded the hills and that was all Malcolm had ever wanted to do.

Malcolm with Bracken and Sweep on the quad bike. The dogs travel in a box attached to the back seat of the bike.

Initially he looked after 500 Cheviot sheep and some cattle while Derek Charlton of Greenside Hill shepherded the 1000 or so blackfaced sheep on Dunmoor. They both walked everywhere.

The first quad bike was shared and bought to use, instead of the tractor, for feeding sheep. It caused much less damage to the land. After melting snow or heavy rain when the ground was particularly wet, the tractor tyres carved deep unsightly ruts that took a long time to heal.

The bike was a great novelty and a timesaver but its capabilities were not initially fully grasped. On one occasion the shepherds went to gather Dunmoor and the bike saved them a good half hour's walk to the bottom of the hill where they left it. After gathering on foot and bringing the sheep home they had to walk back out to collect the bike because they never thought to take it up the hill! When a large parcel of land was returned to the Linhope Estate Derek was made redundant.

Now Malcolm shepherds about 1500 sheep single-handed, 'looking' them twice a day in the summer, once a day in the winter, and sees to the routine worming and injecting which protects them from several fatal diseases. Thanks to the quad he covers a big expanse of ground in a matter of hours which leaves him time for other jobs: the tractor and cattle work, repairing stonewalls and fences, and catching moles.

The ewes are pregnancy scanned and those expecting twins are given bigger rations. Near lambing time they are bought into fields. It has meant an end to the time-consuming task of walking ewes and twins off the hill.

Malcolm's brother Jimmy is also employed by Roly Telford as a shepherd at Branton Eastside, near Powburn. At busy times of the year, when there is clipping, dipping and gathering to do, the brothers help each other out. After the hectic spell is over, Malcolm takes his only week's holiday of the year (although he is entitled to more) to catch up on the housework and gardening.

The modern day hill shepherd is a jack-of-all-trades but Malcolm is still, first and foremost, a shepherd. His interests, apart from playing rugby for Alnwick 'seconds', sometimes the 'firsts', are to do with sheep. He likes sheep and sometimes shows them, and likes talking about sheep. But with fewer shepherds around and usually only one at any place there are not the opportunities there used to be to 'crack' about sheep - except with his brother.

When more shepherds looked after fewer sheep and had more time to do it, they knew or 'kenned' every individual ewe, its mother, even its granny. Malcolm 'kens' his sheep, especially the Cheviots, his favourites, but admits he couldn't tell you who granny was!

9
The Old Road and the New Wood

Below the house at Greenside Hill, on the opposite side of the road, a small burn of the same name flows east and joins the Breamish. In October 1949 it rose to unprecedented heights after heavy rain. Huge sections of the road beside it were gouged out making it impassable for all traffic. The only way through was to walk.

An excavator was bought in and just 10 days later the new road was finished, further up the hillside, away from the burn. Traces of the old road are just visible today, but it is mostly covered over with grass and rushes.

The valley landscape has changed visibly over the years with the planting of several woods. Old black and white postcards and sepia photographs show quite different views without the trees.

The most noticeable is the big coniferous plantation on the hillside below Brough Law. Planted by the Forestry Commission in 1966, aesthetics were not considered, nor were the two 2000-year old archaeological sites consumed within it. A proposal to clear fell the wood and allow it to revert to open hill land is pending.

Close to the wood are the tumbled walls that surrounded an old L-shaped plantation. Some of the original thorn trees still stand today. The plantation was felled during the 1930s by a contracting firm from Blyth. Initial attempts to roll the timber down the hillside were not a success, so lorries were used instead.

After the flood: looking east towards Ingram Glitters.
(© The Nortumberland Gazette)

Another block of conifers was planted, also in 1966, on the steep hillside upriver from Peggy Bell's Bridge. Its location may well present problems when it is ultimately felled.

In the 1920s, Major Basil Bryant who owned Ingram Farm planted a new wood, one mile west of the village, where the car park and toilets are today. The man who actually planted the trees was a "Mr. Bowlby". Over the years the pronunciation and spelling of his name changed to "Bulby". Now it is always known as "Bulby's Wood".

The wood was hit by strong gales on New Years Day in 1970 and subsequently felled. Replanted with a mix of deciduous and coniferous trees, it forms a useful shelterbelt for the adjoining field, which is probably why it was planted in the first place.

The coniferous wood just west of Ingram was planted in 1935, the year of King George V's silver jubilee, hence its name 'Jubilee Wood'. Local lad Jimmy Swanston planted the trees but never lived to see the wood mature. He died on active service during the War. Over the years the name 'Jubilee' has been lost and it now known as the 'Cattle Grid' wood.

The view towards Greenside Hill. (© The Northumberland Gazette)

In March 2000 a large tract of land on the north side of the valley, at Reaveley Ewe Hill, was fenced and planted with trees under a conservation scheme submitted by the landowners, the Allgood Estates.

Extending from the Knock End to the car park at Bulby's Wood the upland woodland was planted to meet 'national targets in bio-diversity'. It attracted grant aid from the Forestry Commission and the Northumberland National Park Authority. The trees are native broadleaves: oak, ash, birch, alder, willow, rowan and juniper. It is hoped they will have positive conservation benefits, at best providing a habitat that will encourage the return of Black Grouse to the area.

Reaveley Glitters, and the archaeological sites within the fence, were not planted. The new wood will change the face of the landscape, again, when the trees mature. At one time, of course, some seven or eight thousand years ago, the entire valley would have been covered with mixed woodland.

Skew Bridge for Major Joicey, in Hennebique Ferro-Concrete, at Peggy Bell's Ford, Linhope, Northumberland.
Span 70 feet. Carries 24 ton Steam Roller Built with river gravel and cement only.
I. C. JOHNSON & CO.'s PORTLAND CEMENT.

10
Peggy Bell's Bridge

The majestic span of Peggy Bell's bridge across the Breamish is a well-known landmark in the valley. Designed on a skew, with a span of 70 feet, it sits below the steep scree slopes of Ingram Glitters, at the site of an old river crossing once known as Hunt or Hunters Ford.

In its day, in 1908, it was a very modern bridge. A picture postcard, which turned up at an antique fair in Morpeth, reveals some interesting facts that are not apparent when looking at the bridge today. The postcard, known as a 'trade' card, was used by I.C. Johnson & Company to advertise "Portland Cement". The Company had cement works at Gateshead-on-Tyne. The card features a photograph of the brand new bridge and says it was constructed in Hennebique Ferro-concrete. This was a new method of reinforced concrete construction, perfected by Francois Hennebique, and introduced into Great Britain in 1897.

Perhaps this explains why it has stood up so well to the ravaging floods and spates compared to other bridges over the Breamish. The card also reveals that the bridge was built with river gravel and cement only and was strong enough to carry a 24-ton steam roller!

Another postcard shows a view of the new road bridge and an old wooden footbridge, 200 yards downstream. Built on two wooden piers, all that remains now is a wooden stump in the river. It was the footbridge and not the road bridge that was Peggy Bell's bridge. Washed away and reinstated on numerous occasions, the footbridge on the postcard was not the original Peggy Bell's bridge but the last of several erected at the same spot, all known by the same name.

The new bridge was commissioned and paid for by Major Joicey of Linhope (See chapter Linhope) but never acquired his name. Initially it was known as the Hunt Ford Bridge. With the demise of the old footbridge (whether it was washed away or fell down I do not know) the new bridge became known as Peggy Bell's bridge.

Who was Peggy Bell? Where did she live, and why were the footbridge, and sometimes the ford, given her name? There are several stories.

One is that she lived at Hartside and raised a public subscription to build the bridge because there was no safe crossing point for pedestrians. The row of stepping-stones beside the ford would be impassable if the water was high.

Another story goes that Peggy Bell lived at Greenside Hill and took tea to the workmen who built the road bridge. This does not stand up because we know from written evidence that the old footbridge was known as "Peggy Bell's" long before the road bridge was built.

Going back to 1893 after a severe thunderstorm on Bloodybush Edge (see chapter The Cloudburst) a correspondent with the local paper reported: "I came to Peggy Bell's bridge which is also wrecked."

Two months later, in the "Glendale Parishes Magazine" we read: "The (road) bridge over the Breamish here (at Ingram) is rapidly approaching completion and when finished it will be a great boon to the district. What is wanted now is a bridge over the ford further up, better known as Peggy Bell's. The cost of a bridge here could not be great all that is wanted is someone to take the matter in hand."

Five years later in October 1898, the Alnwick and County Gazette referred to flood damage following a storm. "Many trees have been uprooted, telegraph wires blown down and much destruction was caused by the large flood in the Breamish. Peggy Bell's Bridge, above Ingram, was carried away (and) a great hole was washed in the roadway threatening the foundations of the new iron bridge at Ingram."

The view upriver showing the footbridge with the new road bridge in the background.

New Bridge, Linhope Road. 8310

More supporting evidence that the old footbridge was connected to Peggy Bell comes in the letter that Jeanie Anderson wrote from Hartside in July 1904 when she referred to "having a picnic at Peggy's bridge."

A commonly held view is that Peggy Bell drowned, either in the vicinity of, or off, the footbridge. We read in Tony Dickens' book "The River Bridges of Northumberland. Volume 1" "Apparently in the winter of 1906, a young maid who was in service at Great Ryle, had decided to make her way home during a storm which had brought the river Breamish into full flood. "Before the present bridge was constructed the river at this point was spanned by a wooden trestle type bridge and, as the young maid crossed this bridge, it suddenly collapsed and pitched her into the river where she was tragically drowned. This young maid was called Peggy Bell, and when the present bridge was erected it was in her memory that it was named."

If this was the case why did nobody living locally remember the incident and why was it never reported in the paper? Such a tragedy, occurring as recently as 1906, would surely have been remembered. Several people who have helped me with my research, and whose families had lived in the valley for many years, were adamant there had never been a drowning.

When Annie Grey drowned at Brandon in 1890 the local paper carried an account of her disappearance and later her inquest (see chapter Brandon Ford). The story of Peggy Bell's 'drowning' contains striking similarities to the true story of Annie Grey; notably that she worked at Great Ryle and was on her way home.

Personally I go with the story told to me by Winnie and Sarah Thompson who lived at Greenside Hill. Their mother told them that Peggy Bell raised a public subscription to build the bridge. It is quite credible because Mrs Thompson's family roots and connections with the Valley went back a very long way, to her childhood days at Milkhope in the 1870s. Perhaps she had heard the story from her mother.

Jack Hope, formerly head warden of the Northumberland National Park, was told, although he cannot remember by whom, that Peggy Bell helped the children to cross the river, presumably on the stepping stones, on their way to Ingram school. (The school opened in 1834). The first bridge, according to Jack, was built with timber from the Collingwood Estate at Lilburn. It hung on chains, rather like a water-gate, and moved with the flow of the river. The two viewpoints, Winnie and Sarah's and Jack's, seem to marry together.

In Ingram churchyard, outside the east window is a big plain headstone now showing signs of weathering. It is the final resting place of Margaret Bell and her husband Andrew who lived at Greenside Hill, where he was a shepherd. Margaret was only 44 years old when she died on April 4th 1849. She had suffered from an obstruction in the bowels for eight days and her death certificate recorded "not certified", in other words she had not been seen by a doctor.

Living locally and taking into account her age and the time the school opened, perhaps, just perhaps, this shepherd's wife was 'Peggy Bell'. Despite many years of research I have not come across any written evidence that could provide a definitive answer to the question everyone asks: who was Peggy Bell?

Just beside the bridge, running along the bottom of Ingram Glitters is a track which once carried the Breamish Valley Railway! It was an affectionate term given by locals to the little quarry line that operated for two or three years during the Second World War.

Scree was raked down the hillside and shovelled into tubs that were pushed by hand along a metal track. The stone was tipped into lorries at a small loading dock, which can still be seen today, at the end of the bridge. The stone was used to build runways at the small airfields that sprung up in Northumberland during wartime, the nearest being at Milfield, north of Wooler. The railway provided good fun for the local lads, when the workmen weren't there, of course. They met up in the evenings and pushed each other in the tubs, and ran off if one tipped up!

The tracks and tubs went long ago but the site is still used once a year for the start of the famous Hill Race on Ingram Show day in September. Bobbie Blain organised and started the race for more years than he cares to remember. When his white handkerchief dropped the runners scrambled up the steep scree slope to the hill fort on the top. After that it was downhill all the way to the finish at Bulby's Wood. Bobbie is now retired and James Shell of Brandon starts the race with a starting pistol.

The route is marked by flags from the top of the hill down to the finish. Originally the marking was done on foot but now a quad bike makes it much quicker. In 2002 the course marker's bike rolled away from the top of the Glitters and bounced down the hill to a sorry end. Luckily for Graeme Nelson he was not on board, unlike Black Tom the huntsman.

In a sporting tale of the Borders entitled "The Shadow on The Moor", Alan Ian, the eighth Duke of Northumberland (1918-1930) tells how Black Tom, the huntsman, became the hunted; pursued by The Shadow to the edge of the Glitters where he plunged, screaming, to his death in the river below.

All that remains of the footbridge today.

11
Early Days in the National Park

The grassland or haughs bordering the river Breamish near Ingram have been a favourite destination for summer visitors for upwards of fifty years.

Post war, as increasing car ownership enabled people to get away from their homes, on Tyneside and the pit villages of south-east Northumberland, many discovered the 'Ingram Valley'. With lovely scenery, clean fresh air and the river to paddle in, it was a cheap day out. Families came year after year.

The favourite picnicking spots were beside Peggy Bells Bridge, Bulby's Wood and further down the valley on the grassland near Ingram Bridge. On fine weekends in the mid to late 1950s as many as 3,000 visitors would descend on the valley.

Such a huge influx of people was not without problems as local farmer James Wilson of Ingram knew only too well. With no public toilet facilities the haystacks in the fields and the bracken beds on the hill were used instead. Few took their litter home. By evening the picnic sites were a mess.

Bill Cook shepherded much of the ground that the visitors used, and regularly ran the gauntlet of unruly behaviour. Dogs ran off leads and chased the sheep. On one occasion he was punched as he intervened to rescue a large lamb being manhandled into a car boot. Air rifles and guns were fired at the scree slopes, so Bill took to doing his round later at night, when the people had gone.

In 1956 a solution to these issues appeared to be just around the corner following the creation, or designation as it was termed, of the Northumberland National Park. It was the ninth, of a total of ten parks, set up in England and Wales between 1951 and 1957.

A report by John Dower, in 1945, first outlined the concept of National Parks.
He defined them as: "an extensive area of beautiful and relatively wild country in which the characteristic landscape beauty is strictly preserved, access and facilities for public open air enjoyment are amply provided, wildlife and buildings and places of architectural and historic interest are suitably protected while established farming use is effectively maintained."

The definition was accepted by the National Parks Committee in 1947 - the year John Dower died - and enshrined by parliament in the National Parks and Access to the Countryside Act 1949. The Countryside Act of 1968 expanded the concept to include "the economic and social interests of rural areas".

The boundary of the new Northumberland National Park extended from the Cheviots in the north to the centre of Hadrian's Wall in the south and covered 398 square miles (255,000 acres, 104,000 hectares). Mainly hill land, a countryside of far horizons and distant views, it included the upper and middle reaches of the valley but not the lower part from Ingram Bridge to the main road.

Now that a statutory body was in place, with responsibility for access and visitors, Mr. Wilson hoped a solution could be found to the problems at Ingram. In September 1956 he met his local M.P., the Conservative Viscount Lambton, to tell him at first hand of the anti-social behaviour and to suggest that a warden service was urgently needed.

Viscount Lambton raised the matter in Whitehall with the Ministry of Agriculture and soon received an answer from the parliamentary secretary, Alick Nugent.

"I am sorry to learn from your letter of 27th September of the trouble your constituent Mr. J. Wilson has experienced from some of the visitors to the Northumberland National Park. "I have a great deal of sympathy with Mr Wilson and I am asking Enoch Powell, whose Department is primarily responsible for National Parks, to pass his suggestion about a warden service on to the Park Committee. I hope it will be possible to provide a warden; I understand that those appointed in the Peak District have been quite successful".

Nugent said he would raise the matter with Mr E.P. Harvey, Clerk of the Park Committee at County Hall, Newcastle-on-Tyne and would "ask the Committee to do everything possible to promote better conduct among visitors".

On 30th October 1956 Enoch Powell wrote from the Ministry of Housing and Local Government (telephone Whitehall 4300) to Viscount Lambton:

"Dear Tony,
"Nugent has sent me a copy of his reply to your letter about the behaviour of some visitors to the Cheviot area of the Northumberland National Park.
"The National Parks Act provides for the appointment of wardens for patrolling land to which the public have been accorded access by an agreement or order made under the Act and in relation to which byelaws have been made.
"Such a warden service attracts grant aid under the Act. There is no similar provision for appointing wardens to patrol land to which there has been traditional freedom of access whether by prescriptive right or by the courtesy of landowners. This is one of the points we shall have to look into when amendment of the Act is under consideration.
"Meantime a system of voluntary wardens has been organised in the Lake District National Park to help in dealing with litter and the North York Moors Park Planning Committee has arranged for the Farndale area to be patrolled by voluntary wardens in the daffodil season. I cannot say whether it would be possible to organise anything of this kind in the Cheviot area, but I am bringing Mr Wilson's representations to the notice of the Northumberland National Park Committee and of the National Parks Commission.

The typed letter from Enoch Powell to Viscount Lambton.

Yours Enoch"

In December, the local county councillor Harry Wardale, who farmed at Akeld Manor, near Wooler, wrote to Mr. Wilson after raising the matter at a Commission meeting.

"The National Park Commission are doing their utmost with other government departments to think out an answer but it is not easy to educate or control some members of the public.

Enoch Powell hits the weak spot as the Act now stands and voluntary wardens in this area would be very hard to find.
"I hope the National Park Planning Committee through Mr Harvey may think of something. I gather the NFU are in touch with them just now.
The only real joy at the moment is the weather. Long may it last."

Mr Wardale's pessimism was justified. It was six years later, in 1962, before there were any real changes at grass roots level. A part-time warden was appointed to help deal with the visitors but he did not stay long.

The job was advertised and two local men, Jimmy Givens and Jack Hope were the only applicants. They agreed to a job share working alternate weekends for the summer season from Easter until the end of October. Although they didn't know it at the time their future careers were to follow very similar paths and they were to spend many years working alongside each other.

Jack was a gamekeeper, employed by a private syndicate that had shooting rights over the Allgood Estates. He and his wife Monica had lived at Reaveley since 1955.

Jimmy was born and bred in the valley, and still lives at Woodbine Cottage in Brandon, home to three generations of his family. His mother worked for the Allgood family at Ingram Rectory. His father Will was a woodman on the Allgood Estates following in the footsteps of his father James who had come to Brandon in 1898.

After leaving Branton School in 1946, Jimmy worked with his father and helped replant the woods at Reaveley Greens and Brandon that had been felled during the war.

In 1961 he started a new job as the first and only pest control operator with the newly formed Aln and Breamish Rabbit Clearance Society.

Myxomatosis had cleaned out the rabbit population in 1948 almost to the point of extinction. However pockets gradually re-appeared and by 1960 rabbits were again widespread. All the old rabbit catchers had either retired or found new jobs.

Share certificate issued by the Aln and Breamish Rabbit Clearance Society.

The Rabbit Clearance Societies were partly funded by the Ministry of Agriculture. It paid fifty per cent of the costs, the biggest being Jimmy's wage and the purchase of Cymag gas. Once a cheap way of controlling rabbits its use is now restricted by health and safety regulations.

Farmers formed their own societies with a committee. The Aln and Breamish extended from Roseden in the north to New Moor House in the south and from Rothbury to East Bolton. Membership was not compulsory but most farmers joined, and paid so much per acre per year. Hill ground cost less than more valuable arable land where rabbits could cause serious damage to crops. There were about 50 farms in the local society.

Jimmy visited each one a minimum of four times a year. He was essentially his own boss and, rather like flexi-working now, managed to combine pest control duties with his new job as warden.

Back in the summer of '62, parts of the valley looked like a supermarket car park. Families and friends met up and one car followed another, rather like sheep, to a favourite spot. The cars were tightly packed, everybody picnicked close to their vehicle and few people walked anywhere.

Initially there were no byelaws and the wardens' powers were limited. People camped overnight and lit bonfires and Jimmy remembers many a late night trying to settle arguments as one family tried to get children to sleep while others had transistor radios blaring.

Many people were confused by the term National Park. They thought, as some still do today, that the land was owned by the nation and they could do as they pleased. They did not realise it was privately owned and that they were there only through the goodwill of the landowner and farmer.

The wardens' main objectives were to spread the word about the Country Code, and to deal with the litter. They did this in an informal but effective way. Each car was handed a strong brown paper 'trash' bag for their rubbish and that gave the wardens the opportunity to speak to the visitors.

An early National Park handbook, price 2/6d, described the Country Code as a "code of behaviour which all who enjoy visiting the country will realise is largely a question of common sense and courtesy, but unless it is observed the beauty and prosperity of the countryside could easily be impaired."

It stated the obvious: that burning matches or cigarette ends could start fires, uncontrolled dogs could cause trouble and loss, especially at lambing time, and litter could severely injure animals and destroy other people's pleasure. And it pointed out that fast cars, on country roads, were a danger to animals and people alike.

Jimmy and Jack prided themselves on the fact that if you came to the valley on a Monday morning you would never know there had been any visitors over the weekend. The picnic sites were pristine.

Visitors did have some advantages. They bought free-range eggs from Mrs Wilson, the farmer's wife, and homemade butter and cream from Mrs Cook, the shepherd's wife. The extra money was most welcome. Local children were quick to catch on that pocket money could be earned. They opened and shut the gate at Ingram, where the cattle grid is now, and were sometimes paid as much as 3d or 6d a time - until Mr. Wilson put an end to their entrepreneurial efforts.

In November 1962 the local National Park planning committee, then part of Northumberland County Council, agreed to buy the old school building and teacher's cottage at Ingram for use as an information centre and warden's accommodation. The school had closed in 1958.

A report to the committee members highlighted the continuing problems with visitors:
"During fine weekends in the summer one of the most popular spots in the National Park is the part of the Breamish Valley around Ingram where large numbers of motorists tend to congregate by the river and picnic on its banks.
"Although the land has little agricultural value, being largely poor pasture with scrub and small areas of naturally regenerated trees, it is nevertheless private property and is used by the farmer as grazing for sheep.
"This leads to a natural conflict of interests and the committee have endeavoured with some success to limit the amount of damage and inconvenience caused to the farmer by employing

Jimmy Givens *(left)* pictured with Jack Hope, his wife Monica and daughter Phyllida at the opening of the Information Centre in August 1963.

part time and voluntary wardens. At the same time they have had to bear in mind their responsibility for ensuring that areas of open country are available for the purposes of recreation."

As a direct result of the continuing visitor pressure it was agreed that a formal access arrangement was now justified and, the following year, negotiations were opened with Ingram Estates and the Duke of Northumberland. Byelaws would be drawn up that would give the wardens legal powers to stop overnight camping.

By the spring of 1963 the school and house had been purchased for £700 and contractors were employed to carry out minor repairs.

The new centre was the first permanent information centre in the Northumberland National Park. It was opened on Friday August 2nd, two months later than planned, by Alderman the Rev R.E. Robson, chairman of the National Park planning committee. Among the guests was Mrs Pauline Dower, OBE, widow of the late John Dower, whose report had been instrumental in the formation of the National Park. She was present in her capacity as vice-chairman of the committee but she was very much a local lady, being a daughter of the late Sir Charles Trevelyan, of Wallington Hall, near Cambo.

The centre was to be staffed at weekends and holiday times by members of the voluntary warden service.

The Whit weekend of 1963 had been exceptionally busy with more than 3,000 people visiting the valley daily and a large number camping. Another report to the committee said: **"An influx of this magnitude raises very serious difficulties for the local farmers who use the land for sheep grazing, and (it) is envisaged that some help will have to be given to them when the proposed access agreements are completed."**

In February 1964 the committee agreed that a permanent warden was needed. The old school house was to be extended, at an estimated cost of £2,800, to form a three bed-roomed bungalow, and a Land Rover was deemed the best type of transport for the new warden. The cost of the vehicle, together with an annual salary, was estimated at £1530.

On May 14th 1965 Jack Hope started work as the first full time warden in the Northumberland National Park. His patch covered the entire Park, 398 square miles, and whilst he alternated his visits to different places much of his time was spent at the Roman Wall trying to placate farmer fed up with the growing numbers of visitors.

Now that byelaws were in place campers could be told to leave. This was not without its problems. Some had used the valley for years and became cross and argumentative when asked to move on. A campsite with no facilities was established in the field next to Jack's house. During the pit holidays some families stayed for two weeks; trying to keep them and the site in order was hard work. Later Monica opened a shop, selling basic groceries and sweeties, in the former school canteen.

The National Park Search and Rescue team was set up in 1963 after two shepherds perished in the snow near Ewartly Shank. The equipment, including a stretcher sledge, was kept at the Information Centre. Jack led the team for many years, and that time it was composed entirely of full time or voluntary wardens.

When gales destroyed the temporary toilets, two huts with Elsan buckets at Bulby's Wood, the committee was pressed by Glendale Rural District Council to build permanent toilets in the valley. Eventually chemical toilets, with tanks underneath, were built at Bulby's Wood and Ingram Bridge. Together with new car parks they cost almost £6,000. The price had escalated considerably because the initial "simple design" did not meet with approval by the National Parks Commission.

In 1974 the county council formed a joint National Park and Countryside Service and appointed Mr. A.A. 'Tony' Macdonald as the first National Park Officer. The move was to herald many changes, not just on the administrative side, but on the ground as well.

By now Jack was head warden following the appointment of a full time warden on the Roman

Jack, in white shirt and tie, studies a map on the bonnet of his Land Rover.

Wall. In 1975 Jimmy Givens became the full time warden for the Cheviot area of the College, Harthope, Breamish and Coquet valleys. Jack was the first to introduce guided walks, initially on Hadrian's Wall and in the Cheviots, but later throughout the Park. He usually went to the top of Hedgehope or Cheviot while Jimmy led short five-mile walks in the valley. Walking was becoming more popular and it was an opportunity to educate visitors about the countryside. There were frequent stops when Jack and Jimmy would point out interesting flora and fauna.

In the late 1970s new staff were appointed to fulfil the aims of the first National Park Plan. All specialists in their chosen field it was their job to promote and develop the key issues of planning, farm conservation and education. High priority was given to visitor services with emphasis on interpretation and information that would give people a greater understanding of the Park.

In 1982, after 18 years service to the National Park, Jack took early retirement and Jimmy stepped into his boots.

Many footpaths and rights of way were still unmarked and one of Jimmy's early jobs was putting in stiles and way markers. What he enjoyed most was leading the High Hills walks. They covered 10-15 miles in the real high hills country of the National Park and often you never saw another soul. The walks required fitness, an ability to get on with fellow walkers and a desire to learn about the countryside.

To walk with Jimmy was a very rewarding experience. He often took walkers to places where there was no automatic right of access but he had asked the landowner's permission first. Thanks to Jimmy a lot of people, myself included, actually walked the far horizons and were introduced to the wealth of flora, fauna and bird life about which he knew so much. Such was the popularity of his walks that he acquired a devoted band of followers nicknamed "The Boghoppers". They rarely missed a day.

By 1982 the Valley was attracting 100,000 visitors a year but the numbers visiting the information centre had fallen from a peak of 15,000 to just 7,700. After 20 years it was in need of upgrading, the display cases of stuffed birds and animals past their best. The National Park officer believed that the large number of visitors to the valley merited the best information centre and facilities that the committee could provide.

In the summer of 1983 plans were unveiled to build a new £153,000 centre at Ingram Bridge with catering, information and conference facilities, a shop, bunkhouse and a big car park. The announcement led to a head on clash between the National Park and the local community. The ensuing fight was to rumble on for nearly ten years.

The justification for a purpose-built centre hinged on two main issues: firstly that the proposed site would be prominent and accessible, the location of the old building, tucked away at the end of a narrow lane, was considered a drawback. Secondly, it would be more cost effective to build a new centre than modernise the old one. It was envisaged that the new centre could attract 40,000 visitors a year.

Locals were furious. The proposals were condemned as a waste of taxpayers' money, environmentally unacceptable because woodland would be felled to create a car park, and the close proximity of the site to the bridge and a 'blind' corner would be a traffic hazard. They argued that the number of visitors did not justify a new centre and called for the existing building to be modernised, at much less cost.

A joint working group was formed but there was little common ground. Residents formed an

Jimmy's daughter Angela presenting a bouquet to the Dowager Duchess of Northumberland at the Centre opening in 1994. Fellow pupils from Glendale Middle School at Wooler look on. Councillor Eddie Teasdale, for many years the chairman of the National Park committee, is pictured beside the door.
(Photo: Jean Givens)

action committee, raised petitions, lobbied National Park committee members and gained a high press profile with numerous stories and letters in the local papers. Legal advice was sought and prominent public figures drawn into the wrangle: the Ombudsman, the Secretary of State for the Environment and local M.P., the Rt. Hon. Alan Beith.

Alternative sites in the valley were mooted but ruled out for various reasons. Wooler was considered by many to be the best place for a big centre to serve all the Cheviot valleys, but that idea too fell on stony ground.

On two occasions the plans were shelved because of spending cuts but never formally withdrawn. After four years of relative quiet they surfaced again in November 1989. The National Park and Countryside committee was recommended to approve them but at the eleventh hour the Duke of Northumberland intervened.

Mr. W. F. P. Hugonin, agent for the 10th Duke, said that Northumberland Estates were not willing to lease the land for the new centre because of widespread opposition to the proposals. "After very careful consideration and taking into account that the views were not only of the local people but were more widely spread than just the valley, it seemed clear that there was a huge swell of opinion against an information centre being built there."

The objectors were delighted. The goodwill of the valley residents towards the thousands of visitors had been severely tested by the confrontation. By 1991 a £200,000 refurbishment package had been agreed. However there was still total opposition to the car park extension and eventually the plan was dropped.

On May 25th 1994 the centre was formally re-opened by the Duchess of Northumberland, widow of the deceased 10th Duke. Ten years later, on August 2nd 2004, exactly 41 years to the day after it first opened, Ralph Percy, the 12th and present Duke of Northumberland officiated at another opening ceremony when the "Decade of Discovery" exhibition, featuring finds from the Breamish Valley Archaeology Project, was unveiled in the old school classroom. (See Chapter "And Did Those Feet in Ancient Times..")

The 2004 opening ceremony (l-r) **National Park archaeologist Paul Frodsham, Alan Voutt, of Brandon, and the Duke of Northumberland beside the Cup and Ring marked stone discovered by Alan in the gravel quarry at Powburn.**

Jimmy retired as head warden in March 1993 after 30 years service to the National Park. His job was becoming more office based, which he did not like.

Both Jack and Jimmy were happiest 'in the field', meeting the public either on a guided walk or at one of the many evening talks and slide shows they gave. Great naturalists and botanists, they are above all true countrymen.

During their careers with the National Park both were awarded the British Empire Medal, Jack in 1976, Jimmy in 1992. The citation to Jimmy highlighted several aspects of his life: as a warden with the National Park Authority, pest control officer with the Rabbit Clearance Society and his 22 years service as a magistrate at Alnwick. It also mentioned his contribution to the local community as secretary of the Games Club and long time supporter of the floral classes at Ingram Show.

In 1997 the National Park became a stand alone Authority, separate from the county council, with responsibility for its own budget. The National Park officer is now known as the chief executive. Administration rests with a big committee of co-opted and elected members, and a staff of over 50 at the Hexham headquarters.

Much water has passed under the bridge since 1962 when just two people in the council's planning department were responsible for organising and promoting the new Northumberland National Park.

Jimmy and Jack live just a few doors from each other in Brandon. In his retirement Jack trains gundogs, while Jimmy still does some part-time work for the Authority, cutting the grass around the car parks at Ingram Bridge and Bulby's Wood.

Today many more people are walking the hills, drawn by the wonderful landscape with its great sense of space and solitude. Others come just to picnic or barbeque beside the river, bringing their children to the same spot they visited when they were young. The wardens are called rangers now but they still deal with the same issues, overnight camping, dogs off leads and the litter. Perhaps 'trash' bags would be a good idea again.

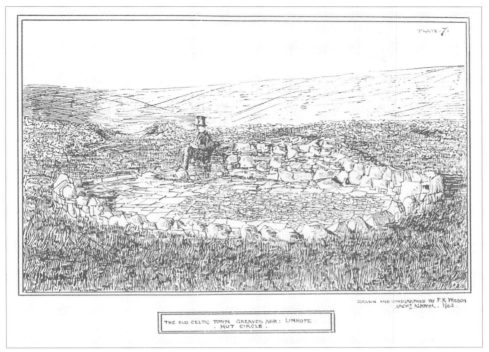

PLATE 7.

DRAWN AND LITHOGRAPHED BY F.R. WILSON
ARCHT ALNWICK, 1862.

THE OLD CELTIC TOWN GREAVES ASH: LINHOPE. HUT CIRCLE.

Lithograph of the Victorian gentleman at Greave's Ash.

12
"And Did Those Feet in Ancient Times..."

The opening lines of William Blake's "Jerusalem" come to mind when walking the hills of the Breamish Valley. Before your eyes, beneath your feet, is a very special landscape rich with evidence of earlier civilisations; of people who lived and walked "upon England's mountains green", who died and were buried with their ancestors.

The Valley has been home to mankind for at least 8,000 years. From Mesolithic man who roamed the hills, hunting and gathering, through to the Bronze and Iron Ages, the Roman, the Saxon and the Medieval eras, up to the present day.

One ponders the intangibles: what languages those ancient people spoke, what they looked like, how they dressed. Who knows for certain? Their tangible legacy is a wealth of archaeological remains that have survived, virtually undisturbed, into the 21st century. Unlike many other historic landscapes the Breamish Valley has, with one or two exceptions, escaped the blight of modern ploughing and large scale tree planting, and is now acknowledged as one of the finest of its kind in England.

The most visible and best-known landmarks are the hill forts so named by the Victorians. Many have remains of roundhouses within their ramparts. Whether they were actually defended military sites or rather symbols of status and power is open to conjecture. With commanding views of the surrounding countryside they are now protected as Scheduled Ancient Monuments. It is a criminal offence to damage or destroy them.

Stepped cultivation terraces contour the hillsides, good examples can be seen on the western end of Heddon Hill and the Ewe Hill above Ingram. They were man made and crops were grown on them as in Mediterranean countries today, when the climate was warmer than it is now. They may have been in use in prehistoric times.

Hidden under the bracken or amongst the tussocks of 'white' hill grass it is easy to miss some of the less obvious archaeology: tumbled heaps of stones and curiously shaped mounds and hollows, often loosely identified on maps as "earthworks" or "homesteads". Other features are best seen after a light fall of snow or when the sun is low and casts long shadows over the landscape: Ancient boundaries and field systems, now just low grass covered ridges, snake over the ground, and broad strips of rig and furrow ripple the terrain, evidence that large areas of hill land were once under the plough.

The first archaeologist known to have excavated in the Valley was George Tate in the 19th century. In Victorian times there was a great desire to learn more about the ancient races, "primeval humanity", as Tate termed them, who had inhabited the countryside. With little knowledge to go on, the only way to find out was by digging "the traces they have left of themselves....their habitations and sepulchral monuments".

From the mid 19th century ancient remains in North Northumberland were excavated on an unprecedented scale. Legal protection was afforded to prominent historic sites, castles and suchlike, from the early 1880s, but no one had yet been enlightened to the protection of more humble antiquities in the landscape.

All that was required for a dig was the landowner's permission and most were agreeable. Archaeology was a fashionable subject amongst educated country gentlemen of the day and there was always the possibility of a 'find' to display on the mantelpiece. However, excavations were often hastily done, quantity not quality was the key-word, the recovery of artefacts the main aim.

Whilst archaeologists sought to learn from their excavations, to others the heaps of stones scatted over the hills were just that. They were of no recognised worth except for building. By the time Tate carried out his excavation at Greaves Ash, near Linhope, in the summer of 1862 much of the ancient Celtic town had disappeared.

"The dilapidations made by man have been more destructive than the elements, for the walls have been a quasi quarry, where stones have been taken to build fences and houses and hence little more remains above the surface, than the foundations of the fortifications and dwellings." He dug at other sites in the valley including the hill forts at Brough Law and Chesters and excavated several burial cairns otherwise known as barrows or tumuli. It seems he was too late. They yielded nothing except burnt wood that led him to conclude they had already been opened. Indeed he knew that an urn had been found in a barrow thirty or forty years earlier, and that large quantities of stone had been plundered to build a wall around a five-acre plantation on Ingram, most probably the South Plantation near the top of Ewe Hill. "The probable inference from them is, that the early inhabitants of the valley disposed of their dead by cremation, and that a tumulus, or funeral pile, was raised over the ashes."

It was to be more than 150 years later that irrefutable evidence was found to support his views.

Tate meticulously recorded his findings in a lengthy report illustrated with fine lithographs and drawings.

Looking north over the ancient landscape of Haystacks Hill, a Romano British settlement on Ingram Farm.

He thanked three local gentlemen for "their occasional aid in directing the excavations" and acknowledged a Mr. Coulson for his "zeal and intelligence in superintending the workmen" who presumably did the digging.

Now recognised as Northumberland's first great landscape archaeologist, Tate forgot to mention two things in his report that would have been of interest to know today. One was the exact location of the barrows he opened and the other is the name of the Victorian gentleman, complete with top hat, shown sitting on the wall of a hut circle at Greave's Ash. Perhaps it was Mr. Tate himself.

Much later, in 1943 and again in 1956, Professor Hogg excavated parts of the settlement at Ingram Hill. An interesting contemporary report, written by Miss Isobel Purvis, the headmistress of Branton School, survives.

"I heard that an archaeologist with students was excavating the site on Ingram Hill. With his permission, the children and I walked over the Fawdon Hills to see what was being done and what a thrilling experience it was for all of us.
"The site lay partly uncovered….I stepped down and stood on the stones - the flat "crazy pavement" laid by hand 2,000 years ago. I saw the post holes of the doorway and the burnt central stones where the fire had been. I held in my hands a fragment of pot that we saw dug out of the rubble - a pot fashioned perhaps by a woman's hands all those years ago. I found it awe inspiring."

By the early 1970s when George Jobey undertook limited excavations at Brough Law and Ingram Hill, radio carbon dating was coming into vogue. Settlements could be dated with much greater accuracy.

During the late 1980s the Royal Commission on Historic Monuments undertook an extensive aerial and ground survey of the upper valley. It revealed hundreds of features not previously recorded, indeed many were not visible on the surface at all.

This survey, coupled with the appointment of the National Park's first archaeologist, Paul Frodsham, provided the springboard for the ambitious Ingram and Upper Breamish Valley Landscape Project, later renamed the Breamish Valley Archaeological Project.

A joint venture between the Northumberland National Park Authority, the archaeology department at Durham University and the Northumberland Archaeological Group, the project started in 1994 and was scheduled to run for five years.

Its remit was to focus on the archaeological landscape as a whole, as opposed to monuments in isolation and it had two main aims: to establish a chronological framework for human activity in the valley from earliest times to the present day, and to interpret the findings in a meaningful way so that visitors could enjoy and understand the archaeology.

As it happened things turned out differently. The project celebrated its 10th anniversary - and its swansong too - in 2003. Its findings have exceeded wildest expectations, evoked memorable newspaper headlines, and were a key factor in saving the valley from inappropriate gravel quarrying.

Dates have been pushed back thousands of years, exquisite artefacts unearthed and great insight gained into the landscape and the people who lived there.

A comprehensive account of the project is expected in 2006 but meanwhile it merits two full chapters in Paul Frodsham's recent book "Archaeology in Northumberland National Park". The book includes reports on numerous excavations but for Paul the Breamish Valley project has been the most exciting and rewarding.

In 2004 a permanent exhibition was opened at the Ingram Visitor Centre. It is fitting that some of the finds are at last displayed in the locality where they were found: to be seen and enjoyed by locals and visitors alike.

What follows is not an exhaustive chronicle of the Project, the finds and excavations, but more a look behind the scenes at the people who made it all happen.

The Roundhouse

Peter Topping making notes in the excavated roundhouse. *(Photo: Sue Brophy)*

The outline of the ancient roundhouse emerged gradually into the dry summer of August 2003. Hidden beneath the cropped turf on Wether Hill for two millennia it was a humbling sight.

Not perfectly rounded, ten metres by nine in diameter, its' shape was clearly defined by angular packing stones set into a trench. The timber uprights of the walls would once have been wedged between them.

Archaeologist Peter Topping contemplated the scene and used his imagination: the height of the roof, how far it overhung the walls, whether it touched the houses next door. Was this semi detached living Iron Age style? Three hollows or scoops on the floor, big enough to sit in, contained a hazel nut and some burnt bone. Perhaps they were early store cupboards or maybe ovens. And the deep hole in the bedrock beside the sandstone hearth: a geological fault or a cooking pit that could be filled with boiling water?

Many questions will never be answered. Whilst the technique of radio carbon dating can age organic material such as charcoal and grain to within a hundred years or so (the variation is excusable when dealing in millennia) archaeology is by nature largely a science of informed guesswork and speculation.

For Peter, an exiled Geordie living in Cambridge, the sight of the roundhouse represented mission accomplished: the culmination of ten years work by the Northumberland Archaeological Group on Wether Hill above Ingram. Since 1994, with the exception of 2001 when the hill was out of bounds during the foot and mouth crisis, the Group's annual dig has focused on the hill fort, a scheduled ancient monument containing 17 roundhouses, and the landscape around it.

For ten days every August the usually quiet hilltop, home to blackface sheep, curlews and skylarks, becomes a hub of human activity.

Before the dig gets underway a vast array of equipment is hauled to the site: wheelbarrows, buckets, stepladders, gas cylinders, measuring poles and plan frames. An excavator is used to strip turf from a secondary trench overlying a nearby palisade enclosure. It takes a fraction of the time that it would by hand. However, its use is forbidden on the hill fort itself and the turf overlying the roundhouse is removed manually with spades.

A makeshift gazebo appears on the skyline next door to 'the kitchen', a weatherproof bothy ingeniously constructed from turves. This is Gordon's domain. A retired maths lecturer, he is the self-appointed chief cook and bottle washer on all the digs. It was, he discovered, easier to do the job himself than explain over and over again the finer points of boiling kettles on a gas stove in a Wether Hill wind.

The car park at Ingram Bridge starts to fill in the early morning as the volunteer taskforce assembles for the dig. Some commute daily from Tyneside, Alnwick and Morpeth while others make a holiday of it and stay locally in cottages. Shoes are swopped for boots, rucksacks swung onto backs. Most walk the mile up to the dig, singly or in twos and threes, taking in some field walking on the way, their eyes quick to spot fragments of flint or pottery lying on the newly ploughed soil.

The four-wheel drive vehicles follow: Peter in his Land Rover followed by NAG president John Nolan and Jenny Vaughan, both professional archaeologists, in a specially hired pick up. Their ageing transit van was thought unlikely to survive another year of the rough hill track.

Some people hitch a lift but the priority cargo is drinking water, plastic containers full of it, for tea and coffee and to prevent de-hydration in the hot summer sun. The number of diggers varies from day to day, usually between 15 and 30; there is no three-line whip. They are everyday people in everyday occupations: teachers, students, an artist, a gun dog trainer, retired businessmen, grannies and granddads. Several rent allotments (an inherent love of digging?) and they all share a common interest in antiquities and ancient remains.

For some the dig has become an annual pilgrimage, an occasion not to be missed, such is their enthusiasm and love for the hill. They know the area intimately and can recall earlier excavations: details of trenches, the prehistoric cord rig ploughing, the cross-ridge dyke and the burial cairn. Others are trying their hand at digging for the first time and get a warm welcome. The sense of satisfaction and achievement at finding pinhead-sized grains of charcoal or excavating a posthole is reward in itself.

The essential attributes of a digger are imagination, required to bring history alive, patience, discipline, a sense of humour and a love of the great outdoors. The dedicated diggers work whatever the weather. On some days cold and soggy, on others shaded by sun hats, there are few concessions to comfort at 1016 feet above sea level on Wether Hill. In the dry windy conditions of 2003 when dust storms blew over the trenches, making digging almost impossible, goggles were issued: a one-off bulk buy from a DIY store.

Most of their time is spent on hands and knees (but sometimes heads down, bottoms up if the trench is on a slope) carefully scraping the ground with a plasterer's trowel (for those who have their own, a cherished possession), working the point around stones, closely examining the soil for any 'finds' however minute. It is slow, methodical work; getting your 'eye in' is important.

Finds suitable for carbon dating must not be touched by hand. Tiny grains of charcoal are slid into small, plastic bags, a label detailing where they were found. At £300 a time Peter is selective about what is dated. The samples are sent initially to East Kilbride in Scotland for washing and then, amazingly, to America because it's far cheaper than anywhere in Britain. The University of Arizona has a response time of three to four months whereas the University of Miami can return a date in less than 30 days.

End of dig party. The curved line of stones in the foreground is part of a series of palisade trenches excavated on the second site in 2003.
(Photo: Sue Brophy)

Prehistoric archaeology rarely throws up the dazzling finds that capture the imagination of the general public. Much of it is quite mundane; charcoal, fragments of pottery and flints, the odd bead or coin.

The single most fascinating discovery on Wether Hill was made quite by chance during the 1998 excavations of a palisade enclosure. At one end of the trench a small rectangular burial pit was uncovered containing broken pieces of decorated Beaker pottery from the Bronze Age. What was even more remarkable was the fact that part of the wooden oak lining was still intact after more than 4,000 years under the ground. This was C14 dated to 2250BC.

The ten days of excavations pass all too soon. As the dig draws to a close there is a sense of urgency to find just a bit more, another posthole, another clue, for 2003 would be the last chance, the last opportunity to dig on Wether Hill. On the final morning, Wednesday 27th August, work continued until lunchtime. At the roundhouse Pete was taking photographs from the top of a stepladder while John was finishing a detailed plan of the foundations, hand drawn and to scale it showed the exact situation of even the tiniest stones. Down at the second site Jenny was puzzling over the intersecting loops of palisade trenches trying to figure out where they started and finished, indeed, what they might have been used for.

At lunchtime, to Gordon's call of "grub's up", the dig came to an official end. With military precision spoil buckets were upturned, kneeling pads and trowels placed neatly on the top. It was time for the very last end of dig party.

Spread out on the grass beside the bothy was a feast of a picnic in one of the most magnificent settings imaginable: Tesco's delicatessen counter on the top of Wether Hill; strawberries, chocolates, tea or coffee to wash it all down. It was time to chat, to reminisce, to walk over the trench for the last time before saying goodbyes.

The following day the roundhouse was carefully backfilled by hand and covered over with turves. It may never be seen again. Whilst Peter could have stated a case for further excavations he believes it is morally right to leave something for future generations to find. Under his expert guidance members of NAG have helped to rewrite the history of settlement and occupation on Wether Hill, a landscape traditionally labelled as Romano British (100-400AD) but now known to stretch back to at least middle Neolithic times, 3500 years before the birth of Christ.

Riding over Wether Hill a month later faces and voices came to mind, a sort of mirage on the deserted hilltop. The cut turves were the only visible reminders of the dig. In time - and given rain - they will knit together finally returning the roundhouse to its past.

The Landscape Jigsaw

The Cast : *Paul Frodsham, overall project director; Max Adams, director, 1994-1998; Clive Waddington, director, 1999-2000; Peter Carne, Field Officer at Durham University, involved from the start as co-director and excavation supervisor and 2002-2004 as director.*

"The Stalwarts": Jane Gosling, museum education officer, Matthew Taylor, teacher, and Rachel Pope, lecturer, all Durham University graduates who have helped as supervisors more or less since the beginning. Also James Whitford, student digger and cook for most of the digs.

On an abysmal March morning in 1994, a group of two, maybe three people could just be made out huddled close to the ground in a bracken bed near the top of Ewe Hill on Ingram Farm. In the torrential rain and thick fog, visibility was poor. What they were doing or who they were was not immediately apparent.

Certainly it was not a day for man or beast to be hanging about, let alone on the hill. And then Max Adams stood up. Instantly the penny dropped. They were archaeologists doing the very first excavation of the Landscape Project, their attention focused on a low turf-covered ridge.

To a casual observer, in a landscape crowned with hill forts, the ridge would not merit a second glance. But archaeologists recognise it as a substantial ancient boundary, running from the back of the hill at Chesters Burn over the top and down to Ingram. It has no local name but appears to divide the fort at Brough Law from its neighbour at Middledean.

It was hoped that by investigating boundary features a framework could be constructed, the outer edge of the jigsaw, within which settlements and field systems could be placed.

In the event, that first trench cut into the Ewe Hill dyke revealed little; only that in its heyday it would have stood as "a low but substantial wall of granite boulders". Over the years it had tumbled, as granite walls do, because the boulders are unevenly shaped and quite unstable.

The three-day excavation merited just half a page in Max's first interim report. And the "appalling weather" got a mention too.

Excavation of food vessel urn containing cremated infant, Turf Knowe, 1996.

Excavations on Turf Knowe in the mid 1990s.
(Photo: Anne Hunter)

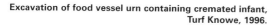

It was an inauspicious start but better was to come that summer when the old boundary again came into play during excavations on Turf Knowe, a shelf of flatish land, part way up the hill, with panoramic views down the valley. The aim was to see whether the boundary at this point was connected to adjacent rig and furrow and a "field clearance cairn".

From the beginning the student workforce has been an integral part of the project. Under Peter's supervision and with help from Rachel, Jane and Matthew, they must take credit for much of its success. Without the 300 or so students who have helped, the sheer scope of the excavations would not have been possible.

For those who found themselves on Turf Knowe it was an unforgettable experience. So great - and unexpected - were the discoveries that the excavations spanned four seasons instead of one.

The "field clearance cairn" turned out to be a sacred monument unlike anything ever seen before. Tri-radial in shape its stone "arms" emanate from a central point and are aligned roughly north, south-east and south-west.

Buried within it were two stone cists, one containing several cremations, a pottery food vessel and a fine iron spearhead. Archaeologists were able to say with certainty that it was used, albeit intermittently, for two and a half thousands years, from 2000BC in the early Bronze Age to 500AD, the Anglo Saxon period.

On the opposite side of the boundary wall a second cairn, barely visible prior to excavation, was discovered. A more conventional rounded shape, it too contained cremation burials, including one in a cist accompanied by a beautiful food vessel and several jet beads. An especially touching story accompanies one particular cremation: the tiny pieces of partially burnt bones placed in a food vessel urn belonged to an infant, about two years old, who had suffered from meningitis a few years before 2000BC.

For Paul the day of that discovery is still vivid. It was the time his second daughter was due to be born and for that reason he likes to think of the infant as a little girl.

The two cairns remain as landmarks on Turf Knowe and can be visited as part of the "Walk through Time", a way-marked trail over the two Ingram hills. Of other excavations, the settlement and field system at Little Haystacks (1998), the agricultural terraces below Brough Law (1999), the beautifully made stone floor at Middledean and the roundhouse enclosures at Fawdon Dean (2000-2002) nothing is now visible. The trenches were all backfilled.

The excavations of the agricultural terraces, extending like giant flights of steps up towards Brough Law, suggested that they were in use in the Bronze Age, but may have been re-used at various times thereafter.

The Fawdon Dean site was most interesting. On a grassy slope, with nothing visible above ground, two ancient enclosures had been identified from an aerial photograph. They stood out because the grass growing above the ditches stayed green during a dry spell whereas elsewhere it turned brown. Nothing was known about the site which had been ploughed in the 1950s with no remains reported.

Excavations revealed that the first enclosure was late Iron Age and contained at least three round houses. The second enclosure dated from the Roman period (circa 200AD) and a single Roman coin was found. This means nothing in itself other than to demonstrate that Roman influence of some kind extended right into the heart of the Breamish Valley.

Tea break at Ingram South on the final morning of the 2003 dig. *(l-r):* Matthew Taylor; Jane Gosling; Joseph Owen; Stewart Gardner; Sue Hackenbeck; Rachel Pope; Peter Carne; Charlotte O'Brien and Paul Frodsham.

The garden at Ingram Rectory, beside the churchyard, is now developed with holiday homes. It was excavated in dismally wet weather in 2001, when access to the hill was not possible due to FMD. Hundreds of sherds of pottery were found, all from the 13th century, the high tide of medieval agriculture in the valley. After the Border Wars broke out in 1296 the emphasis changed, from growing crops to keeping cattle.

During the project's lifetime several traditions have evolved: the archaeologists field teams for the fancy dress five-a-side football and the tug of war at Powburn Show and for three weeks every year are "regulars" at The Plough Inn. Their contribution to the local economy over the years is conservatively estimated at £40,000!

The annual talk in the village hall featured a slide show of the latest excavations and provided an opportunity for people who did not visit the dig to hear about it at first hand from Paul. Sometimes, bravely, he bought prehistoric pots and other fascinating objects for people to see.

Another less publicised event is the get together in the farmhouse conservatory over the now traditional 'glass' of white port! Some wonderful finds have graced the table; beautiful urns, food vessels, the fine iron spearhead from Turf Knowe and polished thumbnail-sized flints. Thousands of years old, quite irreplaceable, it is a humbling experience to hold them, always a relief to hand them back.

On August 15th 2003 the final dig of the landscape project was drawing to a close. The excavation trench in a field overlooking the village hall was unusually quiet and deserted. The 30 students, who as Paul pointed out were just eight years old when the project started, had gone home the day before. Only "The Stalwarts" and one or two others remained.

Under the hot sun, tea was on the boil in the shelter of a field roller, and the team was taking a breather, propped against tipped wheelbarrows, before the final photo shoot from an overhead platform.

Conversation turned to the dig. It had yielded little in the way of 'finds', the most notable being two beads-one polo mint-shaped, the other cylindrical - and a piece of metal that might have been the rowel of a spur or perhaps a brooch.

One feature however was generating much excitement. Overlying an in-filled ditch the archaeologists had found a floor made of clay and stone. Was this the missing piece of the landscape jigsaw, evidence of a "Dark Ages" settlement, 400-900AD, that up until now was tantalisingly absent? The reason for optimism was that the in-filled ditch had a radiocarbon date of 200AD from an earlier excavation. The floor must therefore be later. Further excavations were needed but that August morning time had run out.

Much written work and evaluation is still to be done before the final report is published, hopefully in 2006. With the project almost complete there is a question to be asked about the future of the exhumed cremation burials. Should they be retained for further scientific study or returned to their rightful resting place in the hills?

Today, in the 21st century, the hills overlooking Ingram Farm are still chosen by some as the final resting place for loved ones. With ashes interred or scattered to the wind, the mystical landscape provides a place of quiet remembrance similar, perhaps, to that experienced by our ancestors all those years ago.

Postscript

A final dig took place in the summer of 2004 to have a closer look at the floor. It was not the much-hoped for Dark Ages site, but a multi phase settlement occupied over five centuries from 300 BC - the Iron Age - until 200AD - in Roman times.

The sequence of occupation was very similar to the nearby sites of Fawdon Dean and Wether Hill, indicating that the hill above Ingram was quite densely populated at that time.

Peter Carne wearing appropriate wet weather headgear with Nelson at Ingram South, 2004. The dog accompanied archaeologist Rachel Pope on most of the digs. Nelson died aged 18 just a few weeks after this picture was taken. (Photo: Paul Frodsham)

13
The Hill Shepherds' Homes

On the hills overlooking the valley, quite off the beaten track, are three solitary homesteads, reminders of a way of life that is now just a memory. For generations they were the homes of the out-bye or hill shepherds who worked at Prendwick, Reaveley and Ingram farms.

A view of them all is possible only from the north-west side of Cochrane Pike, the highest point on Ingram Farm. Pause for a few minutes on the footpath and look to the west.

On a plateau high above the Breamish, you can see the two-storey house at The Chesters. Marked on Armstrong's illustrated map of Northumberland, 1769, it is the northerly outpost of Prendwick Farm, three miles away to the south. Traditionally a 'double herding', with a big acreage of ground to cover, two shepherds lived and worked there.

To the north of the river, on a horizon where the hill meets the sky is the cottage at Reaveley Hill Head. A rough track, through the fields and across the heather, links it to Reaveley Farm, a mile below. Beside the garden are the remains of an older house, framed by a stunted Scots Pine. From a distance it resembles a cockerel - or sometimes a camel - depending from where you look.

Looking east, down towards Ingram, is the cottage at Ingram Hill, with fine views down the valley. The least isolated of the three, just half a mile from the farm, it sits on the leeward side of the hill on a terrace of land overlooking Middledean Burn.

In the days before mechanisation it made practical sense for the hill shepherd to live in his workplace. Unlike in-bye shepherds, whose sheep were in fields, the hill shepherd's flock lived on the hill all year round. The ground he covered was often distant from the home farm, the herding done on foot or from a pony.

It was a remote lifestyle accepted by shepherds and their families until the middle of the last century when the tide of social change bought new aspirations. The basic facilities of the old homes were no longer acceptable but modernisation was not an economic option; their remoteness had become a liability.

In the mid 1950s the shepherds closed the doors for the last time. The Hornsby brothers, Herby and Bobby, left The Chesters; Bill and Ethel Cook came to a cottage in Ingram and Lawrence Goodfellow and his mother moved down to a house at Reaveley. The future of the hill shepherds' homes was uncertain.

Schooldays at The Chesters

Margaret Robson was thirteen years old when her family came to The Chesters on May 12th 1939.

The move was done in stages. The two house cows, her mother Margaret and brother Tom aged six, travelled to Prendwick in a wagon the night before. They lodged with friends nearby. Next morning the wagon returned with the second load: furniture, collie dogs, Margaret, her sister Hannah, 12, and father George. The girls helped walk the cows up the hill, and along the winding track, to their new home three miles away. Margaret's mother and Tom got a lift on the horse and cart, sitting beside the family possessions.

The Robsons had lived at Sourhope, a very isolated hill farm near Yetholm, Margaret found the Chesters quite civilised by comparison. From the back of the house, beside the old camp, she could look across the countryside and see other places, Alnham Moor, Hartside and Linhope.

Mr. Francis Octavius Chrisp owned Prendwick Farm. He employed George as householder and a hired man lived in with the family. The parlour, the good sitting room, became a bedroom in addition to another two upstairs. Downstairs the cement floors were as smooth as marble, the legacy of years of wear and scrubbing. Beside the kitchen was a 'bow-le-hole', a small door that coal was tipped through into the house.

It was many years since children had lived at The Chesters. Getting to school was a problem. By rights, because the house is in Alnham parish, Margaret, Hannah and Tom should have attended Alnham School. But it was four miles away, too far to walk twice a day.

The alternative was Ingram School, two miles away, but a tough walk over the hill. Initially there were hopes a taxi would be arranged to collect The Chesters children and others from Alnham Moor and Linhope. After six weeks when no transport had been resolved George decided that, car or no car, the children would go to school.

It was summertime. The children walked the whole way barefoot carrying their sandals and lunch bait in a bag. They had become accustomed to going barefoot at Sourhope, not because George and Margaret could not afford shoes, they just preferred it.

The walk from the house took them downhill to the Chesters burn where they jumped the water. Then a steep climb up the back of Ingram hill to the old plantation. After that it was downhill all the way, past the door of the shepherd's cottage at Ingram Hill, through the fields to the village hall and along the road to school. They followed the same route home but this time there were two climbs and they were often tired. The thought of a hot dinner kept them going.

To begin with much of the way was unmarked, the track from the Ingram end petered out on top of the hill. By walking the same ground everyday the children eventually made a path, which some local shepherds termed 'the school road'. On school mornings they left home at 8 o' clock, by which time Margaret had milked the cows. The walk took about an hour and often they were the first to arrive, Tom having run much of the way.

**The Chesters from the top of Ingram Ewe Hill.
Morning sunlight catches the slopes of Shill Moor
in the background.**

There was no school uniform then. Tom wore shorts, whatever the weather, and the girls' skirts and pinafores. However, there was a very specific rule about sandals that everyone had to wear in school. What the children thought silly was that in wintertime sandals could be left at school, but not in the summer. They had to be carried to and fro every day. From October to May the children wore Wellington Boots. It was a new experience. At Sourhope they had always worn clogs.

The children rarely missed school, only if the weather was bad or they were ill. One snowy morning Hannah and Tom set off by themselves, Margaret having left school by then. In late morning, as conditions worsened and the snow began to drift, George went to meet them out of school. Unbeknown to him they had been sent home early. He bumped into them somewhere on the hill in a 'whiteout', Tom hanging onto Hannah's coat, for fear they became separated. In those conditions the hill is a frightening place.

During term time the children posted letters in the letterbox at Ingram and Cecil Dunn, the postman, left letters at school for them to take home. In school holidays, if the children did not meet him, Cecil pushed his bicycle from Alnham Moor, down the meadow and up the steep narrow path on 'the back braes', now part of Cobden Wood. He freewheeled down on the return journey. It was quicker than walking.

The children's bicycles were kept at the cottage at Ingram Hill. Shepherd Bob Cowens made a special place for them in the 'keb house' beside the sheep pens.

When Margaret went to whist drives at Powburn village hall (upstairs in a granary behind the Plough Inn) she walked over the hill, collected the bike and cycled down the road. Afterwards she biked back to the cottage and walked home. During wartime all lights had to be blacked out at night, even the battery light on front of her bike. The top was covered with black tape making the beam so faint it hardly lit up the front wheel. She knew the road well but a moonlit night was a bonus.

The War made little difference to the children, with just one exception: their father's gun. It stood in the corner of the sitting room, not just any gun, but a 12 bore "Purdey of London", the crème de la crème of game guns. To be avoided at all costs. It belonged to Major Bryant of Ingram who organised the Home Guard. For a while George went to meetings but later the out-bye shepherds were exempted because it was a long way to walk. Major Bryant gave George the gun and cartridges to keep at home. It was never used.

When Margaret left school in December 1939, aged 14, she helped her mother for several months before getting the job as 'between maid' at Prendwick Farm. This involved working between the byre and the farmhouse: milking the cows, doing 'the separating' and helping the parlour maid. On the maid's day off Margaret served in the dining room but, to her great annoyance, when she had a day off the parlour maid did not do the cows. Margaret stayed for nearly three years, until her mother took ill and she was needed to help at home.

It was heavy work. Water for the house was carried from the spring, even after a piped supply was installed. The pipes were so rusty it couldn't be drunk nor used for washing in case it marked the clothes. She milked the cows, looked after the two pigs, and helped her father with the sheep, especially at lambing time.

No tradesmen called at The Chesters. Bread and most necessities were left at Prendwick. When the accumulator battery that powered the wireless needed recharging it was taken down to the farm. A lorry dropped off a full one and took away the empty one. The family's clothes were ordered from the J. D. William's catalogue, still in business today, and delivered by post.

Surplus butter and eggs were collected by the Glendale Stores grocery van from Gracie Oliver's cottage, opposite the school, at Alnham. Margaret walked there and back, five miles, carrying the produce in a big butter basket.

Mrs Robson suffered from recurring ill health. One night, Dr. Patterson had to be called out from Rothbury. George rode his shepherding pony, Jenny, to Prendwick to use the telephone. When the doctor arrived by car, a 12 - mile journey, he climbed onto the pony (she knew the way home even in the dark) and rode to The Chesters. After attending to Mrs Robson he stayed by for a meal before riding back to Prendwick. The next morning Margaret's mother was collected by a horse and cart and taken to the farm. From there a waiting ambulance took her to the Royal Victoria Infirmary in Newcastle.

There was no National Health Service, no routine surgeries and the doctor, together with any medicines he prescribed, was to pay for. It took a long time to get help; the air ambulance was undreamed of.

The family subscribed to the Ingram, Alnham and Powburn Nursing Association and, like everyone locally, supported the fund raising events, whist drives and dances held in various village halls.

When the war ended in May 1945 Hannah was working as a parlour maid at Linhope Lodge and Tom was moving to Brownrigg, a council-run boarding school at Bellingham. Two years later Margaret joined the Wrens, hopeful of seeing more of the country. She got as far as Reading, then a posting to a base on the Solway Firth near Carlisle, when her mother took ill. Again, she had to return home.

In 1949 Margaret got married and her parents left The Chesters. Ticks were starting to appear on the sheep, posing welfare and management problems that George did not want the worry of dealing with.

Postscript

The Chesters stood empty for ten years from 1957 until1967 when it was rented out to the 15th Whitley Bay Scout Group. It is used today by scouts and others as a base for outdoor activities, especially walking and camping. The youngsters stay for weekends and walk out to the house from Ingram or Hartside.

One day, whilst out walking, Margaret called in at her old home. The scouts showed her around. Apart from inside toilets, showers and washbasins, it was largely unchanged.

Reaveley Hill

Belle Armstrong vividly remembers the family's move to Reaveley Hill in May 1950. Her second baby was due in two months time and here she was, sitting on a tractor and trailer beside the furniture, carrying baby Brian in her arms, on the way up the hill to their new home

At the third gate that marked the end of the fields and the start of the hill the cottage finally came into view. It was still some distance off, at the top of the heather. Totally isolated, with nothing else around, just one thought crossed her mind: she knew she would be stuck. It was so different to the house she had left behind.

Belle's husband Bill was a shepherd at Fowberry Park, near Wooler, but the job was not to his liking. It was in-bye and he preferred the hills. Descended from a long line of hill shepherds, his grandfather had lived at Reaveley Greens, a small cottage up the road from Reaveley. Bill's father was born there and so was Bill. When the chance of a job came up at Reaveley Hill he needed no persuading.

Belle had not seen the cottage until the day she arrived. It was primitive even by standards then. The door (it was the only door at the back) opened into a lean-to scullery with a pantry at the other end. The sink had no taps, no piped water. It was to carry from the spring, 200 yards away.

In the living room was an old iron range made by "Henry Moat and Son Ltd Newcastle on Tyne". The centre of daily life, it was lit all year round, even on the hottest days of summer. The family slept together in the only bedroom. When it rained one corner of the room was really wet. Belle dried the wall with towels, and laid hessian sacks on the floor to save the mats.

A zinc tub in front of the fire served as the bath. The netty, a tin hut with a bucket, stood between the cottage and the byre.

Belle never left the cottage until her baby Madge was born in July 1950. At Dr. Bousfield's insistence she went to her mother's at Crosshill near Whittingham, for the birth, the doctor declaring that by the time the nurse got to Reaveley Hill the child would be walking! She came home two weeks later and walked up the hill pushing Madge in the pram. Brian was 13 months old, almost toddling, when Madge was born. Belle's days revolved around the children, the cooking, cleaning, washing and ironing.

She never went shopping. Bill was good at that. He cycled to Hedgeley Store with the monthly grocery order that always included four 6lb bags of Be-Ro plain flour. Like the butcher, the grocery store delivered to Reaveley Farm. Everything was brought up the hill by tractor. The family's food was all home made. Nothing came out of tins. Meals were cooked on the range, either in the oven or in a long-handled black saucepan that sat on a trivot over the fire.

Belle milked the two Shorthorn cows, morning and night, and made butter, washing it in water from the spring. Vegetables grew in the garden alongside the old gooseberry bushes that yielded bowlfuls of golden yellow berries.

Reaveley Hill Cottage from the third gate.

The paraffin stove was Belle's first labour saving device. For the first time she could boil the kettle without having to light the fire. Nappies were boiled in the set-pot beside the fire. Other washing was done in a zinc barrel filled up with buckets of hot water from the range boiler, the clothes pounded with a vacuum posser to get them clean.

The ironing also depended on a blazing fire, and a thick cloth to hold the red-hot handle. Flat irons and heaters were the forerunners of the modern iron, similar in shape but in two separate parts, both made of iron. The hollow outer case or slipper was smaller and chunkier than the white appliance we know today. It was heavy to hold and the iron handle quickly became hot.

A heater fitted inside. It was put into the fire until it glowed red then lifted out with tongs, put into the slipper and held in place by two wires. The problem was soot. If any specks were left on the heater they wafted out the open end and marked the clothes. Belle ironed with two heaters. As one cooled down, the other in the fire was ready to use. Progress came in the shape of a metal ironing box with a wooden handle. The heater was picked out of the fire with a poker and put into the box through a sliding trapdoor at one end. It effectively sealed the unit so no soot could escape. Later came a Calor gas iron.

The stone floors were scrubbed by hand and covered with proggy mats that Belle made from old rags. The light at night came from candles, paraffin lamps and the fire.

Bill herded the sheep on a horse called Polly. When specific tasks needed to be done he gathered them into the pens not far from the cottage. It saved taking the drove down to the farm. Neighbouring shepherds occasionally visited in the evening for a crack and some music. Bill played the melodion and could whistle a good tune.

For days at a time Belle spoke to no one except Bill and the children. It didn't bother her at all. She loved the peace and quiet of Reaveley Hill, the views of the hills and skies that stretched for miles. There were no neighbours, even the farm below was out of sight, but you could see buses and cars on the main road, four miles away, and watch traffic going up and down the valley.

Sometimes Robbie Chisholm the postman called. His visits rather depended on whether there were letters for The Dod or Threestoneburn in which case he passed the door. Otherwise the post was left at the farm. Robbie did his round on a pushbike, all the postmen did, but his was the only one fitted with three speed gears. If there were letters for the out bye places he left the bike and went on foot, often running most of the way.

The mail was delivered from Alnwick to Hedgeley Station by railway van. It arrived punctually at 7.20 in the morning to be sorted and franked at the post office. Robbie's round started at Brandon White House and took in Low Hedgeley, Hedgeley Hall, Crawley Tower, Powburn, Branton Buildings and Fawdon. From there he cycled over the East Hill and up the road to Reaveley Greens.

Robbie carried all sorts in his mailbag: cigarettes and odds and ends that people asked him to get. He always took Belle fresh yeast. Most places got a morning paper with the post. It was usually the Newcastle Journal, posted out daily when it came off the presses just before midnight. The round was nine miles cycling and six walking. Officially it took six hours 50 minutes but Robbie could do it in three.

Belle's pleasures were listening to the wireless and reading "People's Friend". It was always out of date. Her mother saved them, in bundles, often two or three months at a time. With two little children she was virtually tied to the cottage. Going to dances, whist drives even visiting friends were things she never did. The isolation went with Bill's job and she accepted it.

When the children took ill the picture changed. The remoteness of the cottage was worrying. The nearest telephone was at the farmhouse and the doctor lived in Wooler. Mrs Robson, the farmer's wife, had a car and helped when she could by taking Belle and the children to the surgery or to the road end to catch a bus.

Madge was just six weeks old when she developed abscesses on her chest and legs that refused to heal. The doctor referred her to the Royal Victoria Infirmary in Newcastle and Belle took her on the bus. She was admitted to the children's ward and Belle had to leave her because there was no one to look after Brian. She didn't see her baby daughter for three weeks until she made the return journey to bring her home.

Within a matter of weeks Brian was taken to the same hospital critically ill with pneumonia. Dr. Bousfield walked to Reaveley Hill and considered his condition so serious that he should not be moved in a tractor. The doctor walked across the hill to Linhope, two miles away, and arranged for a Land Rover to come around. It brought Brian down to the farm where an ambulance was waiting.

The damp cottage was blamed for the pneumonia. It was no place for children and Bill decided to look for a new job. In May 1951 the family left as they had come, on a tractor and trailer. Their new home was a three-bedroomed house at Stewartshield by Bellingham. Belle was pleased for the children's sake to be going but just a little sad. Despite its drawbacks Reaveley Hill had been a pleasant place to live.

In the churchyard at Ingram two headstones stand close to each other under the trailing boughs of the weeping ash.

The inscription on one reads:
"In Affectionate Remembrance"
"Elizabeth, wife of John Turnbull of Reaveley Hill who died January 22 1880 aged 68 years.
Margaret their daughter died June 15 1863 aged 20 years.
The above John Turnbull died February 12 1885 aged 94 years.
Robert son of Benjamin and Margaret Turnbull and grandson of the above died August 11th
1885 aged 13 months.
Also Elizabeth, daughter of B and M Turnbull died June 15 1902 aged 22 years."

The other says:

"In Loving Memory of Benjamin R. Turnbull, late of Reaveley Hill, died at Glanton January 1
1928 aged 75 years.
Also Margaret Annie his beloved wife died December 16 1933 aged 77 years.
Also their daughter Margaret Annie died June 3 1928 aged 36 years.
Isabella died January 29 1949 aged 65 years."

One can only wonder what life was like then at the solitary cottage on Reaveley Hill.

Postscript

Madge died in December 1963 aged 13. She is buried in the churchyard at Ingram beside her grandparents Thomas and Elizabeth Armstrong. Brian died in 1973 from a hereditary illness.

Belle went back to the cottage just once. Her three boys wanted to see where she had lived. It was no longer a home, just a store for the hill: the front rooms packed with hay bales, the scullery with sheep nets and troughs. She could have cried.

In 1986 a young shepherd, Graham Holmes, chose to end his life at Reaveley Hill just before lambing time. He worked at Reaveley and lived in a cottage at Brandon. A popular lad he herded the hill on horseback and had a flair for photography. The community was shocked.

As each year passes the elements take their toll. The chimney pot has gone, leaving the stack open to the skies, the windows are empty. The very old house is unrecognisable as such but parts of the byre still stand. On summer days the cool stone of its ruined walls provides a refuge for sheep seeking shade from the heat and the flies.

Ingram Hill

The Douglases, the Jacksons and the Cowens - family names synonymous with shepherding in the Breamish and beyond - would find their old home at Ingram Hill little changed.

The broad, latched doors, wooden shelved larder and the old range made by "Rutherford of Coldstream" are just as they were. The black wrought iron fireplaces are still in the bedrooms. At night the tall shutters on the windows are closed, the paraffin lamps and candles lit.

Across the back garden is the netty, its rectangular wooden box seat still intact, and beside it the ash pit, long since filled level with cinders from the fire. Next door is the two-stalled byre with the pigsty attached, the doorways of both framed with fine sandstone quoins and lintels. The vegetable garden adjoins the other side of the cottage. Dog roses and rhubarb flourish behind the stout stone wall.

Ingram Hill is marked on the ordnance survey map of 1897, the outline of the cottage and out buildings identical to those of today.

The cottage at Ingram Hill.

In the early 1900s Bill Douglas, his wife Margaret (an Ingram girl) and their two young children lived at Ingram Hill. Bill was a local man, one of a family of thirteen, whose parents John and Margaret Douglass lived for many years at Alnham Moor. He dropped the final "s" in his surname saying it was unnecessary.

A headstone in the churchyard tells of life cut short. They had been married for less than four years. "Margaret Fraser wife of William Milburn Douglas who died at Ingram 16th May 1904 aged 24 years. The above William Milburn Douglas, Ingram Hill, died 30th August 1914 aged 40 years." After his wife's death, Bill's sister Peg came as housekeeper and when Bill died, his brother Ned took over as shepherd.

In 1921 Jim Jackson moved to Ingram from Goldscleugh in the College Valley; the shepherding for a few years at least was a family affair. Jim was a hill shepherd, and the father of 17 children, the result of two marriages. He came as head shepherd, and two of his sons were hired for the hills. Tommy herded the male sheep, the wethers and tups, on the Wether Hill. From his home at Ingram Hill Jimmy shepherded the Cheviot ewes on the Ewe Hill. The family left in 1927 but Jimmy stayed on until 1938 when he moved to Threestoneburn.

During the war years Bob Cowens lived at the cottage. The family name was well known in the Coquet and Breamish valleys, Bob being one of five brothers who were all hill shepherds. He married Sadie Nixon, nanny to Miss Naomi Allgood at Ingram Rectory. As Miss Nim and her brother James grew up, Sadie did other jobs: cook, housemaid, and ended up staying for 21 years. She was very much part of the family. When she and Bob got married, Miss Nim was bridesmaid and James gave her away. Their father Rev. Roland Allgood conducted the service and their mother Edith played the organ.

Bob and Sadie's daughter Betty is remembered as one of two local girls (the other was Vera Scott from Reaveley Hill Cottage) who passed the 11-plus exam and went to the Duchess' Grammar School in Alnwick. She became head girl and later qualified as a teacher.

By the time the family left Ingram Hill in the early 1950s, a bathroom and porch had been added to the cottage, and water piped from a spring on the hill.

The last shepherd to live there was Bill Cook and his wife Ethel. They moved to Ingram in November 1953 when their son Barry was 12 months old. It was an unusual time to change jobs, May or October was the rule, but the previous shepherd had left through ill health and a man was urgently required for the hill. Bill didn't like his job in the Coquet and was happy to leave.

Ethel remembers it as a quiet, peaceful place to live, the days taken up with cooking, sewing or gardening and the twice daily milking of Jilly, the house cow, a job she shared with Bill. Once a week she went to Wooler to shop. Barry was strapped into a seat on the back of her bike and she cycled to the road end to catch the bus.

Bill shepherded the hill on foot, morning and night, and often brought sheep into the pens beside the cottage. At lambing time any "problems" were brought in to the keb house, a low shed, open at one end, the roof and sides thatched with rushes to keep the rain out. Inside were six pens, each just big enough to hold one ewe and a lamb.

If Bill was needed to help at the farm a tea towel was draped over the thorn bush beside the farmhouse. It was a simple way of communicating and saved someone a 10-minute walk up the fields. The postman called on occasions but often letters were left at the farm. This so annoyed one shepherd's wife that she parcelled up books and posted them back to herself, knowing that the postman would deliver a parcel - which he did!

In August 1955 Bill and Ethel moved down to a cottage at the farm, mainly for Barry's sake. He rarely saw anyone except his parents and had become very shy, hiding from people behind his mother's skirt.

It was a move the family never regretted. The cottage had electric lights and Ethel got her first appliances - a Baby Belling cooker and a Servis washer with a hand wringer. Barry started school at Ingram, and the television at the farmhouse opened up a whole new world.

From the mid 1950s until mid 1960s empty cottages were a common sight on many farms. With increasing mechanisation workers were not replaced. One option was to rent them out as weekend homes to "people from the town". It was usually by word of mouth. A family who found a cottage would tell friends about another they knew of that was empty.

Frank and Florence Baker came to Ingram this way, through friends who rented a cottage on the farm. The Bakers lived at Chester-le-Street in Co. Durham. Initially they took an empty cottage in the row. When it was needed, in 1962, for a farm worker they moved up to Ingram Hill, their furniture taken by tractor and trailer. They gave up the cottage in 1988 when they retired to Rothbury.

Peter and Angela Kellett live in Newcastle and have rented Ingram Hill since the early 1990s. They like it because it offers a complete contrast to city life, its attractions precisely the things that many would regard as drawbacks: no road, no electricity and no mains water. Now that their two children are older, family visits are less frequent, the attractions of town a greater pull.

Peter especially has great empathy with the place, its setting in an ancient landscape, its history and the links with the hill shepherds.

The absence of electricity is perhaps the most influential factor in maintaining those links with the past. Things that 'plug in' invariably emit noise: the television, vacuum cleaner, washing machine. Without them the peace and quiet is preserved.

Quite frequently red reminders arrive from TV Licensing warning of possible prosecution and a fine. When an official from the Office of National Statistics called in 2004 wanting to interview the tenants about their lifestyle, their jobs, family, schooling, and so on, the sight of the cottage took him aback. Noting the fact there was no road and no electricity he left, quite incredulous that such a place could exist in this day and age. Despite that, Peter must still pay council tax.

Doing without is a learning experience: cooking and eating by candlelight, hand washing clothes, tidying the floors with a carpet sweeper. Visitors are curious: the most often asked question "how do you manage without television?" The wind up radio, the sort that is used extensively in rural parts of Africa, is hardly a substitute. It requires winding up 55 times to last 35 minutes. Peter prefers to play his violin.

A lecturer at Newcastle University, he often brings work to the cottage. On fine days examination papers are marked in the garden with skylarks singing overhead. Its unique situation is now valued as never before. The isolation, peace and silence are endearing qualities in today's global, high-speed world.

Old pigsties at Reaveley. They were built back-to-back with the netties that served the cottages.

14

The Pig Killing

As a young girl Hannah Hutton grew up with the annual occasion of the pig killing. Later in life, as the wife of a hill shepherd, she fed and looked after the family's pig until its day came.

Keeping pigs was an age-old tradition in the countryside. It bridged the social classes: the landowner, the rector and farm workers all kept pigs. Unlike a family's house cow or a shepherd's pack sheep, it was not regarded as wages 'in kind'.

The pig was kept near the house in a sty, a small stone-built pen divided into two halves: the back where the pig slept was covered by a sloping roof and the front, where it fed, was open. Pigsties often adjoined the ash pit or the byre but where several families kept a pig the sties were built in a row, like those behind the old farm cottages at Reaveley and Ingram, or, as at Brandon, around a small yard on the opposite side of the road to the cottages.

During wartime, when food was rationed, a licence was required to kill a pig. Families who did so got less meat coupons in their ration book. The maximum was two pigs per household. If you had a third you kept quiet.

By the early 1950s the practice of keeping pigs was beginning to die out although it did linger on at the out-bye, isolated farms. At Ingram, the hill shepherd Bob Cowens killed everyone's pigs. When he moved away nobody wanted the job. Lifestyles were changing. Cars and electric fridges were coming into everyday use. There was no longer a need to lay down large quantities of ham and bacon to last the winter.

I am indebted to Hannah for her personal memories of what is now a bye-gone custom. Although her family did not live in the valley, the pig killing was much the same everywhere.

"My father was a shepherd and also a very good butcher which many shepherds had to be in pre war days.

"My first memory of the pig killing was before I started school. We lived in one of the farm cottages with

earth closet, ash tip and pig sty just across the yard and I well remember climbing into bed and going right under the blankets to shut out the squealing of the pig which no doubt many of my generation who lived on farms will recall. It was part of our way of life and was taken for granted. The pig was our supply of bacon and lard for cooking. Stress was a word that had not been invented.

"The pig killing usually took place any time between November and February, when the weather was colder, which was best for curing the bacon. After it was killed the pig was hung from 'sheer legs', three strong poles tied together at the top (to form a tripod) and left outside all day, to cool. It was always 'cut down' at night after the day's work was finished.

"Ours was always cured outside, on boards supported on empty drums. An old white sheet was put on the boards and, at night when the pig was cut down, the hams and shoulders were laid on the sheet and a mixture of salt, saltpetre [potassium nitrate crystals] and sugar put on. The flakes [sides] were then put on top and treated too. All was then covered with white sheets. Clean sacks were tied over it all and topped with corregated tin sheets, well secured with rope. This lay for 21 days but was turned at 10 days.

"When lifted it was lightly washed down with a cloth and hung up to 'dreep'. When dried off it was put in clean washed bags (often 1cwt sugar bags) and they hung on 'cleeks' [hooks] from the kitchen ceiling.

"The lard came in two white rolls. It was sliced and diced into cubes then rendered in the oven, and poured through a strainer into 7lb stone jars for storing. Crackling that was left from the rendering was chopped up when cold and used in the making of black pudding.

"My parents always believed all the offal meat should be left until the following day. Mother made sausage, white pudding (meat boiled and minced with cooked pearl barley added), potted meat and black pudding. This was made in a roasting tin, and the ingredients were breadcrumbs, pearl barley, milk, dried chopped mint and crackling. Believe me, no 'plastic' black pudding ever had the taste ours had.

"The sausage was the best of the lean pork, minced, that had been taken off the ribs to neaten the spare rib joints.This was also lightly flavoured with chopped mint as no one was keen on sage which many used. Skins for the sausage were the small intestine which were put in cold water overnight, scraped next day on a wood board with the back of a tea knife then put in a bowl of cold water with a small handful of salt to help purify. They were scraped again to take out the water before being filled with sausage.

"We youngsters loved turning the handle of the mincer. It had an attachment for filling the sausages. It was a pipe about five inches long with a flange that fitted to the mincer and pulled the skin on. Mother put the meat in and linked the sausages. Everything was scrupulously clean.

"My father's rue was "those who do not eat flake get no ham either". How we ate all the bacon I can't now imagine, there were six of us altogether at home.

"During the war when meat, like all food, was rationed everyone was allowed to keep only two pigs. One winter my father and a shepherd friend killed and dressed out 36 pigs. Dad would go round his sheep, on foot, then cycle to where ever the job was. He came back home to work again until evening, and then cycled back to cut the carcase down and salt the bacon.

"I also married a shepherd and we kept a pig each year, all our working life, having been brought up with the tradition. One pleasure I have enjoyed so much in recalling all this is the taste of real spare-rib, sausage and black pudding!"

15

The Village of Ingram

A Turbulent Past

The village of Ingram, perhaps hamlet is a more apt description, lies on the south side of the river Breamish at the point where the hills of the upper valley give way to grass fields and pastureland.

Its name and origins date back to pre-Saxon times. "Angr-ham" or "Ingera-ham", a grassland settlement or farm, but also interpreted by some writers as the home of the "in-yore" folk, the people of old.

The ancient church of St Michael and All Angels sits in a quintessentially English churchyard framed by fine trees and a lych-gate. It is now overlooked by a development of holiday homes, built in 2002-3 in a corner of the Rectory gardens. Opposite the church is the old school, opened in 1834 (now the National Park centre) and along the lane the village hall (1929). Of houses the most substantial are the fine Rectory (1700 - 1800s) and the old farmhouse (late 1700s). Set into the garden wall is a red Victorian letterbox, the oldest post box in the district.

In his "Guide to Northumberland", 1889, W.W. Tomlinson mentions the base of a market cross "still standing" on the village green; it is marked on the 1923 Ordnance Survey map as "Cross, site of" opposite the old farmhouse. At that spot some large stones, arranged roughly in a semi circle, are just visible beneath the undergrowth and trees. At the time of writing it is hoped that a small-scale excavation will take place to determine whether it is indeed the base of the long forgotten cross.

The Victorian letterbox in Ingram from a sketch by David Lawrie.

Beneath a canopy of tall trees the Middledean Burn flows beside the road on its way to join the Breamish. On the opposite side of the road is the farm steading, a mix of old and new buildings, reflecting changes in agricultural practices over the years.

This postcard of St Michael's Church and Ingram School, by J.C. Ruddock of Alnwick, pre dates 1905. By then the pitched roof and iron cross on the church tower had been removed. The village hall and a house now stand on the ploughed field in the foreground.

Two delightful watercolour paintings give us a fascinating glimpse of Ingram in the mid 19th century. They hang in a private collection. Both are the work of James Burrell Smith (1822-1897). He lived in Alnwick, and received tuition from Thomas Miles Richardson, senior, one the most highly regarded watercolour painters to hail from the North of England.

The painting of the church was done in 1860, before restoration. It reveals painstaking attention to detail. Smith has captured the differing hues and shapes of the memorials, and a flat headstone, lying askew, is at exactly the same angle today. The date on the other watercolour is 1859. This scene, looking west up the road, shows the old farmhouse, the "model" farmyard beside it, and a horse drinking at the burn. The scene today is quite different, considerably altered by trees and woods.

A few other houses and cottages make up the village, notably the farmhouse (1939), Drive House (early 1920s) and Ingram Folly, a modern house beside the village hall. The row of cottages beside the cattle grid was originally four two-roomed cottages with the intriguing name of "Shiny Row". When the morning sun catches the walls they really do shine.

The watercolour of Ingram Church with the Rectory just visible through the trees.

Rural tranquillity: A cart lies tipped on its shafts in the farmyard in front of the now demolished cart-sheds. The old wood that once stood on Brough Law can be seen in the far background.

Against a backdrop of rolling hills, with sheep and cattle grazing in the fields, Ingram today presents a picture of rural tranquillity. It is difficult to envisage its war-torn past: three hundred years of desecration and destruction at the hands of the Scots, interspersed by only brief periods of peace.

The troubles began in 1296 when Edward 1, the English king, went to war with Scotland.

The following year his forces were defeated and the relative peace and quiet of the Breamish Valley came to an end. For several years in the early 14th century the valley was more or less under Scottish rule.

In 1344 we read that Edward III received a petition from "Angerham", amongst other places, that "their crops and other goods were burned and otherwise destroyed and their animals plundered by the Scots".

Between 1356 and 1360 the township of "Angreham" asked four times for respite from rents because of the Scottish raids, and a document of 1387 speaks of "destruction and burning of the Scots" with regard to "Angreham" and "Revely".

The 15th century was a more peaceful time with the exception of a destructive raid on Ingram in 1436. Serious warfare erupted again in the 16th century and the valley was raided on many occasions. In 1532, in retaliation for an English raid into Scotland, a splinter-group of 300 Scots broke away from the main army and "did run down ye watter of Bremysch, and there take upe 4 towns called Ingyram, Reveyley, Brandon, and Fawdon".

In June 1587, 500 Scots raided "Rile, Preudicke, Revely and Ingrum" and took 500 head of cattle, 300 sheep and 20 prisoners. The following month, "4 men of E. Tevedale took 4 webbes of leed" from Ingram church. A year later the reivers returned to Ingram taking "30 kye and oxen, worth £51 sterling".

Peace came officially in 1603 when James VI of Scotland became James I of England, the Union of The Crowns. However, years of warring had undermined the wealth and stability of the area, and it was many years before it recovered. In 1663 the church was described as "ruinous and destitute". By 1734 the picture of Ingram was of an impoverished place. "The houses are for the most part poor and despicable and the inhabitants....exceedingly poor".

Historian Stuart Davies researched the early history of the valley as part of the Breamish Valley Archaeology Project. I am most grateful to him.

Davies concludes: **"A feeling of lawlessness seems to have continued well into the 18th century. It is difficult to assess how much war changed the society of the Breamish Valley, but it seems seem that the intensity of the troubles in the 16th century left a permanent mark on the landscape, reinforcing livestock over crops and perhaps contributing to the depopulation of the area."**

Ingram was once a much more populous place than it is today. In 1801 the first ever census return shows a count of 66 in the township of "Ingram, Linhope and Greenshaw Hill". This figure peaked at 92 in 1841. By 1901, the population was 77. Today my count of permanent residents, including children, is less than forty.

Ingram Farm

A fine sandstone tablet, set high on the gable end wall of the barn, carries the inscription "WSR MDCCCXXVI". Together the initials and the Roman numerals reveal the identity of the owner of Ingram and the year: The man was William Spencer Roddam, the year 1826.

The farm steading was designed in the shape of a capital E with the barn in the centre. Adjoining were upstairs granaries with housing below for cattle, fronted by open fold yards. At the west end were cart sheds, stalls and a hay house. At the east end, near the farmhouse, was the byre, coach

The stone tablet on the barn wall.

house, harness room and the carriage horse stables.

Towards the end of the 18th century Ingram belonged to the Collingwood and Ogle families. The Collingwood's share passed by marriage to John Tarleton who, in 1802, acquired the Ogle share thereby reuniting the manor.

In 1820 "The Manor or Lordship of Ingram and the Ingram Estate" was put up for auction at Garraway's Coffee House in London. The sale particulars advertised a substantial brick built farm house together with barns, stabling for ten horses and lodges for wagons and carts.

The farm became part of the Roddam Estate and was to remain so for the next century.

The Roddams were an old Northumberland family but the direct line of succession had been broken on several occasions. When Admiral Roddam died in 1808 he bequeathed the estate to a distant cousin, William Spencer Stanhope. He changed his name to Roddam, hence the initials on the barn wall.

It cannot be said with certainty that Mr Roddam rebuilt or remodelled all or part of the farm steading. However, the presence of the stone tablet, blending as it does with the barn wall, would appear to indicate that he did.

At the time of the sale Robert Donkin was the tenant of Ingram Farm. His tenancy ultimately spanned 65 years, from 1806 until his death in 1871. His forebears were well known farmers in the Rothbury area, and his father, an ardent sportsman, kept the famous Tosson Foxhounds.

Robert and his wife Sarah had 10 children, one of them being Samuel who, much later in life, as an old man of 84, wrote his "Reminiscences". His boyhood recollections of Ingram shed interesting light on life in the valley in the early 19th century.

Initially taught by a schoolmaster at home, Samuel went briefly to Branton School and finished his education at Alnwick. After leaving school he was "entrusted with the charge of a hirsel of sheep upon Ingram Hills, carrying in his plaid nook his dinner, a bottle of milk and bread and cheese. He went out with a pair of horses and whistled at the plough, stacked, sowed, mowed (and) reaped with the hook."

In 1826 Samuel moved to Bywell Farm, near Felton. He later became an auctioneer, an occupation that was to run in the family for three generations. His son Robert founded Rothbury Auction Mart in 1871 and together with his son Robert, the partnership of R. Donkin, senior and junior became widely known.

Samuel's father, Robert, was described as a man of "sterling integrity, temperate, frugal and in all things punctual and faithful". A churchwarden at St. Michael's, Ingram, he subscribed to the building of the village school.

A breeder of prize-winning Cheviot sheep, Robert's passion for sheep farming was recalled in an article in the Newcastle Courant:

"Much of his time was passed with the 'clippers', the shearers of his flocks. His flocks and his hills were his delight. He was proud of his sheep and ambitious to excel in the quality of his clip of wool.

"He achieved and long maintained a superiority on the Borders - a superiority which was repeatedly attested by his success at the Agricultural Shows. His prizes, with the sealed envelopes unbroken, he kept in his desk, not regarding them for their intrinsic worth.

"Exact in his accounts, he knew the prices of wool and farm stock for a long succession of seasons, and was not troubled by their fluctuations."

In Robert's day the Cheviot sheep were reared primarily for wool. The quality of the clip was enhanced by smearing or 'laying' the wool with grease, the belief being that an 'unlaid' sheep would suffer in condition.

> "Tarry woo', tarry woo',
> Tarry woo' is ill to spin;
> Card it weel, card it weel,
> Card it weel ere ye begin.
>
> "When 'tis carded round and spun,
> Then the work is haffens done;
> But when woven, drest and clean,
> It may be cleading for a queen."

Samuel tells us that the Cheviot shepherds of the present day, 1886, know nothing of "tarry woo'", nor of the process of smearing or 'laying' the wool. He recalls how it was done at Ingram.

"October, according to the temperature of the weather, which might protract the operation, was the time of its performance. The ingredients were tar and butter, or the best of the grease, the quality of which affected the value of the wool.

"At Ingram it was the practice, when the best of grease was scarce, to mix (or what was called 'menging') the tar with the contents of a dairy of the finest of butter, which placed the Ingram clip of wool in a higher position in the market.

"The cow byre being the theatre of performance, a lot of sheep were housed, the 'laying stools' and tubs of tar of proper consistency placed in juxtaposition, the shepherds 'bratted' in sheep skin, the sheep laid upon the stool, the wool regularly shedded longitudinally, and dips of tar deftly drawn up the sheds, and the work was complete.

"From dark till ten o'clock, light derived from candles looped in a yarn line over the heads of the 'layers', the process went on. The night drave on wi 'sang and clatter', with anecdote and incident upon the fame of sheep-walks, the condition and qualities of stock, of storms which had swept o'er the Cheviots."

One of the worst ever occurred on 18th November 1808. "Drifty Friday" as it was known, was a snowstorm of "unprecedented disasters, unrecorded in Arcadian annals".

"The night previous was calm, clear and frosty; boys sliding upon the frozen pools. The storm without warning (there were no weather prophets in those days) arose about midnight; the flocks all lying abroad. The shepherds, taken by surprise, started off to the hills at Ingram.

"They had been busy 'laying'. A lot of sheep had been left in the byre; there they remained without food for two nights and a day.

"The windows of the farm house were lit up in anxious hope that the master, in his 34th year, in company with his trusty herds, Robert Black and Ralph Buglass, out in the drift, might find their way home. They had made their way to the boundary of Prendwick in anxiety for the lives of the wether flock upon "Cockrain" [Cochrane Pike, a hill on Ingram].

"On their struggles home, the master's faithful collie, "March" got overblown in the drift, the explorers had become bewildered and had lost their 'reckoning' till they had found themselves in a state of exhaustion at Ingram Mill. The loss of sheep was unprecedented, amounting to many thousands upon the Cheviot range.

"Upon the disappearance of the snow, which had lain in wreaths for months, the memory is still vivid of being taken along with a sister to witness the remains of "March" lying as if the dog had died in his sleep, in the ravine at "Ravensheugh", a volcanic formation upon the Ingram and Fawdon boundary.

"The dog, in his attachment to his master, was never absent, except when the master went to church. "March" then demurely lay down upon the mat, not quitting the house till his master's return."

Turning the pages of Samuel's book we glean snippets of history: It was more than a week before news of the battle of Waterloo (1815) reached the vale of the Breamish. The march of the remnants of the gallant Scots Greys, with their tattered colours, through Morpeth and Alnwick was the first that many knew of Wellington's victory over Napoleon.

The Industrial Revolution was bringing sweeping changes to town and countryside, shifting the country from an agricultural to an industrial economy. On the back of this, in 1817, the iron swing plough was introduced in the valley.

"Seeing one upon the premises of a blacksmith named French, at Alnwick, I was ordered by my father to procure one when next there, the wooden plough being so frequently broken in the stony furrow upon the 'breaking up' of Ingram East Haugh.

"Tradition details that Ingram Haugh (area about 300 acres), north of the Breamish and adjoining Brandon and Reveley, was exchanged by an ancestor of the Allgood family, proprietors of the Brandon estate, for a racehorse; that Ingram was occupied by 13 farmers each of whom had a galloping horse; and that the horse of a shepherd was a winner at the races held on Ingram Haugh."

A "Plan of the Estate and Lordship of Ingram in Northumberland" circa 1820 shows the Haugh divided into five parts. Other field names were Goose Croft, Holywell Bank, Broughlaw Brow, Tofts, Ewebright Edge, Shield and Hay Close. Names I couldn't resist mentioning. Today only Shield and Haugh survive. Over the years as large fields were sub-divided they acquired new names: Rectory, Rashery, Bank and Dene. Hay Close is now the Show field, so called because for many years Ingram Show was held there.

Robert Donkin lived to be numbered in the census of Sunday, April 2nd 1871. He died the following morning, in the farmhouse at Ingram, in his ninety sixth year. David Dippie Dixon remembered him in his book "Whittingham Vale", as "one of the most venerable of our Northumbrian patriarchs, the bearer of a familiar and respected name."

Robert was buried at Ingram, beside his wife Sarah, to whom he was married for 69 years. The grave, at the western end of the churchyard, is marked by a fine obelisk erected by their son Samuel

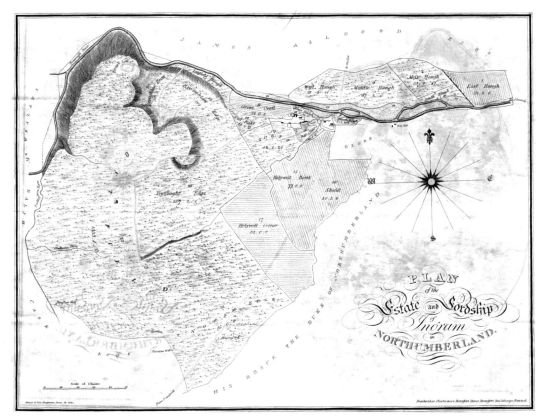

Plan of the Lordship of Ingram. *(© NCRO)*

as a "tribute to parental worth". Beside it a marble headstone records the deaths of eight of their ten children, none of whom lived to three score years and ten.

In 1877, six years after Robert's death, a farm sale was held at Ingram. It included his 1470 Cheviot sheep, (ewes, gimmers, hoggs and dinmonts), 140 half bred ewes, much in fashion then, and 31 cattle of varying ages. In addition were "six excellent draught horses, a clever, useful hackney and implements as usual on a turnip farm".

The sale advertisement drew attention to the general excellence of the livestock.
"The sheep whose genealogy can be traced back for a period of 74 years on the farm of Ingram have been bred with a view of combining size with hardiness and constitution. All the female portion of the flock having been reared without tasting turnips." [A supplementary feed, the first field turnip crop grown in Northumberland, in 1721, was at Reaveley Greens, just up the road from Ingram].

Prospective buyers were advised that Alnwick was the nearest railway station. It was to be another ten years, in 1887, before the station opened at Hedgeley on the Alnwick to Cornhill line.

Exactly when David Hall took the tenancy of Ingram Farm is not clear, but by the early 1880s his reputation as a breeder of pedigree Cheviot rams was well established. Some were given local names: "Breamish", "Pride of Breamish" and "Ingram's Pride". In 1886 we read that a ram called

"Ingram" was one of 15 sold by Mr. Hall at Hawick. It went to a new home in Bahana, Ireland.

That following year, 1887, Mr. Hall and his landlord Mr. Roddam were involved in a dispute with the new rector of Ingram, Rev. Thomas Ilderton.

It concerned the value of "stints" or grazing rights that the Rector had over Ingram Farm. All parties were agreed that the Rector was entitled to 55 units, each unit representing grazing for one beast or five sheep. For many years the rights had been commuted by an agreed money payment from the farmer to the Rector. In a nutshell, Mr Ilderton was after more money. All were agreed that the grazing was over pasture, not arable land, but was it hill pasture, as Mr Roddam contended, or field pasture, as the Rector argued?

The matter was settled by arbitration in 1889 to the disadvantage of the Rector. He was awarded £96 15s, considerably less than the £180 paid in Robert Donkin's day.

Samuel Donkin died at Warkworth in April 1888. He was 86. A local newspaper carried a lengthy report of his interment in Ingram churchyard, the proceedings witnessed at first hand by a "special reporter".

"The remains were taken from Warkworth in the forenoon and conveyed by hearse the whole of the distance, nearly twenty four miles, followed by a large number of vehicles containing private friends. The route taken was by Alnwick and Glanton.

"The funeral was appointed for three o' clock but the party did not arrive until nearly half an hour beyond that, much more time having been taken upon the long journey than was anticipated. After the party had dined at Glanton, a somewhat long turn in the route was taken, and this added to the delay.
"There were two newly dug and open graves to be filled that day, the one for the veteran Northumbrian who had lived long past three score years and ten, and the other for a child whose sojourn had not stretched from one summer to another.
"About two o' clock the burying of the latter brought a break in the monotony, made especially touching by the arrival of the small band of hillside mourners who carried their frail burden down the hill, across the narrow bridge at the ford, and round into the old churchyard. A number of this party remained for the larger funeral.

"About a quarter past three o' clock the funeral cortege was espied in the distance wending its way along the central road of the valley, and as the hearse and carriages drew nearer, there was a distinct rumbling totally abnormal to the place.

"Eventually the head of the cortege was turned to the ford right opposite the church, the hearse horses plunging in right boldly nearly leg deep, and was followed by the other vehicles one by one. The cortege was made up of hearse, five closed carriages, and some half a dozen or more gigs and traps, with one or two gentlemen on horseback. Many of the vehicles including a large number from Rothbury, had joined the procession *en route*.

"On the arrival of the funeral party at the church gates by a circuitous route round the rectory, the whole party alighted, and, on the coffin which was a black cloth-covered one, just bearing the simple record of the deceased's name and age, being lifted from the hearse, every hat was raised, and slowly the procession wended its way into the churchyard."

Another farm sale was held at Ingram in 1904. The outgoing tenant was William Robson of Low Hedgeley. By then the sheep numbers had increased to 2000, together with 100 cattle.

A newspaper report tells of a somewhat disappointing sale, especially with the hill sheep. Cheviot ewes with twins made 38s 6d to 43s whereas the bigger half bred ewes with twins fetched up to 72s.

In 1919, Ingram Farm and outlying portions of the Roddam Estate, including Earle and Earle Mill Farms, near Wooler, were put up for sale on the instruction of Lt. Col. Roddam John Roddam. Perhaps the death of his only son, killed in action at Flanders in 1915, was partly the reason, but a sale of furnishings at his ancestral home, Roddam Hall, would appear to point to diminishing family fortunes. Lt. Col Roddam and his wife, Helen, moved to Greenfield House, near Powburn, formerly the manse for Branton Presbyterian Church.

The auction was held at the County Hotel, Newcastle-upon-Tyne, the auctioneer none other than Robert Donkin, great-grandson of Robert Donkin who had farmed at Ingram.

Mr. Donkin explained to prospective buyers that a sliding scale rent appertained at Ingram. It hinged on the value of the wool clip. At the time of the sale the farm was let to Messrs Rea at the certain rental of £940 a year. Additional rent was based on the value of Cheviot wool as recorded annually by the Teviotdale Farmers Club.

The threshold was 1s 1d per pound. For every 1d that wool was valued above that, an additional rent of £17 10s was due. During the year ended 12th May 1918, the recorded price of Cheviot wool was 1s 7d per pound. Consequently an extra £105 was due (6 x £17 10s) making the rent £1045. (Before decimalisation, 12d equalled 1s, and 20s equalled £1).

Mr. Donkin remarked that the system obtaining at Ingram was a "sound and ideal method…fixed on the basis that the landlord participated in the good times as well as the bad". The sliding scale rent did not apply to every farm, but at Ingram it could work through wool, the most constant source of revenue.

In his great-grandfather's day the lowest price of Cheviot wool was 12s 6d a stone (about 10d a

Ingram farm in the 1920s, from a glass plate negative. Stacks of corn can be seen in the stack-yard where a cottage now stands.

pound) and the highest 55s 6d a stone (3s 11d a pound). During that time the average weight of the clip varied from 251 stones in 1820 to 491 stones in 1866.

[Nowadays wool is no longer such a valued commodity. Demand declined with the introduction of synthetic fabrics, as did the price paid to farmers. The wool cheque from the British Wool Marketing Board is now paid over two years].

Bidding for Ingram began at £23,000 and went up in £100 and £50 bids to £26,000 at which figure the farm was withdrawn. In June 1920 it was sold privately to Basil George Bryant, a businessman, for an undisclosed sum.

The following year Mr G.G. Rea relinquished the tenancy of Ingram and a farm sale was held to dispose of his sheep and implements. We read of Massey Harris binders, two Ransome wheel ploughs, a manure distributor cart and two spring tooth cultivators.

Major Bryant took the farm 'in hand' and initially farmed in partnership with Captain Blackett Ord. In the 1920s considerable money was invested. The open cattle yards were covered, new woods planted and two new houses built: one for the newly married Captain Blackett Ord, the other for the shepherd, Jimmy Jackson and his family. In total three shepherds, a byre man and two hinds were employed. When Jimmy's son Bob left Ingram School he was taken on as "Turnip Dick", the lad who did all sorts, for a wage of 10s a week. At that time the minimum wage for agricultural workers was about 42s 6d a week.

Bob started work at 6a.m. and finished at 6p.m. with some afternoons off. His jobs included grooming the two pairs of horses, harrowing fields, sowing turnips, collecting the coals at Hedgeley Station and driving cattle to Whittingham Mart.

The annual "hirings", where men and women were engaged as farm workers or servants, were held at Alnwick and Wooler. Their importance as livestock fairs had declined following the opening of the railway and auction marts. With sideshows, roundabouts and hooplas, similar to a fun fair today, they were great social occasions, accompanied, for some, by a lot of drinking. Bob remembered going by train from Hedgeley Station, through the tunnel, to the Alnwick "hirings", and his father staying away for three days.

The unlikely combination of singing, poaching and pigeon racing figured prominently in Bob's teenage years at Ingram. He sang in the church choir, attended practices at the Rectory, and throughout his life was a great singer.

Poaching was an autumn activity, when the salmon came up the river to spawn. It was done at night with a "tar light" and involved considerable danger. A heavy sack, filled with tar, was doused in paraffin and set alight. It was carried into the middle of the river, the tar dripping down your back, and thrown into the water. The resulting boiling inferno either stunned or killed the fish. There were no river bailiffs then and the gamekeepers simply turned a 'blind eye'.

The Pigeon Club

Several local men and boys, including Bob Jackson, kept pigeons. In January 1925 a pigeon club was formed. Known as the Ingram Parish Homing Society, the chairman throughout its short existence was the Rector, Reverend Roland Allgood.

A race calendar was organised with prizes for the winners. Membership cost 2/6d and was confined to the parish. At the inaugural meeting Rev. Allgood promised a new 5s bird pannier in lieu of a subscription. Race entry fees were fixed at 6d for 'old bird' races and 3d for 'young birds' that flew over shorter distances.

The pigeons were ringed at The Rectory and taken by car to Hedgeley Station. From there they travelled on the train to the race points of Northallerton, Selby, Doncaster, Grantham, Peterborough and Hitchin, stations on the east coast railway line.

When the pigeons flew home to their lofts they were taken, as quickly as possible, to the timing centre at Ingram Mill. Allowances were given for the time it took, by pushbike, from various places in the parish. From Fawdon the allowance was 5 minutes, Reaveley 4 minutes, Reaveley Greens 9 minutes, Brandon 8 minutes, Branton Buildings 15 minutes, and Branton 12 minutes.

From Ingram the allowance was 5 minutes by foot, or two and a half minutes by pushbike. Bob remembered that. After one race he cycled furiously along the road, head down, clutching a pigeon, and forgot about the gate into the Ingram Mill fields, where the village hall now stands. He went over the handlebars and sprained his wrist. What happened to the pigeon, he never said.

Bob had some success in his first season winning two 'young bird' races from Selby and Northallerton.

At the Club's first annual meeting in October 1925 special thanks were given to Mrs Allgood, Mrs Bryant and Captain Blackett Ord for transporting the pigeon panniers to the station. Few people in the valley had cars then.

The minutes of every meeting were recorded in a ledger. It now belongs to Valerie Burrell, handed down through her late husband Ian's family. They farmed the Mill for many years. Ian's grandfather John Nesbit was the club's first timekeeper, and his uncle, Jack Bell, the secretary.

With a fluctuating membership, and limited funds, the club relied on donations and fund raising events. One year Mrs Allgood gave two young pigs for a raffle. It raised £7 2s and paid for a time clock for Brandon.

By 1930 only a handful of members remained. The proceeds of a dance had helped balance the accounts. The final entry in the ledger is dated November 26th 1930. It reads: "As funds were low and no subscriptions coming in it was decided to have a dance on December 12 in aid of club funds and if this was successful a meeting to be called shortly afterwards when all prize money for the past season would be paid out." From this I can only conclude that the club was wound up.

Changes on the Farm

In 1926 Major Bryant had let Ingram Farm to William Robinson who owned Greenside Hill and Hartside, further up the valley. Bob Jackson left in 1927 to take up a new job as hill shepherd at Philhope in Upper Coquetdale.

The late 1930s saw another new tenant at Ingram and, in 1939, the building of a new farmhouse. It was done in a hurry. The cement was 'green' with the result that walls fell down and had to be re-built. After the War, Major Bryant sold the farm to Paul Gibb, a solicitor with the North Eastern Railway Company. Shortly afterwards the Wilson brothers, James, Andrew and William took the farm tenancy.

More than half a century has passed since James Wilson, his wife Margaret and family left a small farm in Ayrshire, where they hand milked 25 dairy cows, to move to Northumberland. With almost 2000 acres Ingram was a much bigger farm and offered better prospects for their three sons, Frank, Jim and John. The family moved into the new farmhouse on May 12th 1949, the same day that Dallas Allen, the outgoing tenant, moved out.

Much to the surprise of his new neighbours, Mr Wilson bought 300 blackface ewes from Lanark market to stock the Wether Hill. Not only was it a complete change of farming practice - for generations this hill had been grazed solely by wether sheep - the question was whether blackface sheep would thrive, with no peat or heather, on 'white' ground traditionally grazed by Cheviot sheep. They did.

For a few years extra pasture was taken on Alnwick Moor, in the autumn, to give the ewes a change of grass. About 500 were driven on foot from Ingram. Frank remembers the occasions well.

"We would leave at break of daylight. We drove them down the Haugh and through the ford at Brandon, it took them a long time to get across the river. We went straight through Glanton and across the main road, making for Bolton and where the railway bridge is, we stopped there and had breakfast about 8 o' clock.

"It was not a fast job. Willie Scott, he was retired and lived in Brandon, would walk in front so they wouldn't come on too hard. He hadn't a dog. Tom Black, the shepherd at Ingram Hill, was in the middle and I was in behind. We had them in two halves.

"The roads were quiet then. We came round by Broome Park, up the Glen Aln road past Broomhill and onto the Moor. Gates beside the road were often open and on many occasions when sheep got into a field, the dogs had to be put in to get them out.

"I remember we were driving the sheep along the road towards Glen Aln. The first ones went on up the road but the batch in front of me went straight in through the gates and got onto the gravel and the lawn. This woman came out. I have never heard a woman swear like it before. She wasn't very pleased."

When the family came to Ingram only one draught horse remained. It was used to scarify the

Staddle stones in the farmhouse garden.

115

turnips. The ploughing was done by tractor. The first a "petrol" Ferguson, was so called because it started up on petrol, but actually ran on paraffin. During his lifetime Mr Wilson never drove a tractor.

Oats were the traditional arable crop, grown to feed the sheep and cattle, and the flock of free-range hens. The eggs were sold at the farmhouse door.

Before the days of combine harvesters, harvesting was a much slower affair. Just prior to ripening, the oats were cut and tied into sheaves by a tractor-drawn binder. The sheaves were gathered up in eights, into stooks, and left to ripen in the field. Once dry, the stooks were led in on a trailer and built into stacks in the stack-yard. Wheat straw was preferred for thatching. Being harder than oat straw it was more resistant to rain.

Sometime in the past the corn stacks at Ingram were built off the ground, on staddle stones and long metal rods, arranged in the shape of a cartwheel. The central stone, or hub, was multi-grooved. Metal rods radiated from it, like spokes, and slotted into grooves in the encircling stones. When the stack-yard was cleared in the mid 1980s the axle-shaped staddle stones came to light. They now stand in the farmhouse garden, objects of curiosity that few people have ever seen.

Threshing days were amongst the busiest on the farm. Everyone helped: family, neighbours and farm staff. A team of ten or twelve, men and women, was needed to keep the operation running smoothly. The threshing mill belonged to Straughan of Lilburn Glebe. It was towed to the farm by a tractor and usually came twice or thrice during the winter, threshing several stacks at a time.

A belt attached to the tractor engine drove the thresher. Big drums stripped the grain from the straw and a series of sieves separated the oats from the chaff.

Isabel and Janette, two of the seven Wilson daughters, often got the job of cutting the sheaves that were then fed loose into the top of the mill. The grain came down a chute and was bagged into heavy, thick railway sacks. When full, each weighed about 12 stones (75 to 80 kilos) and was to carry up the barn stairs to the granaries. Today 25 kilos is the maximum weight that most people lift.

The straw came out at the back of the mill, ready-tied in bunches. On one occasion Isabel's handkerchief dropped into the thresher and brought the whole operation to a halt. It had jammed the knotting mechanism that tied the straw! The straw bunches were built into stacks or 'mows' in the yard, their height dictated by how high a man could throw them up with a pitchfork. The chaff was blown into a heap. It made good bedding for the hens.

The original threshing mill at Ingram was water powered. River water was drawn off into a leat, or channel, that crossed the fields to the back of the barn. Here it drove a huge water wheel, in an underground chamber, which in turn drove the thresher. The leat was mostly filled in when two fields were merged but a small section is just visible today behind the old farmhouse.

In 1987 Bob Jackson returned to Ingram. We walked around the farmyard together. Many things had changed since his day in the 1920s. Gone were the cart sheds and stables, in their place a big modern shed for the tractors. The old turnip store was now a workshop and a new cottage stood in the stack-yard. The farmhouse had been sold off when the Duke of Northumberland acquired the farm in the early 1960s. Over his lifetime Bob had become accustomed to change.

As a hill shepherd, he was the last to attend a Cheviot Gathering. These were long established occasions when, on appointed days in the year, shepherds met up to exchange sheep that had strayed. The Gatherings were held on July 20th and November 10th near the Cheviot summit. In the late 1950s Bob walked up to the Gathering but found nobody there. A centuries-old tradition had come to an end. Stray sheep were now returned by road.

Bob died in 1988 just before his eightieth birthday. A commemorative stone was laid on Cheviot with the following inscription: "In memory of Bob Jackson (1908-88) the last hill shepherd to attend the Cheviot gathering on this site. From family and friends."

Over the years the Wilson family have welcomed many visitors to Ingram: scouts and guides, schoolchildren, students training for Duke of Edinburgh awards and the North Northumberland Pony Club. From 1984 until

Bob's memorial on Cheviot.

1991 the annual summer camp was held on the farm. The biggest one was attended by 60 children plus their horses and ponies. Granaries doubled up as dormitories, the cattle shed as the kitchen/dining room. The ponies were tied up in lines, cavalry style, in the covered yards.

One very special visitor was Queen Elizabeth, the Queen Mother. She was no stranger to this lovely part of Northumberland, staying on several occasions with Sir Ralph and Lady Carr-Ellison at Hedgeley Hall. On this particular day we knew she was coming to the valley and would stop briefly at Ingram. The drive gates were specially painted. As her car pulled up, she was smiling, as always. Daughter Emma, about seven at the time, had rehearsed a curtsey and presented her with a posy of flowers from the farmhouse garden. An occasion none of us will forget.

This photograph of Ingram Church, from a glass plate negative, dates to the mid-1920s. The wooden cross just visible behind the wall is in memory of Private A.J. Turnbull who died in 1918. It may have marked his grave before the permanent headstone, just behind, was erected.

16
A Walk around St. Michael's Church

Lift the latch on the heavy, studded oak door and step into St. Michael's and All Angels Church. The welcome is one of serenity, beauty and simple dignity, enriched on most occasions by lovely arrangements of flowers and, on a summer's day, by shafts of sunlight that illuminate the mellow sandstone.

Stand in the nave and try to imagine how it might have looked in Saxon times, with a thatched roof, earth floor and without a tower. That came later. This is the nearest we come to the beginning. Exactly when the first church was built, and by whom, is lost in antiquity. But we do know that "in 1060 Ingram Church was restored".

I do not intend to give you chapter and verse of the church's history. It is already well documented. Rather, to take a walk around the church, pausing to look at some of the memorials, and other features of interest.

In a small community St. Michael's was fortunate to have amongst its congregation, not so very long ago, two keen historians. One was Canon A. C. de P. Hay, Charles to those who knew him, team rector, and our vicar for 14 years until his retirement in 1985. The other was Isobel Purves, for many years headmistress of Branton School.

It is thanks to their diligence, and countless hours spent pouring over ancient records, "wonderful old books, time worn and much faded, but most precious" that we know so much about the church and its past. Miss Purves wrote the first history in 1962. Entitled "The Story of Ingram Church" it features some fascinating entries from the registers, sadly omitted in the new history which Canon Hay wrote in the 1970s, the version we read today. It contains but a fraction of his great knowledge of Ingram. Indeed, the old church registers provided him with subjects for many talks, exhibitions and articles during his lifetime. His transcripts have provided me with invaluable background material.

After Canon Hay's death, in 1989, a new font cover was commissioned as a memorial. Carved in oak by local carpenter Peter Challis, of Powburn, the inscription reads: "In memory of Canon Charles Hay, a loving pastor and friend, also his beloved wife Jean".

A memorial on the vestry wall commemorates Isobel Purves (1910-1977) - "whose loving care contributed so much to the church, school and community life of this parish".

On the wall, just inside the door, is a list of Rectors from 1281 to 1958. I shall mention James Allgood 1703-1744, James Allgood II, 1828-1850, James Allgood III, 1852-1887 and Roland Allgood, 1909-1947. The family's long association with Ingram followed the acquisition by Lancelot Allgood, in 1690, of the neighbouring estates of Brandon, Brandon White House and, a little later, Reaveley. Subsequently a fine mansion was built at Nunwick, near Hexham. It is still the family seat today.

Here I will introduce you to a lady whose knowledge of the community, the church and indeed her own family history has provided me with valuable contemporary accounts of occasions and events at Ingram. Mrs Naomi Church is the daughter of Roland, the last Allgood Rector. It is her words I quote as we wander around the church and recall also her childhood days at the Rectory.

On the north wall of the chancel, a stone tablet remembers Barbara Wood. Her husband George was curate from 1830-1847, in the days of Mrs Church's great-grandfather, James Allgood II, who incidentally never lived at Ingram. My interest in George Wood lies in a collection of letters he wrote to the Rector between 1844 and 1847. Nothing was known of them until an antique dealer offered them for sale to Mrs Church's parents. Later they came to the attention of Canon Hay.

Following extensive archive research, he pieced together the background to the letters, So we read in the Canon's manuscript about George Wood of the building of Ingram School, the run-down state of the church, "most unfit for the comfort of the congregation", the levy raised on local "proprietors" to meet the cost of repairs and the building of a wall around the east end of the churchyard. Of George himself, married with six children, we read of his wife Barbara's untimely death at the age of 43, and of his financial ruin and bankruptcy after an investment went horribly wrong. Faced with the valuation and sale of his possessions, his horses lent out for want of food, the curate turned to his Rector for help.

"Will no one be my friend so far as to allow me to keep a part, at least, of the most valuable books, or most difficult to replace of my books. I would suppose £50 or £60 would effect the most part of this object and allow me to keep probably half. Will no one ask the Duke since the old Bishop has refused? The Archdeacon is in the south and I cannot say anything to him on the subject."

There a small chapter in church history ends. Someone must have helped the dispirited man for in 1848 he re-emerged as minister of a church in Perth.

The inscription on the marble memorial, below, tells the story of a terrible accident.

"In loving memory of Isabella Allgood, aged 42, James Charles Allgood, aged 13, David Williamson Allgood, aged 11. The beloved wife and sons of James Allgood, Rector of Ingram who lost their lives in a railway accident at Abbots Ripton, January 21st 1876, and whose remains rest in this churchyard."

Mrs Allgood was taking the boys to their new public school in the south. They were travelling on the Great Northern Railway in the "Flying Scotsman" when it collided with a goods train near Huntingdon. The railway company paid £2,000 in compensation.

"My grandfather was so bowled over by this ghastly tragedy that he hardly spoke for two years. Grandfather had 11 children. My father was the youngest. He was only three or so when it happened. He never remembered his mother.
"My aunt Alice was about 15 or 16 then. She had to take on the duty of being a mother to the family. She had to deal with the servants and shopping and had to cope with everything."

In memory of his wife and sons, the Rector and his sister undertook a complete restoration of the church, the St. Michael's we see today, with the exception of the tower. That remained bricked up, buttressed and in danger of falling.

The "energies and labours" of another Rector, Arthur Vaughan, would seem an apt memorial description for the stone by stone dismantling of the Tower which he undertook and paid for in the early 1900s. Each stone was numbered and put back where it belonged, but on a new foundation. A fine gilded weathercock, a gift from Mr. Allgood of Nunwick, was erected on top of the Tower. At the same time the font, dated March 1662, was restored and set on a new stem inscribed with the arms of the Allgood, Collingwood, Roddam and Percy families. A service of dedication and thanksgiving was held in October 1905. The ministry of Arthur Chicele Chambre Vaughan is remembered on a brass memorial in the chancel, and by an inscription on the lectern, given by parishioners in his memory. A stained glass window in the north aisle is dedicated to Isabel Gibson Vaughan, the Rector's beloved daughter who died in 1901.

Two other features in the chancel merit a look. The relief stone featuring the lower part of an effigy of an ecclesiastic was found when the choir was rebuilt. It might be, because it is so small,

Details of the lovely memorial window featuring Roddam Hall.

Roddam Hall circa 1918.

that it was once placed over the heart of a former Rector who was buried elsewhere. Partly hidden by the carpet are two 18th century memorial stones, one to several members of the Moffit family. Perhaps they were the same that farmed Ingram in the 1700s.

The plaque to Major William James Joicey of Linhope reminds us of his benefactions to the church (see Linhope chapter). One was acetylene gas lighting.

"It was very difficult to see or know when the gas was going to go out. This happened occasionally during evening service. Father would be in the pulpit, the light getting dimmer and dimmer, so mother would rush out to the gas house and remake the gas."

The two memorial windows, next to the door, were given by Mrs Helen Roddam in memory of her late husband, Lieutenant Colonel Roddam John Roddam, 3rd battalion, Northumberland Fusiliers. The Roddam family owned Ingram Farm from 1820 until 1920. Look carefully and notice a house painted on the stained glass. It is their ancestral home, Roddam Hall, three miles north of Ingram. The hall is shown as it was then, with two upper storeys. The top floor was removed in the early 1970s. Oddly, the window records that Lt. Col Roddam died in 1934; his headstone in the churchyard says 1933.

The War Memorials on the wall of the north aisle are much in keeping with the church: simple sandstone tablets inscribed with names of those who gave their lives in the two world wars.

Their Name Liveth for Evermore

1914-1918.

With the passing of time - and generations - the names come to mean less to those who read them. They are just names. I was curious to know more. Who were they? What happened to them? Turning the newspaper pages was a sombre experience. The initial enthusiasm to join Lord Kitchener's New Army gave way to column inches of names: sons, husbands, estate workers, railway workers, agricultural workers, missing, killed in action, wounded. The horrendous loss of lives was brought home to rural Northumberland.

"I remember the maids used to get cards from the men at the Front, funny ones usually, and I remember as a child seeing these cards coming from men in the trenches...they collected these cards and then you'd hear that so and so had been killed."

We read their names:

Christopher Leather. Lieutenant. Ingram. From a well known Northumberland family, he lived with his sister in the old farmhouse. Decorated for services during the Boer War in South Africa, he left the army in 1904. He re-joined on the outbreak of hostilities in August 1914. Christopher was serving with the Northumberland Fusiliers when he was killed during a night attack near Neuve Chapelle, France, in October 1914. He was 32 years old.

In his will he left his "motor car and income from investments" to Olive Marguerite Roddam and personal effects to his sister. The St. Christopher window in the south aisle and a plaque in the chancel are dedicated to his memory.

Walter Potts. Private. Glanton Northfield. He farmed in partnership with his brother. Called to "the Colours", he was granted temporary exemption from service in August

To the Glory of God and in memory of those who gave their lives in the Great War 1914–1918

Christopher Leather
Walter Potts
William Sisterson
George Trotter
Arthur J Turnbull

Their name liveth for evermore

The World War One memorial.

1916 by a county appeal tribunal. In December, the month he married, he again appeared before the tribunal seeking further exemption saying "brother goes with one pair of horses and me with the other". His application was rejected.

In 1918 his death was reported in the paper: "Quite a gloom was cast over Powburn and district when it became known that Private Walter Potts had fallen in the World conflict. The brave lad had seen 18 months service without a scratch until September 24th when, moving forward to the attack, he received his fatal wound, only surviving a few minutes. Being one of Britain's bravest, he asked his comrades for a cigarette, smoked it, and died like a true British soldier on the field of battle. (The) Deceased was one of the most respected young men of the district. He was of a bright and genial nature, always ready for a merry word and joke with all who knew him."

William Sisterson. Private. Linhope. A gamekeeper for Major Joicey, he returned from the War. After de-mob he walked home from Alnwick Station. His new boots skinned his heel and infection set in. He died in 1919 from double pneumonia following blood poisoning.

George Trotter. Private. Branton. Recruited into the 7th Northumberland Fusiliers in August 1915, he went to France in the November. A year later he was severely wounded in the knee and sent home to recover. He returned to France in March 1917 and was killed in action the following month. He was 28. His photograph appeared in the paper with the headline "A local hero's death".

James Arthur Turnbull. Private. Greenside Hill. I know few details except those gleaned from the inscription on his headstone and a memorial notice placed in the newspaper by his family a year after his death. The second son of George Turnbull he died, aged 21, at the Victoria Military Hospital, Beverley, Yorkshire, in November 1918. The cause of death was "pneumonia following influenza". His headstone, a cross on a tiered base, is just behind the churchyard wall.

In the south aisle a memorial window tells of the loss of another young soldier, Robert Collingwood Roddam, the only son of Lt. Col R. J. R. Roddam and his wife Helen. Serving with the Northumberland Fusiliers, Robert was awarded the Military Cross for "gallant and distinguished services" in the field at St. Eloi, Belgium. Promoted to captain just a few days before he died, Robert was killed in action at Hooge, Flanders, in 1915. He was 25. I surmise that his name is not on the war memorial because he lived outside the parish.

The Armistice was signed on Monday November 11th 1918.

"I can take you the spot today where I heard that the War had come to an end. We had a terrible postman in those days, he was called Harry Devine, he was far from it, and had a terrible temper. He was on a bicycle, of course, they wore those hats, they were eyeglass-shaped. Nanny and I were going for a walk. We went over Ingram Bridge and down past the railings when Harry appeared. There was a strong wind blowing, he was pushing his bicycle. All he said was 'the War's over'."

In September 1922, schoolchildren and parishioners gathered in church to remember the Fallen: their names, their faces. The occasion was the unveiling of the memorial stone, and the opening of the lych gate, by the Duke of Northumberland. The dedication service was led by the Bishop of Newcastle.

The Alnwick Guardian reported: "The cost of the memorials has been defrayed by subscription among Ingram villagers and its environs. The lych gate is of sturdy oak with a stone ridge. The front is surmounted by a cross and on a beam is the simple inscription In Memoriam 1914-1918."

The Bishop of Newcastle, Bishop Wild, and Alan Ian, the Eighth Duke of Northumberland lead the procession into church on the occasion of the unveiling of the War Memorials. *(© Newcastle Chronicle Ltd.)*

1939-1945

Relatives and friends of the men who died have recalled memories of the local lads, who swam in the river, went to dances together. Close friends. Their deaths were a dreadful loss in such a small community.

1939 ✝ 1945
James Allgood M.C.
Robert Holywell
William Purvis
Blain Stephenson
James Swanston

Friends who died.

We read their names:

James Allgood M.C. Lieutenant. Ingram Rectory. An army gunner, James was Mrs Church's brother. Awarded the Military Cross for services in the desert, he died in Italy while attempting to reach Allied troops. He had escaped from enemy captors and stepped on a landmine.

Robert Holywell. Ingram. An estate worker he died after contracting an illness and was buried in the churchyard. The inscription on the military headstone reads: 2659496 Guardsman R. Holywell, Coldstream Guards. 7th December 1940 aged 23. "Greater love hath no man than this, that a man lay down his life for his friend".

William Purvis. Ingram. Commando. Royal Marines. Billy returned home wounded in 1944 after D-Day. He married Ella Little, of Reaveley Greens, and went back to the war. Advancing into Holland, he was one of nine marines killed while attempting to take an island in a river. It was mistakenly believed to be safe. He died on January 28th 1945, five days after his 27th birthday. Billy was buried in a war cemetery south of Eindhoven.

Blain Stephenson. Powburn. Served with the Army Reconnaissance Regiment attached to the 7th Armoured Brigade, working behind enemy lines. Wounded in Normandy, Blain was put on a hospital ship that was torpedoed in the English Channel in August 1944. He was 19 years old and posted as "Missing at Sea".

James Swanston. Served in the 51st Highland division of the Black Watch. A gamekeeper at Broome Park his family home was at Ingram. Jimmy was married with a young baby that he never saw. He died early in 1940 on the retreat to Dunkirk. Aged 27, he was buried in Belgium.

God's Acre

In the 14th century the church was much bigger than today. It had wide north and south aisles, a longer chancel, evident on the ground outside the east window, and two chapels: the Clinch, or south chapel, and Reaveley or north chapel.

In those days of prosper, soon to be numbered by raiding and warfare, St. Michael's had two distinguished Rectors: William de Montfort, Dean of St Paul's, London, and his successor, William Reginald, chaplain to Edward 1, tutor to Edward II and later Archbishop of Canterbury and Lord Chancellor of England.

A survey by dowsing, undertaken by H. D. Briggs in 1986, located the foundations of the once much larger church. The accompanying sketch plan gives you some idea of how it looked then.

The old steps on the north side of the churchyard puzzled me. It seemed a strange place to have steps, who would use them? Bobbie Blain, the present day sexton had the answer. For many years the church heating system was dependent on a coke-fired boiler (until a severe frost wreaked havoc in 1982). The coke was stored in a stone shed outside the churchyard, beside the steps. They were a handy short cut to the boiler room, and saved the sexton carrying heavy sacks roundabout.

In 1983 four students from Alnwick Duchess High School carried out a survey of the churchyard under The Community Task Force initiative. One was Valerie Anderson whose family lived at Ingram. Their finished research was bound into a book, now in Bobbie's care.

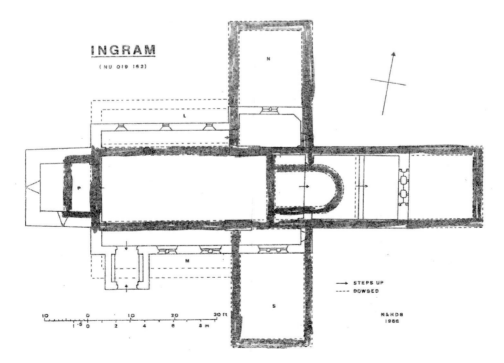

Church foundations as revealed by dowsing. The sketch plan features in a book entitled "Dowsing and Church Archaeology" of which H.D. Briggs was a co-author.

For the survey the churchyard was divided into six quadrants or areas, and each headstone plotted on a scaled map. The survey is in two parts: part one lists, in alphabetical order, the name of every person buried in the churchyard, except where the headstone was unreadable. After each name there is a quadrant number, a grave number and the date of death. With this information it is quite easy to locate specific graves. Part two details all the graves in each quadrant, together with the name(s) of those buried and, if known, where they lived. The burial book, without a shadow of a doubt, is an important parish archive. I have referred to it on countless occasions. As headstones weather, and lichens and moss obscure inscriptions, it is reassuring to know that the story they tell has been recorded for posterity.

Over the centuries many people from outside the parish have been buried at Ingram. The churchyard is now almost full so burials are generally restricted to parishioners. The question as to the future, where a new churchyard might be sited, has been asked but not answered. An area of ground on the southern boundary is now set aside for the interment of ashes.

Personally, I never tire of looking around the churchyard. My research has bought me into contact with so many people interred there, most of whom I have never met, but whom I feel I have come, in a little way, to know. Sadly, place names are omitted on several recent memorials; they often provide a valuable reference for historians.

On top of the church tower you can see the splendid weathervane. Declared unsafe, in the mid 1980s, it was taken down and languished for many years in a storeroom in the village hall. Thanks to financial assistance from the Northumberland National Park Authority it was restored to its rightful place in March 1999.

The Rectory

The Rectory stands at the western end of the churchyard, close to the Allgood family burial plot. It is most probable that it occupies the site of a former tower, the first reference to which dates back to 1509. The next reference occurs in a survey of 1542 in "A Book of the State of the Frontiers and Marches betwixt England and Scotland" to be found in John Hodgson's "A History of Northumberland".

"Ingrame a little towre decayed. At Ingrame ys a lytle towre w'ch ys the mansion house of the p'sonage there & for lacke of contynuall necessary repac'ns ys fallen in great decaye in the Cov'ynge & Rooffes there of. Also a lytle by west the said towre of Ingrame the ryv'or water of Brymshe by rage of floodes hath worne sore upon the southe banke thereof that except there be shortly made a were & defence of the same yt is very lyke in continuance of tyme to were awaye both the said towne of Ingram & tower aforesaid."

Another reference to the tower comes in 1734. "There are the remains of an old tower called Lumphaugh, at the distance of a pistol shot from the church".

The earliest reference I have found to the Rectory is in David Dippie Dixon's book "Whittingham Vale". In the "annals" we read of a fire in June 1775.

"The Rectory House at Ingram was entirely consumed by a chimney taking fire and communicating to the roof, which was thatched. Most of the household furniture, which belonged to Rev. Mr. Dixon, was saved by the uncommon spirit and activity of the neighbours, from the suddenness and violence of the flames. The whole misfortune is said to have arisen

from the nest of a jackdaw, which first took fire in the chimney."

Clearly the Rectory was re-built, or at least the damage made good, but exactly when I do not know. The house today is of two distinct architectural styles, Georgian and Victorian.

In 1804 when the church spire and steeple were taken down, being too ruinous to repair, permission was given to the Rev. Mr. Ion to remove the stone "for what purpose he may want them for the use of Rectory of this parish." Whether it was used to build a new Rectory, or re-model the old one, is not clear. What is more certain, however, is that the Victorian house was built in 1852, the year that James Allgood III became Rector. We know from Mrs Church that her grandfather wanted a house with "large windows and doors". In the Post Office Directory of Northumberland, 1858, we read: "The living is a Rectory value £480 a year with 40 acres of glebe land and handsome residence erected in 1852."

James III was the archetypal sporting rector. Perhaps his best-known feat was as an undergraduate at Oxford when he jumped a horse bareback over a table in the upstairs dining room of an Aylesbury tavern!

A follower of the West Percy Hunt, James III is remembered in C. M. Fergusson's book "Border Sport and Sportsmen" as "an outstanding sportsman and gentleman of the old school. A first class shot, an A1 breaker of retrievers, a good cricketer and a first rate Rector. Having an inherent love and knowledge of all that country life means, he is liked by all his hill farmers and shepherds who are his people."

His son Roland was also well known as a sporting rector. One of the best game shots in the north of England, he adored fishing and was a lifelong supporter of the Trinity Foot Beagles. His association with the pack went back to university days at Cambridge. It was partly through his

The Rectory circa 1900. The same view is not possible now since the land in the foreground was planted with trees.

involvement, whipping-in for four seasons in the early 1890s, that the pack was invited to hunt in Northumberland. The first visit was in 1895. Hounds and hunt staff travelled to Hedgeley Station in a horsebox coupled to a train and stayed in the farmhouse at Reaveley. It marked the beginning of an annual tradition that, with the exception of the war years and one or two others, has continued to the present day. The Trinity Foot is one of several beagle packs invited to Northumberland in September for the annual festival.

Roland and his wife Edith moved to Ingram in autumn 1908. The following year, when he took up the reins as Rector, the parish was considerably enlarged by the addition of Brandon and Branton, formerly part of Eglingham parish.

We read in the Glendale Parishes Magazine: "By the kind permission of the vicar of Eglingham, the Rector of Ingram has obtained the privilege of administering to the spiritual needs of the people of Brandon and Branton. He hopes to complete his round of visits there shortly." The two villages have remained part of Ingram Parish ever since.

From the outset the Allgoods worked wholeheartedly for the good of the community; bringing people together, supporting charitable causes and broadening the social fabric of valley life. Between them their talent for organising all manner of activities and occasions became well known: Mrs Allgood for her work during the First World War sending parcels and comforts to the troops, with the nursing association, the Sunday school, the Girls' Club, the Mother's Union and the church choir. The Rector is remembered as the founder of the parish tea and sports, the pigeon club, and the motivator behind the new village hall.

Shortly after taking up office Canon Allgood was walking on the Fawdon hills when he came across the still-warm body of a wild goat, partially hidden in deep snow.

"It had obviously been thrown out of the herd. You often saw them at Threestoneburn, The Dod or up the valley. Father had the head sent away to a taxidermist. The skin was given to old Jack Wilson, originally our gardener, and he had the skin as a mat."

Affectionately known as "Goaty", the fine head was mounted and hung in the entrance hall at the Rectory. In 1914 an article by "Rambler" appeared in the Newcastle Journal.

"The wild herd I saw last week on the Cumbrian border edge were fine beasts, yet not one can equal the "billy" I went to see in a charming house up the Breamish two days ago. "Some while ago I had taken a photo of his head and horns, but this did not content me. I got a tape and measured this on Saturday night. From tip to tip I found 31 inches; the right horn went up to quite 32 inches, the left to 31inches, both horns wrinkled like that of an ibex and having 18 rings, probably told his age, as the circles inside the bark do that of a tree. I believe this specimen makes a record for the finest goat in Northumberland."

The wild goat population is now greatly diminished largely because of drastic, some people would say unnecessary, culling. The nearest herd today lives on the hills near Kirknewton.

When the Allgoods left Ingram in 1947, Mrs Church and her husband gave Goaty a new home. *"We were always very fond of it but when we moved to Glanton there just wasn't room. He went to the Hancock Museum."*

Roland and Edith Allgood both died in 1948. They are buried at Ingram. The Rectory was sold off in the early 1960s when Ingram was amalgamated into the Glendale Group of Parishes headed by a team rector, based at Wooler.

The Church today.

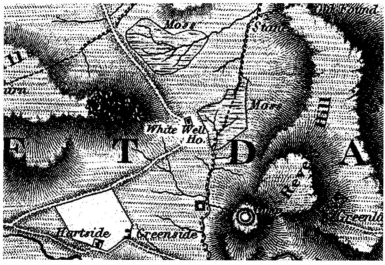

White Well House as shown on Greenwood's map of 1828

17
Ingram School

The school, a single classroom with the teacher's cottage adjoining, served the scattered community of Ingram parish for more than a century: from its opening in 1834 to closure in 1958.

During my research I have heard mention of a school at White Well Walls, an abandoned medieval village near the foot of Dunmoor hill. Only Winnie and Sarah Thompson could provide any evidence. They told me that when they lived at Greenside Hill, in the 1920s, an elderly man visited the farm. He told them that his father or grandfather (they couldn't remember which) had lived at Hartside and walked to school at the White Well Walls. On Greenwood's map of 1828 a dwelling known as "White Well House" is marked. I have delved no further but would surmise that perhaps a shepherd gave elementary tuition in his home. Its situation would have been quite central for the hill children from Linhope and Hartside, Ilderton Dod and Reaveley Hill.

Thanks to Canon Charles Hay's research in the church registers we know when Ingram School was built, and a little of its early history. An entry in the vestry book, 1833, details "subscriptions for the erection of a school and cottage, intended to be built on the Glebe at Ingram."

The subscribers were local landowners, and the Rector, Reverend James Allgood II. His disproportionately large subscription of £200 would seem to give the church considerable influence over the new "Free" school. [It eventually became a Church of England Controlled School]. Others who subscribed £20 each were the Rector's brother, Roland Lancelot Allgood, owner of the Reaveley and Brandon Estates; the Duke of Northumberland, Fawdon and Clinch estates and William Roddam, Ingram estates. The trustees of William Weallans Esq, Hartside and Greenside Hill, and Bishop Crewe's trustees (as owners of the Glebe?) each contributed £10.

A later note in the vestry book adds: "The above sums were expended according to the several

130

receipts, given by the builders, who undertook the work, and which are deposited in the iron box chest. More than thirty shillings were paid, in addition to the original subscription, for work not included in the stimate."

An advertisement was placed for a schoolmaster, the cost of 6s 6d being met out of vestry expenses. For many years the same landowners paid an annual subscription to help augment the schoolmaster's income. The first mentioned was in 1834. We read of the Duke paying £4.0.0, Mr Allgood, three guineas, William Roddam, two guineas, I.N. Weallans £1.10.0 and an unspecified amount of £10.0.0, most probably from the Rector.

In 1855 the school was described as "a neat structure possessing accommodation for 50 pupils". The schoolmaster was a James Sutherland who combined his job with that of parish clerk.

A picture of day-to-day life at the school emerges on reading the logbooks. The earliest in existence begins in 1876 and ends in 1916. The second covers the years from 1916 - 1956 and the third, 1957-1958.

One senses the frustration felt by successive teachers: the difficulties of actually educating children, who for various reasons, illness, truancy, the weather, the long walk, did not attend regularly, and the disruption caused by "the flittings" in May, the customary time when farm workers and their families uprooted, often on an annual basis, to new jobs on other farms. Continuity of learning was hard to achieve.

The school curriculum was limited, and rather dull. Pupils were taught the 'three R's', supplemented by botany, geography and history. Strong emphasis was given to scripture, religious instruction in line with Church of England teaching. Throughout its history the school maintained close links with the local clergy. They visited on a regular basis to examine the children in Bible knowledge.

Until the 1950s the school lacked even basic facilities: no kitchen, no electricity and no piped water. The children drank from 'the well' in the playground. Not a well in the accepted sense of the word, but a trough continuously filled by a piped supply of spring water that drained away into the burn. An open fire in the classroom was the only source of heat; wet clothes were hung beside it to dry and drinks warmed up on the hearth. Everyone sat at desks, the youngest pupils aged six or seven taught alongside older peers. By the time the school closed the leaving age had been raised to 15.

The logbooks, Inspector's reports and former pupils tell the story.

Sir Edwin Landseer's famous painting of the Chillingham Wild Cattle featured on the cover of the Glendale Parishes Magazine for many years.
(© NCRO)

1893 - The average attendance was 8.1 boys and 16.6 girls. In the parish magazine we read: "It is gratifying to note that the parents of scholars have contributed 19s 8d for coals."

1894 - Inspector's Report: **"The children passed fairly but much remains to be done. The reading should be much more animated and the reading lessons should be explained. I shall hope some day to see the cold stone floor replaced by a wooden floor."**

1899 -

May.	Admitted two new pupils from Heddon, James and Arthur Harbottle.
June.	The above removed from school because it was too far for them to walk.
July 21.	Poor attendance due to bad weather.
August 4.	Poor attendance owing to Wooler Show.
September 22.	Attendance very poor this week, several children have not returned since the holidays. May Davison will not be back to school until the spring owing to distance.

1900 -

January.	Emily M. Crawley commenced duties as teacher.
February 23.	The average attendance is 7. The state of the roads makes it impossible for those who live any distance to attend.
March 16.	Some of the children from the hills have attended this week for the first time since Christmas.
March 30.	Measles has broken out in school. Accordingly it has been closed until 23 April by the doctor's advice.
May 4.	The school is at a great disadvantage owing to the prolonged absence of more than half of the scholars. Many have attended (only) a week since Christmas and some only one day.
May 11.	Thirteen children have attended this week and in consequence the work is more satisfactory.
November 9.	All the children helped to finish and make garments preparatory to sale of work which took place today. The sale was well attended and all but two pinafores were sold. The takings amounted to 25s 6d half of which will be used to buy new materials.
December 14.	The timetable was altered to give sufficient time for examinations in reading, writing, recitation, dictation and arithmetic.

Inspector's Report: **"The children are industrious and considering the poor attendance caused by very severe weather have made satisfactory progress."**

1901 -

May 1.	Fifteen children present. Two are away from school with whooping cough.
May 10.	Six children are leaving the school because their parents are leaving the district.

1902 -

March 7.	I have taken James Sisterson's name off the register as he has only attended three days since mid-summer.
March 14.	James Sisterson returned to school on Monday and has attended this week.

Inspector's Report: **"The order and instruction in this very small school are quite satisfactory, especially considering the broken attendance during the last few months owing to the severe winter and the long distances the children have to walk."**

September 15.	School opened today with 11 children.

1903 -

May 8.
: Several pupils are leaving the school this week. One has been obliged to close the school today for a week on account of the many changes taking place in the district.

June 19.
: It has been decided to take the mid-summer holidays now instead of in August. The school closes today for 5 weeks.

September 18.
: The result of the half-year examination held last month is fairly satisfactory. All subjects were weak in standard 4, the children being careless and thoughtless. None of them show an intelligent interest in their work or any desire to improve. The great drawback to a school of this kind is the constant changing from one place to another, as it is impossible for the children to get merely interested and desirous of improving.

1904 -
: The Inspector's report urges the Managers to consider boarding the floor.

May 13.
: A half (day's) holiday was given on Monday on account of the Ingram Farm sale.

May 6.
: I received notice that Mary Shell being over 14 years of age has left the school as she is needed to help in the house. Eleanor Porteous leaves today for the summer half year. She is to be employed in agricultural labour until November. Average attendance this week is 17.

1906 -

January 19.
: Average attendance for the past week is 6.7. The weather has been boisterous and some children are absent because of epidemic sickness.

October 19.
: Severe storm today, no children attended school.

1907 -

January 11.
: The hill children have not returned.

January 30.
: Storm. Two children attended. Register not marked.

March 4.
: Obliged to send children outside and open windows from 9 o' clock to 9.25 as the fire was smoking.

March 16.
: The week has been very stormy. Severe weather threatened on Wednesday afternoon. School was closed for the afternoon. On Friday no children attending, school was closed for the day. As I consider that the attendances made by many of the children might have been better, facilities being given for the changing of wet shoes and stockings, I have sent several names today to the attendance officer.

May 15.
: The hygiene inspectress visited the school this week on behalf of the Education Committee who wish lessons on food to be included in the yearly syllabus.

May 28.
: Form No. 39 sent from West Lilburn School stated that John Redpath is aged 13 years. He himself states that he will not be 13 until July 15 1908.

1910 -

January 14.
: School closed for a fortnight by order of the Medical Officer. Sickness in the District.

May 20.
: School closed today for the funeral of the King. [Edward VII]

1911 -

March.
: The accommodation of Ingram School is capable of holding 44 pupils, on a basis of allowing not less than 10 square feet of floor space for each older child and 9 square feet for each infant.

May 4.
: Attendance officer called and took names of two boys who have been absent over a fortnight, lambing.

May 5.
: Owing to heavy rain frequently this week the Linhope children have attended badly. The children have learned a new song today for the Coronation.

June 16.
: Closed school today for Coronation week holiday. The children had tea, sports and fireworks and each received a medal.

July 25.	All the hill children are absent from school today owing to a bull being in the vicinity. It is a source of danger and all the children are afraid. Steps have been taken to have it removed. I myself have written to Mr. Robson at Hedgeley to remove it. Attendance only 13.
September 8.	School closed half an hour early in order to allow children to go to Major Joicey's tea party. (at Linhope)
November 3.	The hill children are not able to get down the Hartside road, it being flooded by the Breamish.
1912 -	
September.	Medical inspection of children. Only five presented for inspection owing to some parents objecting.
1913 -	
October 2.	Every child was present at school today - 20.
1914 -	
January.	George Bell fell in the stream during play this afternoon. I accordingly sent him home to get dry things on.
July.	Miss Evelyn Scott came to the school to take charge temporarily but there were no children present.
November.	The Sisterson family at Hartside have got scarlet fever. All the children from the hill district absent owing to that disease.
1915 -	Miss Rebecca Morton commenced duties as teacher.
December 10.	The average attendance for the week has only been 5.9. The weather has been bad for the hill children to come the long distance. I hear the boys are bush beating at 4 shillings each per day.
1916 -	
January 25.	Only four children present and on enquiring I learn there was shooting at Linhope so probably the hill boys are bush beating.
February 17.	The attendance both last week and this have been poor. I received instructions not to take names off the register and to be most careful of omitting to mark for poor attendance.
March 9.	No children attended. I have been reading this logbook through and find much the same state of things. Have also practised on the organ.
April.	Bad attendance is the rule not the exception here…the position is quite hopeless when managers and parents conspire to put the teacher under the children's rule rather than vice versa. The teacher resigned.
May 15.	Three Oliver children admitted. A welcome addition to my very backward school.
29.	Little Adam returned to school this afternoon after being off nearly two weeks turf cutting. He and John Little took the morning in going to the stores at Hedgeley for their parents.
December.	Mrs J.E. Stuart commenced duties as teacher.
7.	We took our first nature walk under my supervision. It is a bright frosty day. 7 children present.
23.	The children gave a concert in school. The profit of £1 5s 1d to be devoted to the establishment of a basketball team.
1917 -	
October 26.	Two boys when on cycles collided and were severely hurt. They were bandaged and sent home in Mr. Nesbit's cart.
1918 -	
November 10.	Influenza epidemic. School closed. Re-opened on December 2 but closed again until after the Christmas holidays.

1919 -

February 27-March 17.

School closed again. Influenza.

August 25.   Admitted George James Anderson [of Linhope] for the first time.

"We had a wonderful teacher. We never really appreciated how good she was. She taught the whole school, about 20 of us. She did far beyond what was reasonably required to do her job. If we got wet she would make sure we got dried and would lend us clothes." George Anderson. Linhope.

1922 -

September.   Children attended church for unveiling of the war memorials.

"I got terribly wrong when the Memorial was unveiled. The Bishop had an impediment in his speech and there was a great gushing of words and then a long, long silence and you know what bairns are, I happened to look up and saw Jim Jackson. He was smiling and we both burst out laughing. Mother never stopped fighting to us all the way home from Ingram. The next day at school the teacher gave us an awful dressing down for laughing in the church." Betty Anderson. Linhope.

1929 -

February 8.   Holiday today so the children can attend the opening of the village hall.

"We watched the hall being built, the roof going up. The teacher sat at the front beside the fire. The older you got the further back the room you went. We sat at a desk, one desk between two of us with two inkwells. We wrote with scratchy pens. I remember getting the water from the well to make the ink. It was mixed with black powdery stuff and put in a big stone jar. We did scripture, sums, reading, dictation, history and geography. When Rev. Allgood came into school we had to stand up and if there was a funeral we were kept in." Mark Purvis. Ingram.

Ingram School pupils 1922. The photograph was taken in the churchyard. George and Betty Anderson are circled.

Back row (l-r): Donald McLean, Reaveley; George Anderson, Linhope; John Thomas Sisterson, Hartsid; Robbie Sisterson, Linhope; Alex Armstrong, Reaveley Greens; Alf Armstrong, Reaveley Greens; Johnny Glendinning, Reaveley; Jimmy Swanston, Ingram.

Middle: Jean Sisterson, Linhope; Ellen Jackson, Ingram; Betty Anderson, Linhope; Mrs J.E. Stuart with daughter Irene; Winnie Thompson, Greenside Hill; Agnes Jackson, Ingram; Edith Nesbit, Ingram Mill; Elvia Glendinning, Reaveley.

Front: Dick Sisterson, Hartside; Gabriel 'Gib' Swanston; Jackie Stuart; Robbie Swanston (holding ball), Ingram; Adam Jackson, Ingram; Jimmy Sisterson, Hartside; Will and Eddy Armstrong, Reaveley Greens.

1930 -
September 1.   Miss Eva Maclean, a local gamekeeper's daughter, commenced duties as teacher.

1935 -
Marriage of Miss MacLean. She returned to school as Mrs Proudlock.

1936 - Christmas party in the hall.
"The children of Ingram School, with their baby brothers and sisters brought along by their mothers, met at the Parish Hall for a delightful afternoon. Games were played to suit all ages then they all sat down to a Christmas tea, complete with crackers. After tea the children entertained their visitors by singing etc. Miss Opie Robson [now Mrs Opie Telford of Mile End, Glanton] **played a very pretty piece on the piano…by this time a huge pond complete with humped monster had been arranged and from this pond each child drew a present. Mrs Proudlock received a pair of gloves and an afternoon cloth from the scholars. Bags of sweets, apples and oranges given by Mrs Bryant, Mrs Robson and Mrs Allgood were distributed."**
Alnwick and County Gazette and Guardian.

1939 -
April.   Fifteen pupils on the register.
September 1.   Evacuation Order issued. School closed for three days.
September 3.   War declared. School closed until the 11th. Several evacuee children attended
                 school during wartime: two stayed privately with the Bryants of Ingram and
                 others with local families under the Government's Evacuation Scheme.

1940 - Instruction given on air raid precautions and gas mask drill.

Bobbie Blain was 11 when he first went to Ingram School in 1941. He provides the personal recollections of schooldays during the War years.

"If there was an attack the church bell was to be rung by anyone near at hand. It was rung once after a report of an invasion in Lincolnshire.
"The school windows were all taped up to stop the glass shattering. At various times we had to have a drill to see how quickly we could put our gas masks on, it was to get you used to them because they were quite uncomfortable. If you forgot your gas mask it was about 100 lines."

1941 -
February.   School cut off from village by snow.
April.   Fire-fighting practice. Use of sand and stirrup pump.

"There were buckets of sand in school and a hand-manned stirrup pump. We had to put it in a bucket of water and then pump like anything. There were no taps in school. It had a long hose, the harder you pumped the more pressure you got. Someone would be responsible for putting it into the bucket and someone was responsible for the nozzle. We had these practices outside about once a month. Then we had to pretend there was a fire in the loft. One of us stood on a desk with a smaller one on your shoulders, below the trapdoor. The older ones went up into the attic. A bucket of sand was passed up and we had to wear our gas masks when we were doing this."

November.   Several boys are helping Mr. Allen (the farmer) to lift potatoes.

1943 -
January.   Heating oil stove put in classroom at 8.15a.m.and together with the fire the
                 temperature rose to 45 at 9.30a.m.

1944 -
January 26.   The temperature in school this week has been nearly beyond endurance. Children
                are sitting with scarves & coats on.
*"You couldn't write because your fingers were so numb. We used to love to get out at playtime and have a
run around to warm up.*

*"The older ones had to knit socks and scarves for the Forces. I had to knit a pair of socks, dark blue, for a
navy chap. They were on three needles and a spare one that you knitted onto. We only did our knitting once
a week and my hands were always sticky. It was so cold and damp the needles used to rust over the course
of the week. I would take them with the knitting to the lych gate wall. You had to transfer the knitting from
one needle to another, and rub the spare needle on the wall to get the rust off."*

Bobbie left school in 1945 aged 14.

1947 -
February.   School closed. Snow,
1949 -
January.   Reassembled after Christmas vacation. Temperature in school is 41 degrees.
            Everything is damp and really unfit to be in as the children all have coughs and
            colds.
            As I began to feel shivery and faint during the morning, caused by the smoke and
            dampness, the school was closed during the afternoon and a large fire left to dry
            the room out.
May 12.   Children taken to the farm sale at Ingram.
May 16.   Admitted James, Janette and Isabella Wilson from Fenwick Farm, Scotland. Fifteen
            pupils on the register.
1950 -
March 9.   We have had our first meal served in school from the new canteen. A most
            enjoyable and appetising meal served to 10 pupils and myself.

Hedley Wilcox badly burnt at his home on Sunday March 26. [Hedley was the Rector's son. He was
14. On Sunday afternoons the Alnwick Motor Cycle Club used to scramble bikes on Fawdon hill.
Hedley had been watching, with other local lads, and got grass stains on his trousers. When he got
home he went into the garage and used petrol to try and remove them. As he lit a cigarette the
fumes ignited. He suffered fatal burns and died in hospital a few days later].

June.   Nine children on the register.
October 18 -   The school got a wireless.
1951 -
May 21.   Admitted Robbie Cowens, Linhope.
1952 -
January 8.   Admitted John Wilson, Ingram.
May.   Mrs Mame Bell appointed as cook.
October.   Twenty-two pupils on the roll aged between 5 and 15.

Ministry of Education report: **"This small country school consists of only one room. There is no
artificial lighting, no running water except in the built on kitchen canteen and no surfaced
playground. The rough patch on which the children play and have their physical education is
often unusable. The head mistress has worked single-handed since 1930.**

**"In an assessment of the work, due consideration must be paid to the fact that every year there
is a coming and going of pupils due to the May Hirings. Of the 8 seniors now in attendance**

only three have spent all their school life here. Some of the children have had several changes
of school and their work has suffered accordingly."

1954 -

February.	Schoolroom let to the hunt committee as a supper room.
	During the summer holidays the roof was re-slated, the porch cemented and a new stove installed.
October.	Schoolroom and canteen painted. Washbasins fitted in porch.

1955 -

April.	School and canteen water in "filthy condition containing live creatures."

1956 -

May.	The new Secondary Modern School opened at Wooler. 10 juniors and infants on register.
	Mrs Bell retired as cook after 4 years but carried on as caretaker.
September.	New floor laid at a cost of £83.13, exactly 52 years after the first wooden floor of 1904.
	Electric light installed in the school and canteen at a cost of £97.15s 4d.
	The Clerk to the School Managers is the new Rector, Rev. P. G .M. Dennis. His salary was £11.10s 0d

1957 -

May 31.	Managers Meeting re-proposed closure of school and transfer of children to Branton County Primary School.
June.	Ten pupils on register.
	Local people signed a petition opposing the closure plans.

The Christmas Party in the Village Hall. 1955. *Clockwise:* **John Tunnah, Violet Tunnah, Ingram; Robbie Cowens, Linhope; Mrs Eva Proudlock; Betty Tunnah; Billy Goodfellow, Reaveley; Heather Cowens, Greenside Hill; Michael Hope, Reaveley; Sheena Telfer, Linhope; Johnny Wilson, Ingram; Margaret and Angeline Goodfellow; Thomas Tunnah; Laura Goodfellow; Jake Wright, Low Blakehope; Isabella Wilson; John Hope.**
Foreground (right) **Ethel and Barry Cook, Ingram.** *(© Northumberland Gazette)*

The Newcastle Diocesan Education Committee reconsidered the question of closure and was "anxious" that the school should not be closed but retained for as long as possible.

July. - Diocesan Inspector's report: **"Every one of the eight children is receiving Church of England teaching which is given regularly by the Head Teacher. The vicar is a frequent and interested visitor to the school. The catechism is being well taught and learnt. ...it was a genuine pleasure to be with pupils who were so obviously interested in what they were learning and doing."**

October 7.	Notice of closure posted on the school this morning. "The Northumberland County Council being the Social Education Authority propose to cease to maintain the Ingram Church of England Voluntary School."
	Two fire extinguishers supplied to school.
November 8.	Managers agreed to lodge objection to closure.
December 20.	Christmas Party.
	Mrs Proudlock noted in the logbook: "It was the wish from all present that the school would still be in being for many more Christmases to come."
	Attendance for the month was 100%.
	The Nature Prize "The Observers Book of Butterflies" awarded to William Goodfellow who brought in 74 wild flowers out of the total, for 1957, of 156.

1958 -

April 28.	School closure confirmed in a letter from the Director of Education to Mrs Proudlock.

"I should be grateful if you would kindly let the Managers know that it has now been decided that the school should be closed at the end of the summer term and that the children should transfer to Branton School. Further particulars about the arrangement will follow later."

"I started when I was 5 and left when I was 11, when it closed. There was compulsory drinking of warm milk that had been heated beside the fire. In the winter the milk froze in the bottle and the ice came out the top. The food was very good. We always had creamed potatoes and tomato relish on a Monday.
"The school trip was to Spittal beach, one year we went to Bamburgh. The highlight of the year was the Christmas party in the hall. There was a big tea. The Christmas tree was at one end and there were decorations. Santa Claus came with presents. I remember getting a tin drum. It was hung on the tree with my name on it.
"We used to knit. It took me two years to knit a sweater but I did get a prize for it at Ingram Show.
"There were nine pupils at school when it closed. There was no closing ceremony. We got some books and bits of things, old cricket stumps that didn't go back to county hall." Johnny Wilson, Ingram.

July 17.	The attendance officer took medical cards, books, sewing, craft materials and PE equipment.
July 25.	All the canteen equipment was taken away this afternoon by the county meals service van. Miss Ina Bell finished today as temporary canteen cook and will finish on July 31 as caretaker.
	Desks and other equipment still remaining are to go to Bamburgh Church of England and Branton County Primary Schools.
	Visit of Dr Reid to say goodbye and collect medical equipment.
	Mrs Proudlock wrote and signed the final entry: "Closure of school and the termination of my duties after 28 years."

In 1963 the school began a new life as the National Park Information Centre. (See Chapter Early Days in the National Park).

Mamie Wilson and Robert Little were married at St. Michael's Church on August 2nd 1930. Following the service the newly weds walked under an archway of hockey sticks formed by the Hedgeley hockey team of which they were members. Their wedding reception was held in the parish hall where over 100 guests were entertained to tea.

The couple are pictured outside the hall with Mamie's family - her parents Jack and Jane Wilson, of Rectory

---

18
The Parish Hall

During the summer of 2004, two simple signing ceremonies took place at Ingram: one in church, after morning service, the other at a parish council meeting. Together the occasions marked the start of a new, hopefully brighter future for the parish hall, now sorely in need of major refurbishment.

The signing of a new trust deed and constitution represented the formal transfer of the hall from the church to the community for whom it was built 75 years ago. Most importantly, it opened the door for applications for external funding. This is seen as vital to help meet the high cost of restoration, and ensure the long-term future of the building.

When the hall was opened on February 8th 1929 it was cause for celebration. A large crowd gathered to watch the Rector's sister, Mrs Straker, of Angerton, perform the ceremony.

"In the evening everyone adjourned to tea in the school after which entertainment was given in the parish hall. It consisted of some clever conjuring tricks. At the close Col. Roddam proposed a comprehensive vote of thanks. Afterwards the hall was cleared for dancing when a large company danced to excellent music composed by local violinists." Alnwick County Gazette and Guardian.

For the first time parishioners now had a meeting place other than the church or school room. It had taken several years to gather enough money together. Thanks largely to the energies and endeavours of the Rector, Canon Roland Allgood, the £100 residue in the war memorial fund was gradually augmented by public subscriptions, sales of work, a legacy grant and help from diocesan funds.

With almost £500 in hand, building work started in 1928 on a plot of Glebe land next to the school. The builders were Beatties of Wooler. Constructed of rock-faced concrete and lit by piped acetylene gas, the hall with its wood panelled interior became a great asset to the small community. Under its roof dances, social occasions and meetings about all manner of things were held; the Girls' Club, the Show, the Men's Club and the Women's Institute, to name but a few.

Unfortunately, in 1929, nobody thought to write anything down or draw up an official deed. Informally the Rector and churchwardens were the trustees, the day to day running administered by an ad-hoc hall committee.

It was not until the 1970s when the committee applied for a grant to improve the toilets (chemical buckets in the old earth closets) that a major problem became apparent: the hall had no legal owner.

By then Canon Charles Hay was team rector. He took up the cause of the ownerless building - for which no rent had ever been paid - and after great personal effort, hours of research and negotiations with the Church authorities, a solution was found. The hall was transferred to the Newcastle Diocesan Society who held it in trust for Ingram Parochial Church Council.

Canon Hay said at the time: "The PCC has always looked on this project as a means of preserving the only community facility in the entire parish, the only meeting place other than the Church building itself. It has not sought ownership for its own ends but because there seemed to be no other way of preventing the hall from falling into complete ruin."

The Ingram W.I. outing to Keswick, 1953.
Pictured (l-r) **Mrs Renee Telfer, Linhope; Babs Cowens, Linhope; Mrs Jean Beattie, High Blakehope; Mrs Annie Goodfellow, Reaveley Hill; Willie Scott, Brandon; Mrs Jemima Smith, Alnham Moor; Mrs Janet Taylor, Linhope; Mrs Ivy Cowens, Greenside Hill; Jimmy Davison, the bus driver.**

Teas are served in the hall on Ingram Show day. This photograph was taken in the late 1990s.

Because of uncertainty little in the way of maintenance had been done for many years. After its formation in 1979 the parish council agreed to help in whatever way it could, and to organise fund raising activities towards a new floor. In the mid 1980s, with the help of a National Park grant, the original window frames were renewed and the floor replaced. Subsequently new toilet facilities were added and the kitchen refurbished at a cost of about £5,000, the money raised by local efforts, including a grand auction, and grant aid.

In the new millennium, with no money to effect major repairs, the PCC unanimously agreed to hand over the building to a new hall management committee, with charitable status, thus making it easier to attract outside funding.

After almost three years of complex legal negotiations the hall was transferred to Ingram Parish Council, as custodian trustees, on a 30-year lease with effect from July 1st 2004. Henceforth the building will be known as Ingram Village Hall, rather than church or parish hall.

The main priorities of the new hall committee are to replace the windows and doors, modernise the kitchen and provide facilities for the disabled. Canon Hay's words still ring true today: "It is a community asset which has been kept alive though the years by community effort."

19
Ingram Show

The origins of Ingram Show can be traced back to the early autumn of 1909 when the new Rector, Canon Roland Allgood, organised the first "parish gathering". It was very much a local affair, connected to St. Michael and All Angels Church. Parishioners were invited. Outsiders were not.

That a record of the occasion survives is thanks to the Rector who wrote an account for the Glendale Parishes Magazine.

In the issue of September 1909 we read: "With regard to the Parish Gathering: I would only say that at present the main object will be to give all parishioners an annual opportunity of joining together in friendly intercourse and enjoyment.

"We hope that there may be games or sports for children. We hope to be able to supply an excellent tea for all, at the small cost of 6d per head, just to defray its' own expenses.

"Following this we hope that there may be a musical entertainment which will of course be free of charge followed by other games for all and perhaps a few dances to wind up with because a more definite programme will be issued later on.

"In conclusion, to avoid disappointment afterwards, I would remind you that this entertainment must be exclusively Parochial (that is including both Brandon and Branton) and we cannot on this occasion invite our friends from elsewhere.

"Herewith then let me extend the heartiest of invitations to all parishioners, and may a hearty acceptance and fine weather contribute to the success of our First Parochial Gathering".

In the November issue Canon Allgood wrote: "Not only have we successfully held our first annual Parish Tea and Social Gathering but thanks to the generosity of Major and Mrs Joicey, let it be known that we have become possessed of a Parish Tea Set of our own.

"If our room was small our "company" at any rate was large, and I hope everyone enjoyed themselves. And let me say how very grateful we were for the willing hands who helped in the various arrangements which were necessary for the children's Games, Tea, Concert etc.

"I only hope that next year all those who come to our Parish Gathering will also make a point of being present and joining in the Service on our Dedication Festival Sunday. "Our church being the church of St. Michael it is proposed to hold this gathering on or about St. Michael's Day."

The Parish Tea was held on the green beside the school until 1914 when it was "indefinitely postponed" owing to the War.

Canon Roland Allgood, founder of Ingram Show.

It was revived as part of the Peace Celebrations, most probably in 1919, the Armistice having been signed the previous November.

In 1923 it took on a new dimension when another of the Rector's innovative ideas came to fruition: the formation of a sports club. Since then, the two events - sports day and the parish tea - have run hand-in-hand, evolving over the years into Ingram Show, traditionally held on the second Saturday in September.

The first meeting of the Ingram Sports Club was held in the school in July 1923. About 25 people were present to hear Canon Allgood outline his ideas for sports day. A committee was formed, officials elected and the proceedings written up in a ledger. It survives to this day, in the care of Jimmy Givens, of Brandon, a fascinating record of the parish tea and sports from 1923 - 1945.

At the inaugural meeting it was agreed that the sports be confined to the Parish, just as the first Gathering had been in 1909.

"Any man is eligible to compete in the sports at Ingram Parish Tea who has been regularly resident in the Parish or who has regular employment in the Parish or is resident in the Parish owing to his employer being a householder in the Parish."

Several resolutions were carried: that the Parish Tea committee be asked to "manage the teas as in previous years", the sum of 1s to be charged for the same. That the committee of the Girls' Club be asked to run the children's and ladies' sports, and that money prizes only be given for all events. Subscribers to be asked, and anyone giving 2s or more to receive a free admission ticket to the Tea and Sports.

A further five meetings were held before the first sports day on September 16th 1923. The field behind the stack yard at Ingram was chosen as the most suitable venue, the green beside the school being too small. A tent was borrowed from Major Browne of Callaly Castle, for the tea and a dance in the evening.

The programme of sports included serious field and track events, and many novelty races: an obstacle race which included changing clothes, drinking a bottle of lemonade and smoking a cigarette, a ladies 'air ball' race, bumping in sacks, pillow fight on a pole and an old men's handicap for over 50s. For 1d you could try 'cutting down the rabbit' - and keep it if you succeeded!

"It was simply and utterly a parochial event. It was known as The Ingram Parish Tea and Sports, that was what it was called and it was absolutely and completely just for the parishioners. It was an event and gathering of everyone together, no televisions or cars or telephones in those days. It was organised by my father. He started it.
"There was always a very good tea which my mother ran with various helpers who came every year to help her. We didn't have industrial departments, or sandwich cakes and the largest potatoes and writing, and all that business....just the tea and sports.
There was a wheelbarrow race, a tug of war, bolster and bar and 100 yards....just for the parish and they had a wonderful day." Mrs Naomi Church.

Included in the sports programme for 1923 was a Hill Race, the Rector's idea. He had seen a similar event at Grasmere Sports in the Lake District. Word of mouth has it that a version of the race was run before the Sports Club started. But 1923 was the first year that runners competed for a magnificent silver challenge cup.

The Rector and churchwardens of Ingram Parish were appointed 'ex officio' trustees of the cup. The Minutes Book does not reveal who gave it but Bobbie Blain, whose association with the show goes back many years, believes it was Mr. Annandale. A wealthy businessman, he farmed at Brandon, and was the first secretary of the Sports Club.

The race was run over Ingram Glitters above Peggy Bell's Bridge. The course was fixed "from the Ingram side of the water at "Knock End", over the Old Camp and finish at the gate into the "Night Fold." The route is the same today. Initially the race was confined to residents of "Ingram Parish and Upper Breamish Water".

"The runners, the first time that I went, were taken up in a horse and a cart to just above Peggy Bell's Bridge. We started from the same place that they do now. You went up the Glitters and there was a pole, way up on the top. We had to keep to the right of that. If I remember rightly there was somebody standing up there to see that it was carried out properly.
There was an old wood up there on the hillside. We came down there and finished at what they called the Night Fold, past Ingram near Bulby's Wood." Adam Sisterson. Linhope.

In 1926 the hill race was opened to adjoining parishes, perhaps to attract more entries. The prize money was set at £1, 15/-, 10/- and 5/- providing there were at least nine runners. Three years later, after another lengthy discussion about the confined nature of the sports, some novelty races were opened to outsiders.

The first vegetable and industrial show was held in 1929 (the flower show followed in the mid 1930s) and that year the dance was held in the newly opened parish hall to reduce the cost of hiring marquees.

In 1932 Canon Allgood put the future of the sports to a vote. Should they continue or cease? It was unanimously agreed to continue, and seventeen sports including boxing in barrels and a motorcycle obstacle race were planned.

An advert inviting people to the 1936 Ingram Sports appeared in the Alnwick and County Gazette and Guardian.

"A full programme of athletic sports and novelty races from 2p.m. until dusk including the famous Hill Race on the foothills of the Cheviots. Most Picturesque Setting, Most Enjoyable Day. Come and Join in on Saturday, September 12th at 2p.m."

As it turned out, the day was marred by incessant rain. Only part of the sports programme was held and the children's events were postponed until the Monday night. It was a financial disaster. The sports ran at a loss of £12 13s 6d.

R. Swanson Winning The Barrel Boxing Event.

Barrel boxing 1936 *(© Northumberland Gazette)*

Three successive deficits, when money was taken from the tea account and the hill race subscription fund to balance the books, eventually forced the opening of all the sports events in 1938. People from the parishes of Alwinton, Kirknewton, Ilderton, Eglingham, Whittingham and Alnham could now take part. A sheep dog trial was held for the first time.

A year later, following a public general meeting in June, posters and schedules were printed for the 1939 Ingram Parish Sports and Industrial Exhibition. Mrs Holderness-Roddam's offer of a silver challenge cup for the dog trial was accepted. [It is still competed for today]. A suggestion was made that the show be insured against bad weather, and the sports club secretary was instructed to write to BBC House in Newcastle about broadcasting the "famous hill race". It would have been interesting to know the reply but War intervened, and a committee meeting arranged for August 24th was never held.

Sheepdog trial competitors in 1950. *(l-r)* **Joe Scott, Reaveley Hill; Jimmy White, Low Blakehope; Herby and Bobby Hornsby, Prendwick Chesters; Les Dixon; John Smith, Alnham Moor with Queen (The Winner); Gib Smail, Prendwick, and the Hunter brothers of Puncherton.** *(© Northumberland Gazette)*

In July 1945 Canon Allgood called a meeting to "discuss the present and future" of Ingram Parish Tea and Sports. Only eleven parishioners attended. In the Minutes Book we read: "It is definitely a Parish Thing - it is - and it is hoped - will always remain Ingram Parish Tea and Sports. The Canon gave a resume from as far back as 1909."

It was decided not to hold the usual sports; no serving men were home, the usual field was under cultivation, posts were unobtainable owing to war restrictions and the tent had been commandeered by the military! A few sports were held in the September as part of the Victory Celebrations but it was a very low-key affair. Here the Minutes Book ends.

So far as is known there are no surviving records from 1945 until 1973. The Minutes Book(s) were lost. For those years, only word of mouth recollections, snapshots and newspaper accounts remain.

Over the years events have come and gone, mirroring the times and the interests of successive generations. The hound trail and wrestling are no more, their place taken by pony sports and a dog show. The sheep show that began in the 1950s still flourishes, with a reputation as one of the best. Whilst much reduced, the sports programme still includes the old favourites: the tug-of-war and the bolster-and-bar (a pillow fight on a pole). The famous hill race has stood the test of time.

The start of a hound trail in the early 1970s.

Below: **John Hope (right) knocks Jimmy Givens to the ground in the bolster and bar competition.**

It was always a men-only affair until the mid 1980s when one or two ladies took up the challenge. However the day is still to come when a lady wins the overall race, or the cup. To this day the cup is still awarded to the first local runner home, not necessarily the overall race winner. Spectators must do a quick turnaround to get from the start to the finish because the race is usually won in under 10 minutes.

Past winners *(l-r)* **Bill Telford, Stuart Nelson, Tom Shell, John Shell, Ross Wilson, Arty Hunter, John Hope, Ian Swanston, Charlie Oliver and Paul Brown line up with Lord James Percy (right) at the prize giving. Stuart and Arty are holding replica cups awarded belatedly for three consecutive wins.**

On show day in 1998 a reunion of past winners was held to mark the 75th anniversary of the presentation of the cup. Thirteen past winners attended with Bob Martin travelling the farthest from Yorkshire. The oldest veteran present was Ian Swanston who won the cup from 1947-1949 when his family lived at Ingram. He had the honour of handing over the trophy to that year's winner, Stuart Nelson of Low Blakehope.

Left: **Flashback to 1936 when Ian's brother Gib won the cup for the second year running. He was followed home by two other brothers Robbie** *(left)* **and Charlie** *(right).* **Ian was 6th that year.** *(© Northumberland Gazette)*

Centre: **Ian pictured with the 1998 winner Stuart Nelson shortly after the end of the race.**

Bottom: **19.9 The motif on the parish tea service given by Major and Mrs Joicey in 1909.**

Only 27 individual names are engraved on the trophy, several runners having won it on more than one occasion. Tom Shell holds the record for ten consecutive wins from 1972-1981. The race was not held during the War years and was cancelled because of Foot and Mouth Disease in 1952, 1966 and 2001.

For about thirty years, until the late 1970s, the show was held in the field beside Ingram farmhouse. It is still called the Show Field today. From there it moved to its present home, the field beside the village hall.

It is often said as Show Day comes around in September, that Ingram Show 'just happens'. That is not quite literally true, but everyone knows the format, predictable from one year to the next. Beforehand, a team of men set up the show field: posts and ropes for the sports ring, pens for the sheep show. On show day a team of ladies serve home-made teas in the village hall. Of the original Parish Tea Set, given by Major and Mrs Joicey of Linhope, only some side plates now survive. Each one features a blue belt-like motif inscribed with the words "Ingram Parish Church".

Subscriptions to the prize fund are still most welcome, although collectors no longer knock on doors in the parish. The weather remains the single unpredictable factor but the show always goes on. Newspaper headlines recall some wet years: "Ingram Show hit by weather but is voted a great success", "Rain fails to dampen spirits of show". In 1983 when it rained the entire day as a television crew filmed the show for the "About Britain" series it prompted researcher Roy Deane to write: "I think we managed to capture much of the atmosphere of the day, and the feeling that everyone enjoyed themselves, despite the rain, came across strongly."

On a fine day an average of 800 - 1000 visitors file

A study in concentration - horticultural judge, George Lee, of Yetholm, assessing the best collection of vegetables at the 2004 show and below, judging the gladioli exhibits.
(© Dean Chapman)

Blackface gimmers caught up for judging at the 2004 sheep show. They were shown by Malcolm Elliott, of Hartside, *(pictured centre)* **with help from Stuart Nelson, Low Blakehope** *(left)* **and Richard Irvine, Yardhope.**
(© Dean Chapman)

through the gate to sample the delights of a traditional country show. Many have long associations with the valley, having lived or worked there in days gone by. They return to meet up with old friends, and to see the show. In a huge marquee, the array of home grown vegetables and flowers, handicrafts, baking, dressed sticks and photographs draws a crowd throughout the afternoon. Nowadays the show classes are open to everyone although several cups and special prizes are confined so only locals can win them. Prize money is paid out but taking part, supporting the show, is what really matters.

With the centenary approaching Canon Roland Allgood will be remembered. He would surely note with approval that the sports, the horticultural and industrial classes, quoits, the sheepdog trial, live on today. And, of course, the excellent tea, which is how it all began in 1909.

Judge Gordon Leitch, of Jedburgh, casts a critical eye over entries in the stick dressing classes.
(© Dean Chapman)

A local landmark - but not for much longer. The only photographs I have come across of the Nurse's Cottage, which stood in Branton for almost 60 years, all date from the time of demolition. Unfortunately I have been unable to trace any photographs of the nurses themselves. *(Photo: Sandy Hunter)*

20
The Nursing Association

The founding of the Ingram and Alnham Nursing Association in May 1918 brought improved standards of health care to everyone in the community who was willing to pay. In return for a 3/- annual subscription, members and their families were entitled to the services of a qualified district nurse, free of charge.

Based in Branton, firstly in lodgings and later in a cottage, the nurse's duties were that of midwife, health visitor and nurse rolled into one. For many years she covered the far-flung district on a bicycle, during the day and night, in all weathers. Often she walked part of the way because many of her patients lived at remote shepherds' homes. On some occasions a car was hired, but it was not until the early 1940s, when the nurse drove her own, that the bicycle was finally given up.

Caring for expectant mothers was an important part of the nurse's job. An additional fee of 7s 6d, over and above the subscription, was payable for maternity cases. During confinements, when babies were born at home and mothers stayed in bed, the nurse lived in with the family for ten days. In the 1930s, under the new Midwives Act, maternity fees were raised to 10s and the nurse lived in for a fortnight.

The first nurse employed by the association was Nurse Wilkinson. Her "salary, coals etc" amounted to £27 11s 4d for the year, board and lodgings £49, and uniform £5. That many people were willing to pay for her services is born out by the subscriptions and donations received, £103 5s 9d. No subscribers' list exists for 1918-1919 but the nurse was in great demand: she paid 2070 visits - a record never surpassed throughout the association's history - 25 night visits and attended six maternity cases. It is no wonder that repairs to her bicycle that year cost £14 5s 6d!

In its first year the association received two grants, each of £25, from the county council and the local government board. These helped towards a final balance in hand, at the end of a busy first year, of £48 11s 1d. Until 1933, when the first Ministry of Health grant was received, the association was self-funding, heavily dependent on voluntary efforts to augment its income.

The nurse's cottage was built in 1924 at a cost of £200. Other associated expenses were for a joiner, £27 8s 8d, fencing, £3 12s 9d and a rain-barrel, £1 1s. It is generally believed that the cottage was funded by "public subscription". However, no such item appears in the accounts. Instead we read of a "jumble sale and free gift" that raised £159 12s 2d. Without this, the huge expense of the cottage would have plunged the association into serious debt. Some people today will still remember the cottage, in the centre of Branton, next to the church stables. Built around a timber frame, the corrugated iron walls were covered with fine mesh and rendered in pebbledash. To begin with it offered little more than a roof over the nurse's head. With two rooms and a kitchen it had no piped water. The facilities were basic.

A committee of local women, including the Rector's wife Mrs Edith Allgood, was in charge of the day-to-day running of the association. From her home at Ingram Rectory, Mrs Allgood co-ordinated the nurse's visits in addition to her duties as honorary secretary and treasurer, a post she held from 1918 until 1947. It is thanks to her meticulous record keeping - statements of accounts and lists of subscribers - that the early history of the association survives to this day.

Two ledgers document its fortunes from 1918 to the birth of the National Health Service in 1948, when its work effectively ceased. One is devoted to the annual statement of accounts and also notes the number of visits made by the nurse. In the other is recorded, to the last penny, the association's income from 1934 - 1947. Every year Mrs Allgood wrote down each individual subscription and donation: who had made it, how much they gave and where they lived. The printed annual reports from 1935 - 1946, with the exception of 1941, are paper-clipped to the pages.

These together with the ledgers provide a contemporary insight into a chapter of social history now largely forgotten. The accounts tell of a continual struggle to balance the books: several entries of "owing bank" are underlined in red pen. The association walked a financial tightrope for most of its life, with the committee, ever grateful of donations, both in cash and kind, and of special fund raising efforts, always urging subscribers to dig just a bit deeper into their pockets. Wholehearted support was required at the jumble sales, dances, whist drives and concerts to keep the association - and the valuable services of the district nurse - ongoing.

Reading the annual reports one senses the great community spirit fostered by the association. Its survival was important to everyone at a time when the drugs, antibiotics and medicines of today were undreamt of. The community rose to the challenge.

1935 - Subscribers 111. Visits paid 966.
The association became the "Ingram, Alnham and Powburn District Nursing Association". After nine years of service Nurse Wigham resigned to get married. She was presented with a suitably inscribed clock.
"This year has seen many changes. Two farms have changed hands, and many of our old subscribers have left and we are sorry to lose them. We welcome the newcomers and as time goes by, hope that they will all realise the value of a nurse in a district such as this and all help to keep the Association going by becoming members, a step which we are sure they will never regret."

1936 - "The visits that she (Nurse Turnbull) has paid this year are nearly a record for our district and we heartily congratulate her. Such work means wear and it may be because of these twelve hundred odd visits she has paid that her bicycle, which has done 8 hard years of work, has worn out! The association have had to supply her with a new one.

"We have also been faced with the cost of re-painting the Cottage at Branton after 5 years. It is very unfortunate that both these heavy items of expenditure should come in the same year, but we hope that all subscribers will help in showing their appreciation of the Nurse's services by subscribing just a little more this year."

1937 - Subscribers 116. Visits paid 1240. Maternity cases 4.

"The committee are most grateful to Mrs Kidson (the President) and her Powburn people for handing over to the Nursing Association the sum of £41-5-2 raised by a bazaar in the Jubilee Hall. This wonderful effort on their part, which must have entailed much thought and hard work, enabled the nursing association to pay for the painting of the Nurse's Cottage and also to buy a new bicycle, both of which were very necessary.

"They also thank Mrs Chrisp for raising £11.5.0 at the Alnham whist drive and dance and Mr. J. Bell for £12.0.6d at Ingram, also for a whist drive and dance. These three wonderful efforts have placed the Association in a sound position for another year, but we want all subscribers to realise that the expenses of the association are much higher than they used to be and the new Midwives Act which comes into force in July will add to the expense."

1938 - "This year has seen the introduction of many new rules and regulations with regard both to the Nurse and patient. One rule that the committee would like every member to know is that in the case of pneumonia, if the Doctor so orders, a temporary Nurse may be had free of charge to the patient, to live in, as long as needed. Another rule, also of great benefit, is the Compulsory Pension Scheme for all nurses, to which both the District Association and the Nurse have to contribute, the County Council also.

"Nurse Ockleford has now been with us a year, and in spite of very bad weather before Christmas, when there was much sickness, she paid 1653 visits. The Committee wish to add their appreciation."

1939 - Visits paid 1265. Night visits 11.

"The association has weathered its 21 years well, and those of its members who have been subscribers and friends from the beginning, must feel proud of its achievements. Year by year its usefulness, and the work of the nurses during that time, has, we feel sure, been appreciated by the members".

Special thanks were given to P.C. Winter for selling his vegetables, and handing over £1.12.0., and to the President Mrs Kidson for her kind gift of a new Maternity Bag all fitted out for the nurse.

1940 - Subscribers 125. Visits paid 1216.

"In many ways it has been the most difficult year, especially from the financial point of view which we have so far experienced. War, when ever and where ever it comes is a ghastly and terrible thing and demands sacrifices of which we know but little in normal times.

"With our Nursing Association, the effect has been disastrous. We rely so much on special efforts in our various Halls and Parish Rooms. These, owing to the "Black Out" and commandeering for Military use have been impossible to run - a dead loss of very many pounds. The balance sheet speaks for itself. We began the year with a good balance of £57.12.8. We ended it with a balance of £13.11.3 and would draw your most earnest attention to the fact that this meagre balance has to keep us going till the new subscriptions come in.

"The minimum subscription is 3/- and the committee want subscribers to realise that smaller sums, although very welcome, do not entitle them to be members and have the free use of the Nurse's services.

"We know how grateful many members are for the splendid service that Nurse has rendered in the district. It has been a very hard year for her but in spite of a terrible winter and impassable roads, her work was always freely given and courageously carried out.

"Mrs Dryden of Branton must also be thanked for many occasions on which the Hon. Secretary has used her telephone and always received most kindly help in conveying messages to Nurse in case of need."

1942 - "Through the great generosity of Captain J. Carr-Ellison, who has been a very good friend to us, water is being laid into the Nurse's Cottage, with the idea of putting in a bath and basin. We have wanted to do this for years, but up till now it has never been possible; and now our dreams are coming true, as through the kindness of Miss Houseman, the bath and basin are being given to the Association. We also wanted a sofa and easy chair, and Mrs Kidson also ever ready to help, has offered to give these; and other kind friends of the Committee have all helped to make the cottage more comfortable. The expenses of running the Association are very heavy now, and we will have to make every effort we can.
"The Ingram whist drive and dance had to be put off owing to the storm...and Alnham could not have one owing to the Hall being taken over.
"May we appeal to all to help in every way they can. We shall probably have to buy a new stove to heat the water. We have had to paint the cottage and mend it externally. It really wants painting inside, but we cannot afford that yet."

1943 - Visits paid 1724. Maternity cases 2.
"The County Nursing Association and County Council, under whom we serve, have decreed that the minimum subscription in future, must be 4s 4d or we do not get our grant of £50.
"Members will see that the visits paid have gone up by 600 to 1724. The installation of the telephone, and her car, has made it much easier to visit patients more regularly.
"The Nurse's Cottage has been modernised in every way and the committee can never be grateful enough for all kind people who have helped to bring this about by their various gifts. Since the beginning of the financial year, a bath and hand basin with hot and cold water and a kitchen stove have been installed; the telephone put in; a sofa, with most useful box-seat, given. The cottage has been repaired and painted outside and also colour washed and painted internally." [The bath was in the kitchen. It had a fold down wooden top that served as a table.]

1944 - "The members subscriptions show an increase, and after all 1d per week as a minimum, is very little in return for the nursing we receive. We owe a tremendous debt of gratitude to our President, Mrs Kidson for raising, all by herself the wonderful sum of £100 10s 6d without which we simply could not have carried on.
"We are also most grateful to Mr. Waite of Hedgeley Garage for having a box there for the Funds. Please remember it when waiting for a Bus!"

1945 - "Our Nurse continues to give every satisfaction, and has paid 1,158 visits in all weathers (some very severe storms) during the year - as well as helping neighbouring Associations during the absence of their nurses- this being possible with the help of her car. The committee hope now - after the Victory in Europe - and with Petrol Restrictions easier and the "Black-Out" gone, that every effort will be made to help the good work of the Association by some really good, voluntary efforts because without such help it would be difficult to carry on."

1946 - Visits paid 1580.
Tribute was paid to the late Mrs Kidson, of Breamish House, President for thirteen years and a member of the committee since 1918.
"The committee wish to thank all those who helped in any way to raise money - especially Mrs Shell of Brandon, Mr. Cresswell of the "Plough Inn" and the promoters of whist drives and dances at Ingram and Alnham - a total in all of £82 7s 6d -also all subscribers, who, by giving just a little extra, have raised the subscriptions this year by £10."

In 1947 Mrs Allgood wrote, in green ink, her final set of accounts and list of subscribers. It must have been with some sadness: by now Nurse Bell's salary was £352 16s 4d and her car expenses £40 5s 2d, including for the first time a £10 licence. The bank was owed £32 9s 11d and the association had just 6d in hand. Later that year she and her husband moved to Scrainwood on his retirement as Rector.

By March 1948 the bank was still owed £12 8s 2d. Soon afterwards, with the coming of the National Health Service, the Nurse's Cottage was sold to Hedgeley Estates for £350, and the furniture to Northumberland County Council for £71 15s 6d. The cottage was demolished in the mid 1980s.

After 30 years the work of the nursing association had come to an end with, ironically, the biggest sum ever of £347 16s 3d in the bank. During the 1950s the association was re-named the "Ingram, Powburn and District Care Committee". Small gifts were given to hospital patients at Christmas and occasional donations made, all noted in Mrs Allgood's original accounts ledger. In March 1978 the committee was wound up. The final entry, signed by Mrs Opie Telford, whose father Mr. William Robson audited the nursing association accounts for many years, records the donation of £395.54 to The Journal newspaper's "Fight Breast Cancer" appeal.

21
Ingram Mill

Many years ago, three corn mills stood in the valley, all close to the River Breamish, their origins linked to the old townships of Reaveley, Fawdon and Ingram.

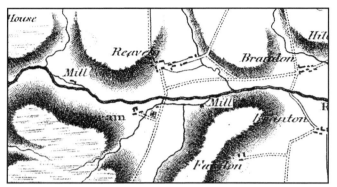

Figure 21.1 Fryer's map of 1820 showing Reaveley and Ingram mills.

Reaveley Mill was situated west of Ingram, on the north bank of the river, a few hundred yards upstream from Bulby's Wood. Records exist dating back to the mid 1600s. Much later the mill is shown on Fryer's map of 1820. Its demise came sometime after that. Fawdon Mill stood further down the valley, in the vicinity of Brandon Ford, at the foot of East Hill. A note of its site is recorded on a mid 19th century map as "this was Fawdon Mill but was destroyed".

The last surviving mill was at Ingram. Marked on Armstrong's map of 1769, today it is merely tumbled stones, the outline unrecognisable as such. However, we are reminded of its existence in the name given to the three houses and random collection of buildings that now make up Ingram Mill, half a mile east of the village. The miller's house, the granary and a single storey row of buildings, which once incorporated a cottage and blacksmith's forge, still stand today.

Old maps reveal that the mill stood almost directly in front of the house, its foundations on a level with the leat, the stream that drove the water wheel. The mill formed part of the Glebe Farm that went with the "living" of Ingram Church. In the 1850s it covered 40 acres and included fields close to the present day village hall and, a finger of land around the mill itself. One Andrew Waugh was farmer and miller for many years. By 1858 Joseph Carr is mentioned as his successor.

The arrival of the Nesbit family in 1873 would appear to coincide with the decline of the mill. The census described Thomas Nesbit as an agricultural labourer, no mention of miller. He lived with his wife, Mary Ann, and young family in the two-roomed cottage. Four children were born after the move to Ingram, the eighth and last a daughter, Sarah, in 1880.

Handed down over the years is the story of baby Sarah floating in her cradle when the mill leat flooded the cottage. She was carried to safety across a plank but Mary Ann, her mother, contracted pneumonia from which she never recovered. A headstone in the churchyard records her death, in 1881, aged just 36.

By then negotiations were underway regarding an exchange of land that would substantially enlarge the Glebe Farm. The parties to this were the Rector Rev. James Allgood and His Grace Algernon, 6th Duke of Northumberland (1867-1899), who owned the adjoining farm of Fawdon.

In a nutshell the Rector agreed to relinquish two six-acre portions of glebe land - Priest's Meadow and Priest's Bog - that lay on Fawdon ground and, his rights to "stintage and sweepage". These were terms used to describe his entitlement to grazing rights ("stints") over the farm, and the cropping of hay ("sweepage") from the glebe lands. In practice the Rector did not exercise these rights but received rent instead.

For his part the Duke ceded some 47 acres including the lower part of Fawdon Hill, overlooking the Glebe Farm, and six acres of "gravel beds and bed of the River Breamish". Before the exchange took place the land was surveyed on foot, the square measurement calculated in acres, roods and perches, the linear in chains and poles.

"I hereby certify that I am not the agent of or connected with either of the parties to this exchange; and having personally examined on the ground and valued the land and heriditaments proposed to be exchanged, I further certify that they are correctly represented on the Map annexed…
"The proposed exchange is just and reasonable and will be materially beneficial to the parties interested.
"The land given in exchange to Ingram Rectory to be free from payment of Tithe Rent Charge, to be fenced in when required by the Rector of Ingram, two thirds of the expense to be paid by the Duke of Northumberland and one third by the Rector of Ingram, the fence to be maintained in the same proportion viz two thirds by the Duke and one third by the Rector of Ingram. W. B. Wilson, Blagdon. Umpire and Valuer."

After the new boundaries were in place the Glebe Farm remained largely unchanged until well into the 20th century. In 1928 the Rector Roland Allgood gifted a small parcel of land near the school for the new parish hall. Periodically, as the river shifted its course, land disappeared and the boundary fluctuated.

Some very ancient boundary stones still stand today. They are marked on the 1865 Ordnance Survey map. One, near the site of the mill race is inscribed with the initial 'N', presumably Northumberland. The other three can be found on a small

Haymaking was a busy time when everyone including the Rector, his maids and servants lent a hand. These photographs were taken on the Glebe Farm in about 1920.

Above: The pikes were carted on a low hay bogey to the main haystack. For the children, hitching a ride was the best part of it all.

Loose hay was built up into a pike using long handled pitchforks. Molly Ross is on top of the pike. She milked the cows and looked after the goats and pigs at the Rectory. The Rector has his back to the camera.

triangle of land beside the gate to the farm. On close examination the letters 'N' and 'G' can be made out. Perhaps the 'G' stood for Glebe.

In 1954 the historic ties between the Church and the Glebe Farm ended. By now the farmhouse and the old mill buildings were in a very poor state of repair, so poor that the buildings were condemned following an inspection by the County Agricultural Committee. The house had no electricity, piped water or sanitation. With capital expenditure in excess of £1,000 required to modernise the house, the Church Commissioners decided to sell the farm.

It was bought by the sitting tenant, John 'Jack' Nesbit for £1500. Born at the farm in 1873, as a boy of twelve, in the 1880s, he remembered the mill being demolished. The Nesbit family's long association with Ingram Mill continued into the fourth generation. Jack's grandson, Ian Burrell, took over the tenancy and subsequently inherited the farm when his grandfather died in 1963, at the age of 90. A new bungalow was built for Ian and Valerie after they married. The farmhouse at the time was occupied by Ian's widowed aunt, Molly Bell, one of Jack four daughters. After she died the house was sold.

In the late 1980s parts of the farm were sold off in parcels. The Duke of Northumberland bought some of the original 40 acres of glebe - today it is farmed by the Nelson family of Low Blakehope - and the best of the land exchanged in the 1880s. It is once again part of Fawdon farm. Another piece of land was sold to Mr. and Mrs Cyril Fierman, who built a new house beside the village hall.

A boundary stone inscribed with the letter N.

Jack Nesbit pictured beside his beehives in the farmhouse garden, circa 1952.

Ingram Mill as it looks today. The restored granary is far right.

The almost derelict granary and row of outbuildings, together with some hill ground, was bought by Mr. and Mrs Paul Lemeunier. Sympathetically converted and incorporated into a new house, the granary retains some original features including the exterior stone steps to the upper storey. The row of old buildings, condemned years ago, has also been restored.

The derelict granary in 1990.

In 2001, Ian's widow Valerie sold the bungalow together with the remaining land and buildings. Two paddocks now belong to Mr. L. M. Glen-Davison, the remainder of the holding to Mr. and Mrs David Whitehead. In 2004 the bungalow was completely encased within a much bigger new house. At the same time a new extension was added to the old farmhouse which is owned by Mr and Mrs Conrad Clayton.

Although sixty years have elapsed since the glebe was sold, its ties with the church are not forgotten. Two covenants are still legally binding on all who have a stake in the former glebe farm. Fearful perhaps that, post war, the 1950s was heralding a more liberated society, and mindful of the effects of drink, the Commissioners ensured that the decorum and setting of the nearby church and rectory would not be compromised in the future.

In the deeds we read: *"That neither the property nor any existing or future building shall at any time hereafter be used as or for a place of amusement, hotel, tavern, inn or public house nor shall any spirituous or fermented liquors at any time be sold in or upon the same property."*

In addition *"No act, deed, matter or thing shall at any time be done suffered or permitted which may be or become a nuisance, annoyance or disturbance to the Minister for the time being conducting, or the congregation attending, divine service in the Parish Church of Ingram or the churchyard surrounding the same."*

With no aspiring publicans or theme park developers in its midst the future of the old Glebe Farm looks set fair, the land as for generations still grazed by livestock. Within its bounds the church fete is held every once in a while and, in September, Ingram Show.

22
The Valley in Wartime

In May 1940 following the evacuation of troops from the beaches at Dunkirk, mainland Britain was braced for a German invasion.

Nationwide, on government orders, a massive construction programme got underway: pillboxes sprang up across the countryside, huge concrete blocks were moved onto the beaches, and anti-tank roadblocks became a familiar sight in many villages. A force of Local Defence Volunteers was mobilised; drilling and exercises began in earnest.

Basil Oliver was ten years old when the war broke out. His family lived at Hartside and his father Alex was one of the first to join the LDV, or as the local lads termed it, "Look, Duck and Vanish".

In July the LDV were incorporated into the new Home Guard. Detachments were formed at Powburn, Ingram and Wooperton, all three joining up for exercises. The LDF armband was replaced by uniform, and initially the men were armed with shotguns. Later, they were issued with Canadian Ross rifles with bayonets attached. In use during the First World War, the barrels were badly bullet-worn, and their firing capability dubious, to say the least.

The Ingram Home Guard was comprised mostly of farm workers and shepherds, both reserved occupations. (Older men served with Air Raid Precautions checking that 'blackout' regulations were complied with). The men met most Sunday mornings in the field behind the stack-yard at Ingram for parade, marches, and instruction from regular army officers. Everyone cycled or walked, some from several miles away.

Captain Teddy Robson, headmaster at Branton School, was in overall command of both the Ingram and Powburn detachments. Dallas Allen, farmer at Ingram, held the rank of Sergeant and Basil's father, Alex, was a Lance Corporal.

During the early years of the war, two wooden look out posts were constructed and manned at night by the Home Guard. One was on the western end of Heddon Hill, built into the bedrock, with a commanding view of the valley road. The other was set against the garden wall of the house at Greenside Hill. The open front faced down the valley. Inside, a wooden plank served as a seat. At night the Home Guard did 'road checks', stopping passers by with 'Halt, who goes there' before returning to the seat for a smoke. In daytime children used it for a 'breather' on their way home from school.

A little further down the road, scooped out of the hillside at the Knock End, was a gun pit. It was screened by whin bushes and big enough to hold two men.

"I remember going past there and hearing a "psst, psst" and here was Jimmy Straughan and me Dad in this gun pit. Jimmy was a Bren gunner. They told us to cycle down to Ingram to see if there was any action. When there was an exercise the different detachments wore different coloured armbands. We had to come back and tell them, but if there was, we weren't to stop as we went past, in case we gave their position away." Basil Oliver. Hartside.

The firing range was just past Peggy Bell's Bridge, at the foot of Hartside Hill. Long poles, with circular targets, were set into the ground in front of a terrace of land. Two men, the spotters, sat in a dug out trench below to check for hits: bulls eye, inner or outer circle or total miss.

A Northover that fired mortars, and took five men to carry it, and an anti-tank Blackett Bombard were stored in the open cart shed at Ingram. Most weaponry, however, was kept in a room underneath the village hall at Powburn, mortars and hand grenades, all quite visible through the window.

Had German infantry ever reached the Breamish Valley, they would have encountered tank traps. These were barriers formed by slotting long lengths of rail into three-foot deep sockets in the ground. The tank trap at Brandon was constructed between two high walls built to narrow the road. Another, at Branton, was beside the former church. Its site is marked by saucer-shaped depressions, clearly visible in the tarmac today.

A pillbox stood beside both barriers, at Brandon in the corner of the stack yard, and at Branton behind a wall. They were well recognised as potential death traps, so were never used.

The search-light battery at Reaveley was operational in the early 1940s. Manned by regular soldiers, it was one of many set up in the countryside to act as homing beacons, guiding returning British aircraft towards local airfields. Beams were directed upwards from three huge lights, fitted with arc lamps and mirrors. The soldiers who operated the lights lived in nearby barracks, the foundations of which can still be seen today, in the Townhead Field, at the west end of the farm.

"Us laddies used to pester them to put the lights on. The sergeant would say 'we'll put them on at eight o 'clock', sometimes they did. Sometimes they didn't." Basil Oliver.

Basil remembers the sight of a huge, partially deflated barrage balloon wobbling over Fawdon Hill, cables trailing underneath. The boys thought they might catch it but it moved on over Ingram Mill before coming down at Roddam Rigg.

The War brought several new faces into the valley: evacuee children from Tyneside; a mother and her children from London; land army girls at Reaveley and Ingram, and later two Prisoners of War, an Italian and a German, who worked in the woods at Linhope.

One of the most mysterious was "the spy" who rented a flat above the garages at Linhope. A pleasant man, who rode a bicycle, his sudden disappearance, overnight, accompanied by much vehicle movement on the valley road, was never explained. Nor was he seen again.

By 1943, with the threat of invasion over, the searchlight battery and tank barriers had disappeared; the look out on Heddon Hill, no longer in use. Several shepherds in the Ingram Home Guard who lived farthest away at out-bye farms, were stood down. Those lower down the valley joined the Powburn detachment.

Stephen Shell was 19 when his family moved to Brandon Farm in 1943. Having served with the 90-strong Home Guard at Chatton, the only man who didn't smoke, he joined the Powburn platoon. It was expected of you.

The men, about 32 of them, met every Sunday morning and Tuesday night in the yard at the Plough Inn. Square bashing and drill was supplemented with hand grenade practices at Callaly and weapon firing in the quarry, now Powburn Show field.

When exercises were held, usually in and around Powburn, they drew a following of local lads, always ready for a laugh at the exploits of their fathers and friends. On one occasion "German" soldiers, in uniform, were defending the gravel crusher at Hedgeley.

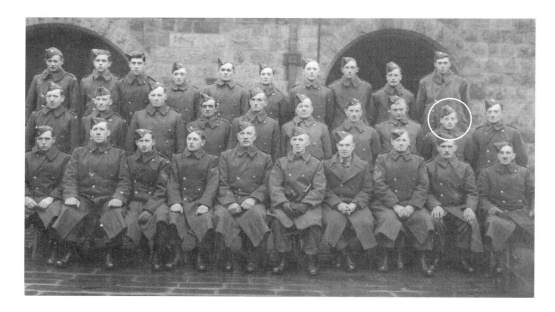

Powburn Home Guard pictured outside The Shambles in Alnwick circa 1944.
Stephen Shell is circled.

Back row (l-r): **Jackson Shell, Brandon; Terence Scott, Powburn; Joe English, Fawdon; Unknown; Unknown; Unknown; George Whillis, Brandon White House; George Taylor, Percy Cross; Jim Clark, Crawley; George Charlton, Fawdon.**

Middle: **Bob Foggon, Brandon; Willie Smith, Branton Middlesteads; Jack Bell, Ingram Mill; - Hodge; Will Givens, Brandon; Billy Dunn, Hedgeley Station; Tom Mills, Middlesteads; Jack Blain, Reaveley; Stephen Shell; Unknown.**

Front: **Dallas Allen, Ingram; Eddy Ord, Branton; Jack Scott, Powburn; Tom Whillis, Brandon White House; Dan Easton, Fawdon; Lieutenant -; Eddy Houston, West Hedgeley; Tom Usher, Powburn; Unknown; Charles Eungblut, Glanton Station.**

"We were advancing down the river to attack it. The men were running down and I had been told that I had to be a casualty, I think because I was light to carry on a stretcher and the stretcher-bearers could run with me.

"The army had laid controlled charges and as you passed they exploded and nearly blew you off your feet. I can perfectly remember getting onto the main road and there were kids watching. They came running forward saying 'It's Steve Shell', thinking I was hurt. They were so disappointed when I got up."

Memories of "Dad's Army" abound: of the chap who forgot to look through the sights before firing his gun; of the guardsman who became entangled with a washing line during an exercise in Powburn; of the Sten gun that rocked you backwards, almost off your feet when it fired; and of spending a night in a ditch near Breamish House with only five rounds of ammunition - all you were issued with.

Despite this Stephen remembers the Home Guard as a fairly professional set up. *"It was the cheapest army that this country ever had. One million men and they didn't have to feed, house, transport, or pay them. The whole idea of the Home Guard was that it was expendable. It would have a nuisance value in terms of the enemy. The men who were in it knew the countryside and that was their main advantage. The best thing we could have done was to block Crawley Dene. We could have dealt with wagonloads of soldiers and small armoured cars but I don't think we could have dealt with tanks."*

Most Home Guardsmen were stood down in December 1944. Stephen's certificate of commendation from the King reads:

"In the years when our Country was in mortal danger John S. Shell who served 13th August 1942 to 31st December 1944 gave generously of his time and powers to make himself ready for her defence by force of arms and with his life if needs be."

During the war years the civilian population was under the jurisdiction of Police Constable Jack Inchmore, of Powburn, 'policeman, judge and jury' of the district. Initially he rode a bicycle but later drove a car. He was known to enjoy a drink with locals at The Plough until ten minutes before closing time when he slipped away home, only to return in uniform.

Licences were required for all manner of things: to kill sheep or pigs on the farm, to move imported Irish cattle and for any extra collie dogs that a shepherd might have, over and above the permitted two, which were exempt. Jack Inchmore made it his business to go around checking that all was in order. Often it wasn't. Any misdemeanour earned a ticking off but the threat of fines and further proceedings were usually allayed by a bag of oats, a bit of bacon or 'something in kind' into his hand.

The pillbox in the stack yard at Brandon stood until the 1960s. Of no use as a store (the interior was dissected by a floor-to-ceiling Y-shaped wall) it took contractors with pneumatic drills the best part of a week to demolish.

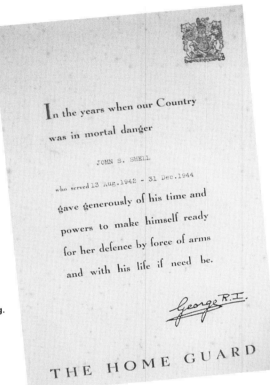

Stephen's commendation from the King.

Ingram Bridge in the 1920s with the sandstone pillars at either end.

23
Ingram Bridge

For more than eighty years a plaque on the parapet of Ingram Bridge reminded passers by of when it was built and by whom: in 1893 by the Cleveland Bridge and Engineering Company.

The two-span lattice girder bridge was constructed upstream from the ford crossing near the church. A great boon to the district, horses and carts no longer had to use the ford nor were pedestrians dependent on the wooden footbridge that was frequently washed away.

In September 1891 we read in the Alnwick and County Gazette: *"The River Breamish was very high on Sunday night and on Monday morning so much flooded in fact that the water had washed a pier of the County Bridge away [at Hedgeley] and consequently all vehicular traffic is stopped on the main road to Wooler.*

"The wooden footbridge over the Breamish between Brandon and Branton was also carried away. Surely something will now be done to get stone or iron bridges built at Ingram and Brandon."

Moves had already begun. Correspondence in 1890 - 1891 between the Rector of Ingram, Rev. Canon Thomas Ilderton, and the county surveyor, Mr. Kynnersley, reveals that the county council had agreed to grant a sum of not more than half the cost of a new bridge, but not exceeding £635, providing that regulations were complied with and the work carried out to Mr. Kynnersley's satisfaction.

In the event the new bridge cost £1,500. I surmise that local landowners dug into their pockets to make up the balance. One in particular, Captain Carr-Ellison, of Hedgeley Hall, wholeheartedly promoted the project.

The bridge was completed in the autumn of 1893 with fine red sandstone pillars at either end.

Since then it has faced continual threat from flooding and scouring, the force of the water eroding the gravel bed and weakening the foundations. Over the years, copious quantities of concrete have been poured into the riverbed.

One of the biggest problems faced by the County Bridges Engineer is that the river is continually shifting its course. In the 1950s gabeons (stone-filled cages) were constructed on the banks, up and downstream of the bridge, in an effort to stabilise the river's course. Most have now disintegrated through lack of maintenance.

Some of the worst damage occurred during heavy flooding in 1984 when the abutment on the southern approach to the bridge sheared and slipped into the river. Emergency repair work costing £35,000 was needed to prevent it collapsing completely. Following major strengthening and underpinning, the deep swimming pool below the bridge disappeared.

At some point in the late 1970s or early 80s I remember noticing the above-mentioned oval-shaped metal plaque hanging by just one pin, and wondering if I should remove it before someone else did.   The next time I looked that important little piece of the bridge's history had gone: taken, I suspect, as a memento.

The sandstone pillars are long gone and today signs at either end warn drivers of a weak bridge. When it was built of course no one could have envisaged the volume and size of vehicles it now carries: tractors and trailers, tour buses and huge, articulated lorries.

The damaged abutment.

Floodwaters cover the southern approach to the bridge in November 1984.

24
The Roadman

The sight of workmen filling in potholes in the valley road, one summer's morning, brought to mind George Bell, long time roadman in the parish.

George in uniform.

George was one of 'the old school' the last of a generation of roadmen who lived locally, and personally tended to the day-to-day upkeep of the roads and verges. The youngest of three sons, he was born on December 26th 1904 in one of the now derelict old cottages at Reaveley.

As a boy George attended Ingram School. His memories of it are vague. He suffered from bad asthma attacks and was frequently absent. His father George was the roadman then. In those days the roads were just earth and stone. As the stones worked their way to the surface they were picked off and put into heaps. With the appearance of tar macadam the roads were gradually transformed. Tarring was done manually, the tar boiled in a black pot suspended from 'sheer legs' over a fire. Mr. Bell often came in from work 'black as the ace of spades'.

George was the cattleman at Reaveley until he took over his father's job as roadman in January 1934, employed by Glendale Rural District Council. By then tarring was more mechanised. Wagons brought in a gang of workmen to do the job with the help of a steamroller. Most of the roads in the valley were by now surfaced with tarmac, apart from the cart track to Alnham Moor and the private drive to Linhope.

Usually George worked on his own, starting at 7.30 a.m. and finishing at 4.30p.m. His round was much the same as in his father's day: Ingram to Hartside, round by Reaveley, up to Reaveley Greens, along to Ingram Mill and down to Brandon. Sometimes he walked, sometimes he took the pushbike. Most days were spent edging the verges, cleaning out the water cuts and sweeping the roads with a brush.

In 1940 George was appointed sexton of St. Michael's Church. He dug the graves, and rang

July 6th 1945 board Empress of Australia
" 7th . Sailed from Liverpool 10 ᴀᴍ.
" 13th entered Saragossa Sea
" 15 Passed China Straights into Caribbean Sea
" 18 Docked at Cristabal 11·ᴀᴍ
" 21 Pass through Panama, Enter Pacific.
Aug 3ʳᴰ Arrived Pearl Harbour 09·30
" 4ᵈ Visit Honolulu.
" 6ᵗʰ Visit Honolulu. Waikiki
" 8ᵗʰ Sailed from Pearl Harbour
" 11ᵗʰ Cross International Date line. 22.04 hrs
" 12ᵈ this day did not Exist
" 15ᵈ VJ day
" 16ᵗʰ Arrive Eniwetok. Marshall Islands
" 20 Sailed from Eniwetok
" 23ⁿᵈ Cross the Equator 09·50 hrs
" 24ᵗʰ Arrived Manus, Admiralty Islands
" 27ᵗʰ Sailed from Manus
" 28ᵗʰ Passed Malucca Straights
" 29ᵗʰ Passed Celebes Sea Approaching East Indies
" 30ᵗʰ Run into monsoon

Extract from George's diary written on board ship to Hong Kong. Just one month after disembarking, on September 5th 1945, he sailed for home. The voyage took him via Singapore, Madras, Colombo, the Gulf of Aden and the Suez Canal. After passing through the Mediterranean and the Bay of Biscay, George arrived at Southampton on November 9th.

the bell on Sundays. A year later he joined the Royal Air Force and saw service in England and the Far East. In July 1945 he was posted to Hong Kong. On both the outward and homeward voyages George kept a diary, in a small notepad, of the ports of call and notable events at sea. It survives today, a fascinating account of a round the world trip and a remarkable contrast to his life at Ingram.

The French Oak Leaves. Cast in metal, each measures about two inches.

At some time during the War he rescued a free French pilot from a blazing aeroplane. His daughter Ina does not know where or exactly when, her father was a quiet man who never spoke about the War. She still has the French Oak Leaves awarded to him for gallantry, and a certificate of commendation from the British Government. It reads:

"By the King's Order the name of Aircraftman 1st Class GW Bell Royal Air Force Volunteer Reserve was published in the London Gazette on 1 January 1944 as commended for brave conduct. I am charged to record His Majesty's high appreciation of the service rendered. Archibald Sinclair. Secretary of State for Air."

In November 1945 George returned home to his wife Mame and their two young daughters, Ina and Cathy. Mame was his cousin. She had come to the valley in 1928 to keep house for the family following Mrs Bell's sudden death. She and George were married on August 4th 1934 at Ingram Church.

George's most vivid memories are of snowstorms, of casting snow manually with a shovel, often with a gang of local men. During one bad spell he opened the road on Ingram Haugh nine times. The wind kept blowing it in. In the winter of 1947 the drifting was so deep at Greenside Hill that the men hung their jackets on top of the telegraph poles.

"The bank was cast out with machines. The road above Greenside Hill was never opened up for eight weeks. We got up at the finish but it took weeks. In places the snow was 40 to 50 feet deep. Someone from Ingram would take a horse and sledge down to the main road to collect supplies, the lower part of the road was open and bread and butcher meat would be picked up at Brandon White House."

On several winter mornings, if there had been a light fall of snow or frost, George started work earlier. This gave him time to get up to Greenside Hill and sand the banks before the postmistress Lorna Chisholm came up with the van.

After the flooding of October 1949 when the road below Greenside Hill was washed out, George helped to build the new road higher up the hillside. In later years when responsibility for the roads

Snow clearing near Greenside Hill, 1935. *(l-r)* **George Bell, senior; Mark Purvis, Ingram; George Bell, junior, and Robbie Holywell, Ingram.**

was devolved to Northumberland County Council, he became one of a gang of men working on roads throughout the district, no longer just locally in the valley.

In August 1974 George and Mame were given the keys to a bungalow in Wooler. It coincided with their ruby wedding celebrations, and George's retirement after forty years as a roadman and seventy years a resident in the valley.

25
Ingram Haugh

Between Ingram Bridge and the small bridge eastward that crosses the Reaveley Burn lies a big expanse of grassland; ridged and furrowed by the plough, grooved by ancient river courses and ditches. Many years ago the rasping call of the corncrake was heard here, sadly, no more.

Today it is the haunt of other lovely birds: lapwings flock over its turf, now grazed by sheep and cattle, while snipe favour the damp, wetter ground. At dusk, barn owls hunt the perimeters. Towards its centre a collection of tumbled walls, in the shape of a cross, is said to be the remains of an ancient sheep shelter.

Near the beginning and the end of the last century the public gaze was drawn to Ingram Haugh for two very different happenings: one a spectacle to behold; the other a spectre that, had it come to pass, would have blighted the valley landscape forever.

Figure 25.1 The Yeomanry Camp from East Hill.

The Yeomanry Camp

In June 1909 the rows of white military tents and lines of horses, massed near the top of the haugh, drew visitors from far and near to the valley. The occasion was the annual summer camp of the Northumberland Hussars Yeomanry. It made an impressive sight.

Before the First World War, the yeomanry - and their horses - were an integral part of the nation's militia. Indeed the N.H.Y. were among the mounted troops who played a decisive role in the South African Boer War (1899 -1902). Regiments, aligned to counties, were comprised of volunteers with officers drawn from the gentry and landed families.

Among the officers at Ingram were Major Lord Armstrong, Major Viscount Ridley and Captain W.M. Burrell, family surnames still familiar in the county today.

Men serving in the Hussars were drawn from all parts of Northumberland and Durham. They were attached to one of four Squadrons depending where they lived: "A" squadron (Newcastle and Gateshead), "B" squadron (County Durham east of the N.E.R. main line), "C" squadron (North Northumberland) and "D" squadron (South Northumberland and County Durham, west of the N.E.R. main line).

As the squadrons were based in different towns, the annual summer camp provided an opportunity for men from all four units to train together. For several years the camp was held at Walwick Grange, near Chollerford. Other venues included Rothbury and Blagdon (the Ridley family seat near Stannington) and, one year the regiment travelled to Otley in Yorkshire.

Ingram was used on only one occasion. How or why it was chosen I do not know. Three archive sources - and a few photographs - survive. All give a slightly different perspective on those nine days, in June 1909, when the hills rang with the bugle call.

The day-to-day routine, coupled with military rules and regulations of the day, is detailed in "The Regimental Standing Orders", a heavy foolscap ledger that was actually brought to Ingram. It is now kept with the regimental collection at The Discovery Museum in Newcastle-upon-Tyne.

Turning the pages was a great delight. Each day's orders, issued by the commanding officer Colonel C. Loftus Bates D.S.O. (an honour he gained in the Boer War), were written up in the hand of the adjutant, Captain H.R. Milvain of the 12th Royal Lancers. He lived locally at Eglingham Hall and was seconded to the camp as right hand man to Colonel Bates.

So we read of an advance party of men, from towns across the North East, arriving at Ingram on Wednesday June 2nd, three days before the camp officially started. Whilst not specifically stated, I think many men and horses would travel by train to Hedgeley Station. Tents for officers were set apart from the main camp. The horses were tethered in lines between the troopers' tents. Of the bigger tents, we know one was used as the hospital and another by the regimental band. The camp had a resident doctor, Surgeon Lieutenant H. Drummond, and a veterinary surgeon, Veterinary Major Elphick.

The orders for Saturday June 5th list the daily routine; it varied little over the duration of camp. Exercises or 'schemes' were arranged around mealtimes and stable duties. The welfare of the horses had high priority.

So we read of Reveille at 5.30a.m., stables and water, 5.45a.m., feed and dismiss, 6.45a.m., breakfast, 7a.m., parade, 7.50a.m., midday stables ("orders will be issued on return from the field"), dinner, 1.30p.m., evening stables, 5.30p.m., teas, 6.15p.m., guard parade, 7.30p.m., First post, 9.30p.m., watch setting, 10p.m. and lights out at 10.15p.m.

On arrival at camp each horse was inspected by a Board of Officers. Some troopers had their own horse. Others were hired or lent by officers' families.

"Stables: On "Stables" sounding all men and grooms must turn out at once (unless a whole Squadron has left stables) and when their horses are groomed they can shew them up and, if passed, they can be dismissed from Stables. It is part of the orderly officer's duty to see the horses watered. Horses will be watered always at the beginning of stables in order that their legs maybe properly dried. [They would be watered at the river]

"The sick horses will parade at 7.30a.m, at the sick lines. All horses not yet inspected will parade with the sick horses."

"**Picketing:** No men are to picket their horses out of the lines without leave from their squadron commanders and all sick horses will be placed in the sick lines and under the orders of the NCO in charge for feeding and watering.
"The lines must be kept properly clean and a tent orderly told daily to keep the tents and surroundings tidy."

"**Daily Sick:** The Medical and Veterinary Officers must be most particular to note whether the man or horse is fit or not fit for duty."

"**Parades:** Squadrons will parade for Drill under Squadron Commanders at 7.50a.m. Signallers will parade with their squadrons. Machine guns section will parade under the orders of Lieut. Charlton for drill."

Turning to the pages of the Alnwick and County Gazette, Saturday June 12th, under "Military and Territorial", a regular column in the newspaper then, we read:

"**The town of Alnwick had quite a military appearance on Saturday, with the passing through it of detachments of military on their way westwards to the camp. One trooper passed through with his head and nose swathed in bandages, and only one eye on view, he having come to grief with his horse on top of him. His injuries had been dressed at Warkworth by Dr. J. S. Forrest.**"

A separate report appeared entitled the "Northumberland Hussars at Ingram". It listed, by name and rank, the 21 officers in camp at Ingram.

"**About 500 men of the Northumberland Hussars went into camp at Ingram on Saturday morning for their annual training under excellent auspices. For a few years the regiment has been encamped at Walwick Grange, and the change to the charming uplands of North Northumberland will no doubt be much appreciated by the men of the regiment, which is under command of Col. C. L. Bates, D.S.O.**"

"**The camp was pitched on the long green haughs which border the Breamish, and the surrounding country was admirably adapted for the military operations that have been carried out during the week.**"

As the men settled in to the routine of camp rules concerning non-military matters crept into the Regimental Orders:

"Men are warned that they must not go into the whin bushes to the south of the road on any pretext whatsoever except on duty. Anybody found doing so, will be severely dealt with."

"**Clothing:** In many cases the clothing and equipment have been returned to stores in a very dirty condition. All ranks are warned that it is part of their duty to keep their clothing and equipment clean and in good order."

Note also: "No washing in the River above the Red Flag".... "All civilians employed in camp must wear badges".... "All NCO's (non commissioned officers) batmen will be accommodated in tents set apart for them."

The Regimental Orders contain no details of how or where the hussars trained in the surrounding countryside. Someone, however, wrote a report for the paper. It appeared on Saturday June 19th a week after the camp ended.

"Interesting manoeuvres were carried out by the Northumberland Hussars at Ingram on Saturday. The scheme was that the hill tribes (represented by B and D Squadrons under the command of Major Backhouse) had been raising the low-lying country round Hedgeley and Glanton. A force consisting of A and C Squadrons, under Maj. Selby-Bigge, was despatched to punish the tribe, and was ordered to destroy Linhope. The operations were carried out successfully by the punitive force.
"During the afternoon the men had a holiday, and proceeded to Alnwick."

Only two photographs of the camp are held in the regimental archives. One is of men seated on the ground, around a horse, perhaps having a lecture. The other records a visit to the camp by Henry, the 7th Duke of Northumberland. (1899-1918)

"**Parade:** The Regiment will parade for Divine Service at 9.45a.m., turn out 9.25a.m. The Lord Lieutenant of Northumberland (His Grace the Duke of Northumberland K.G.) will inspect the Regiment at 12pm and will present Territorial Officers Decorations to Veterinary Major G. Elphick and Captain C. Cowell and long service good conduct medal to Sgt. A. Cook-Jones."

The newspaper also carried the story: "On Sunday the Duke of Northumberland visited the camp and inspected the regiment, and presented long service decorations to Veterinary-Major Elphick, who has served for 35 years in the regiment, and to Captain and Quartermaster Cowell. Long service medals were presented to Sergeant Cook-Jones of A Squadron, who also holds the South African medal and four bars, and Sergeant Charlton of D Squadron."

Troopers in camp.
(Photo: Northumberland Hussars Museum Collection)

The Duke of Northumberland, centre, inspecting the ranks. Notice the rope tethers for the horses and the saddles and saddle cloths laid out in typical military style.
(Photo: NHMC)

Additional orders were issued as to procedure when the camp ended on Monday, June 13th.

"Beds will be emptied in the rear of Band Tent (the men slept on straw) and palliasses and bolsters will be handed in to the Quartermaster's Store by Squadron Quartermaster Sergeants at 7a.m.
"Tents will be struck (brought down) at 7.15a.m. and will be loaded with other baggage as soon as ready and all lines properly cleared up. Transport under Lieut. Charlton will move off at 9.30a.m. and will march via Mile End, Eslington Hill, Yetlington, Follions, Trewitt and Snitter."

After spending nine days at Ingram, the Hussars trekked on horseback to Ponteland, staging a mock attack on Rothbury on the way south.

The Gazette and Guardian again: **"The work of "striking" was performed with a celerity that was very creditable. While the convoy kept closely to the road, the remainder of the regiment engaged in a running fight that took them over wide tracts of country. The "hill tribes" were supposed to be busy again, and reports had reached that several raids had occurred in the Rothbury district, and that the tribes were collecting in force to attack the town itself.**

"Major Backhouse handled his men admirably in the endeavour to check the entry of the larger force into the town, holding position after position, and gradually retiring. He found, however, that he had too wide a front to cover, and Lord Ridley's command was held to have succeeded in getting through in time to save the town from too close attention by the tribesmen.
"The long journey to Ponteland was resumed, where the remainder of the training was largely taken up with patrol work."

A first hand account of the yeomanry camp, probably written by Canon Allgood, the recently appointed Rector of Ingram, appeared in the July issue of the Glendale Parishes Magazine.

"Not for a long time has Ingram's peace been so rudely awakened as it has been this month and that by His Majesty's Hussars: and not perhaps since the days of Douglas and the Percy (long life to them) have the grand old hills rung with the bugle call.
"The tramp of Cavalry and all the accoutrements of war, and watched over and guarded by the Gallant Yeoman, The Flower of England, we slept sound indeed - and what an attraction The Yeoman Camp especially on Sunday - Motor cars, Bicycles, Carriages from far and near carried sightseers to

Looking west towards Ingram - the Camp from Heddon Hill.

our peaceful valley in spite of its' aloofness: we could not help feeling how easily the distance of mile is overcome in these days."

It was many years later, in 2000, that I first saw a birds eye view photograph of the camp. It surfaced at a postcard fair in Leeds. Taken from Heddon Hill, of interest is the pencilled note on the reverse, written by a trooper who was there.

Addressed to Miss M. Morton, 13 Westbourne Grove, Ripon, and franked Powburn, Alnwick. June 7 1909, it says: "My Dear Mo, Do hope you are well. It is a glorious hot day here. My tent and horse is marked X (on a simple plan of the horses and tents which he drew). Had 4 hours squadron drill on the hills this morning. Quite well. Fond love, yours H."

The following year another different view of the Camp, taken from East Hill, turned up at a fair in Birmingham. It had nothing on the reverse. Credit must go to Richard Westmacott for finding the cards, just two of many he has sourced for me since the mid 1980s.

The Regimental Orders Book spanned the years from 1905 until 1914. The final page is taken up with embarkation details as the men of the Northumberland Hussars Yeomanry prepared to board ship at Southampton bound for the battlefields of France and Belgium.

One cannot help but feel a sense of sadness, knowing what lay ahead. That some or maybe most of the men and horses, camped in the peaceful surroundings of Ingram, would soon be pitched into the appalling carnage of the Great War. Many never to return.

S.T.R.I.V.E

Eighty-seven years on from the Yeomanry Camp, Ingram Haugh was again the focus of public and media attention.

In the spring of 1996 Northern Aggregates, a subsidiary of Ready Mixed Concrete, unveiled plans to quarry 1.5 million tonnes of sand and gravel from the haughland and three prime agricultural fields close by. The sites, collectively termed "Brandon West" were to be a sequel to existing workings at Branton, scheduled to finish in 2002.

Although the valley has a long history of aggregate quarrying, the workings had, until now, been confined to the eastern end, in the corridor of land bordering the river between Brandon and Branton.

Since the 1920s, when gravel was dug manually from the riverbed, a rolling programme of extraction had continued. By the mid 1980s, when fields on the north side of the river were exhausted, attention turned to the south side. Despite widespread public opposition, and the county council's decisive rejection of the plans, RMC was given permission, on appeal to the Secretary of State for the Environment, to open new workings. A few years later an extension was granted, again on appeal, bringing the quarry pits to within a few hundred yards of Branton. What had once been green fields bordering the village were reborn as lakes.

Now the unique, impressive landscape of the Breamish Valley, adored by so many, faced a similar threat: ten years of quarrying with the land "restored" to six lakes. The 138-acre site lay just outside the National Park boundary. One field at Brandon was owned by the Allgood Estates, the remainder of the land, on Ingram Farm, by the Northumberland Estates.

In June irate locals came face to face with Northern Aggregate bosses, and county councillors, at a packed public meeting in Powburn. At the time John Davies, general manager of N. A. described the reaction as "fairly typical".

"Invariably such applications for mineral extraction do provoke that sort of response to which I can only say that sand and gravel are only available in certain parts of the country."

The company attempted to justify the plans as of ultimate benefit to the valley. The creation of lakes would provide "a new feature of significantly enhanced nature conservation value" and form an "attractive addition" in terms of recreational potential.
It was well known that RMC was under intense pressure to remove its bulldozers from the coastal beauty spot of Druridge Bay. The company was continuing to remove 40,000 tonnes of sand annually from the beach, despite having agreed with the county council, in 1993, to leave - providing alternative sites were found. One site at Wooperton already had planning approval. Now it seemed the valley might be sacrificed as part of the deal.

The Logo.

Against this background S.T.R.I.V.E. was born: initially styled as a "residents association" it became apparent that a more meaningful name was needed; a name that would strike a chord. An acronym of Save The Real Ingram Valley Environment, STRIVE was to become synonymous with the fight that lay ahead to save the valley. Car stickers, letterheads and T-shirts were to carry its name and the specially designed logo depicting trees, hills and a river.

The group co-ordinated grass roots objections to the plans by organising petitions, letters and so forth, and emerged as a highly motivated environmental pressure group, challenging not only RMC strategy and policies, but ultimately Northumberland County Council's draft Minerals Local Plan.

We were fortunate to have in the community some dedicated individuals, wholeheartedly opposed to the quarrying plans. From within the STRIVE committee, under the chairmanship of Graham Stephenson of Ingram, emerged a core of people who were to become experts in technical fields: planning, geology, the gravel land-bank and the minerals plan. Having mastered 'the language' of the aggregates industry, they proceeded to analyse every sentence and argument of the application. Their ability to continually demand answers to questions, to continually highlight inconsistencies, to scrutinise planning documents and statements emanating from County Hall took a great deal of commitment and much personal time.

Other STRIVE volunteers helped in different ways: a rota of people was on duty in the valley every weekend, handing out specially printed petition forms that most visitors were pleased to sign. As we discovered, the valley had thousands of friends.

Support for STRIVE, protest letters, even donations, came from groups and individuals, locally and nationwide. Objectors included the Northumberland National Park Authority, the Council for

National Parks, the Northumbria Tourist Board, the Council for the Protection of Rural England, local MP the Rt. Hon. Alan Beith and, most importantly, two organisations that, by law, had to be consulted before any decision on the application could be made: one was the Farming and Rural Conservation Agency, the other English Heritage.

In July 1996 archaeologists working on the Breamish Valley Landscape Project discovered a Bronze Age burial ground, 4000 years old, on Turf Knowe, above Ingram. As a direct result of the project a wealth of evidence was coming to light about ancient civilisations in the valley. Dates were rolled back and the landscape in its broader context hailed as one of the finest of its kind in the country.

Following a personal visit to the valley and a climb to the hill fort at Brough Law, at the invitation of local archaeologists Paul Frodsham and Max Adams, English Heritage inspector Mr. Henry Owen-John concluded that the landscape would be "detrimentally affected" by a gravel quarry.

His five-page letter of objection to Northumberland County Council included the following comments: "The outlook from a number of scheduled ancient monuments and other sites of national importance will be circumscribed by both extraction and after use.

"The weight which attaches to the need to preserve nationally important archaeological remains and their settings is very clearly set out in planning policy guidance. This constitutes my principle objection to the proposed development."

These remarks were in sharp contrast to the RMC appraisal which simply stated: "There are no known archaeological sites of national, regional or local importance within or adjacent to the site."

In recommending that the application be refused Mr. Owen-John added: "If your members are minded to approve it, I would be very grateful if you could let me know in advance so that English Heritage can decide whether to request call in by the Secretary of State."

Hardly a week went by without media coverage of STRIVE or allied issues; letters and news stories appeared in the local and regional press, on local radio and, fleetingly, on television. The highlight was a report on Radio 4's flagship early morning news programme "Today".

In August a walk took place around "Brandon West" to see the damaging effect that quarrying would have on the landscape, the wildlife habitat and existing recreational areas. It was led by Jimmy Givens, retired Northumberland National Park head warden and a valley resident for most of his life. More than 50 people joined the walk, including Stewart Bonney, editor of The Northumbrian Magazine and Veronica Heath, a regular contributor to The Guardian newspaper with her "Northumberland Diary". Both were to keep STRIVE in the public eye.

A Road Show was put together to tour the local summer shows. Consisting of a simple three-fold board it featured photographs of "Brandon West", petition forms and so on. The first visit was to Powburn show followed by Glanton, Glendale, Ingram and finally Alwinton. It generated much interest and, most importantly, many signatures.

By October, with no date announced for a formal hearing by the county's environment and planning committee, STRIVE was informed that RMC was considering amending its application.

For the first time the group held talks with the Druridge Bay Campaign to see how they might help one another. A joint statement was issued condemning RMC for its attack on two "Northumberland beauty spots" and accusing the multi-national of "greed" by continuing to exploit Druridge Bay when it had already secured vast reserves of sand at Wooperton that would

last until 2022. The company, they said, had 26 years to find a non-controversial, alternative source of sand.

In November, with changes to the "Brandon West" plans expected at the end of the month, the two campaign groups fired off another salvo at RMC. Both were headline events. The DBC for its part nailed a big notice to a board at Druridge Bay. It read simply: "Greedy. Ruins Magnificent Countryside". For STRIVE it was the moment to hand over a record-breaking petition to Northumberland County Council. Containing almost 5300 signatures, including several from around the world, it was the biggest petition ever received by the council in response to a planning application. Together with the 1420 letters of objection, already lodged at County Hall, it was an indication of the immense public opposition to the quarrying plans.

Having had little television coverage since the campaign began, STRIVE agreed to take part in a documentary programme for "North East Tonight" hosted by Mike Neville. It would feature reports from Druridge Bay and RMC plus interviews with STRIVE chairman, Graham Stephenson and archaeologist, Max Adams.

The STRIVE committee meeting was brought forward to Monday, December 2nd, to accommodate filming. Events that day turned out very differently from planned. In a shock announcement during the afternoon came the unexpected news: RMC was halting commercial sand digging at Druridge Bay and withdrawing its application for "Brandon West".

The official reasons given were the need to respect the requirement for high-grade agricultural land, and the acceptance of the "archaeological significance of the valley and site".

Our meeting went ahead that evening with the film crew present. Amid a general air of elation and euphoria, glasses were raised in a champagne toast to "STRIVE and The Valley".

The first, and as it happened only STRIVE newsletter, just hot off the press, was over-printed with "VICTORY" to reflect the good news. Extra copies were ordered for family and friends, and to send out with formal letters of thanks to organisations which had opposed the application.

A ceilidh on December 13th, originally planned as a fund raiser, became a night of celebrations instead. The three musicians, who played free of charge, were each presented with an inscribed framed photograph of the valley. Another was gifted to the village hall, where it hangs today, as a reminder of the STRIVE campaign.

Musicians at the celebration ceilidh in the village hall.

A few days later the group received a letter from Mr. Christopher Hampson, chairman of RMC, confirming his company's decision to withdraw the application. He wrote: "Our commitment remains to submit substitute proposals for mineral extraction on a site outside the Breamish Valley. I take this opportunity to wish you a very happy Christmas".

Whilst the imminent threat to the valley had been lifted, its long term security remained compromised by the inclusion of "Brandon West" as a "preferred site" in the draft Northumberland Minerals Local Plan. Unless it was removed, once and for all, the possibility would remain that, in future years, another aggregates company would do exactly what RMC had done.

Many individuals and organisations, including STRIVE, had already lodged letters of objection to the site's inclusion in the plan. However, getting it withdrawn was not straightforward. Formal legal processes had to be followed.

Northumberland County Council, having included "Brandon West" in two draft plans, was now recommending it be deleted. The change of policy was due to the overwhelming objections to the RMC application, its subsequent withdrawal, and the fact that the company did not object to the site's removal from the plan.

Following a local public inquiry in November 1997, a government inspector accepted the council's explanation for its change of mind. Importantly, he was satisfied that the county had adequate reserves of sand and gravel to meet national land-bank requirements without the inclusion of "Brandon West".

With the fight to save the valley over, it was agreed that most of the money in the STRIVE bank account should be given to the local community. The village hall received £400 and Branton County First School, £200. The account however remains open.

Today the legacy of gravel extraction is plain for all to see. Within a few miles of Ingram are lakes at Roddam, lakes at Branton and lakes at Hedgeley. Thanks in part to STRIVE, this unspoilt part of the Breamish Valley escaped the blight.

A comment made by Jimmy Givens during the campaign, is worth remembering: "My greatest concern is that if quarrying goes ahead it will destroy a landscape formed 10,000 years ago and future generations will never know how beautiful it once was."

26
The White Bridge

The valley road, the C54, crosses the Reaveley Burn at the White Bridge. For many years it had white wooden railings, which is how it got its name.

We forget now, in an age of motorised transport, that it was once a ford crossing. Horses and carts had this ford to negotiate and, further down the road, another two through the millrace that fed Brandon farm.

In 2003 the White Bridge was strengthened, and the deck reconstructed. Ironically, the old foundations were so sound and solid that breaking them up took much longer than anticipated. The road was closed for almost four months with traffic diverted via Reaveley. Inevitably, the wooden railings disappeared, to be replaced by a modern barrier of dull grey steel. However, this little local landmark is still called the White Bridge.

The Reaveley Burn flows into the river a few yards below the bridge. Once, it meandered its way eastward, sandwiched between the road and the river, and joined the Breamish near Brandon. Over the years, as the river changed course, land that had separated the two waterways disappeared. Ultimately the burn was breached. Today, in places, the river is uncomfortably close to the road.

Heddon Hill

The cottage on the side of Heddon Hill commands fine views east, south and west and, of the daily comings and goings on the valley road. It was built around the beginning of the 19th century as a shepherd's house for Reaveley Eastside. Reaveley then consisted of an Eastside and a Westside, each farmed by different tenants.

Over time, Eastside became part of Brandon farm and the name died out. Jock Hedley was the last shepherd to live at Heddon Hill. After he retired in the early 1970s the cottage became a weekend home.

By the time Susan Cable rented it in 1974 it was little more than a roof and four walls. Windows had fallen out and there was no electricity or running water. The generator had been taken to bits and, although the well had a pump, it never worked. When poll tax was introduced in the mid 1980s the very basic facilities did not justify payment of the £600 bill. The cottage fell empty and, for several years, nature took over.

Jock Hedley and his wife Florence pictured after the presentation to mark his retirement as secretary of Ingram Show.

A new lease of life came in 1996. On one of their regular visits to the valley Susan, and Anne Timlin, were asked if they would be interested in 'doing up' the cottage as a permanent home. Their reply, which they later regretted on several occasions, was "yes".

The restoration work took two years - and many frustrating days - to complete. A utility room and bathroom was added on, electricity and central heating installed. An electric pump brings water uphill from the well. The transformation from semi-derelict cottage to the lovely modern home of today is recorded for posterity in a photograph album given to Susan and Anne when they moved in, in 1998.

Heddon Hill Cottage.

27
The Brandon Estate

Leaving the hills of the Breamish behind, and High Blakehope nine miles distant, our journey down the valley brings us to Brandon. The road at this point departs from the river to wend its way up and over "the banks" towards the main road.

Perhaps best described as a farm and hamlet, Brandon is also a thoroughfare; people passing through, on their way into or out of the valley.

Approaching from the west one is struck by the presence of stonewalls and the mix of old and new buildings. The road divides the farm - and the steading - into two. On the south side, the elegantly proportioned, Grade II listed farmhouse has fine views across the river. Close by are the old farm buildings, also listed. A stone tablet records the name R. L. Allgood and the date, 1831. Arranged in traditional style around yards, they were built in an un-mechanised era but skilful adaptation has enabled their continuing use today. A hay barn (1955) with a modern lean-to shed (used to house ewes at lambing time) occupies part of the former stack-yard.

To the north, set back from the road, are two large multi purpose sheds. Of recent construction, they provide housing for cattle over the winter, and storage space for the big round bales of hay and straw, all tractor-handled by virtue of their size and weight.

Their size contrasts with the neat row of single storey cottages, adjoined at one end by three small hemmels (their open yards now covered) and at the other by Woodbine Cottage. This two-storey

Mrs Jane Givens and her children *(l-r)* **Alf, John and Bella outside Woodbine Cottage, early 1900s. Her grandson Jimmy Givens and his wife Jean live there today.**

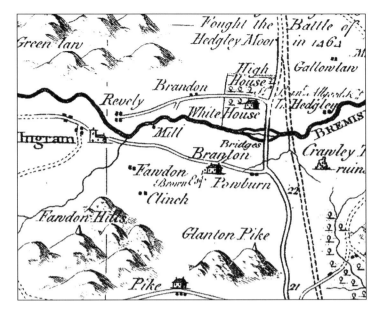

Armstrong's map showing the White House.

not-quite-detached house features a circular "insurance" plate on its front wall. It may possibly have been an inn sometime in the past. The blacksmith's forge, the eastern-most building, is largely unchanged since the days when draught horses stood outside waiting to be shod. It is now the farm workshop, dwarfed by the combine harvester when it comes in for repair.

Formerly part of the extensive Collingwood lands, the Brandon Estate, which included Brandon and the adjoining property we know today as White House, was acquired by Lancelot Allgood in 1690, when Collingwood fortunes were at a low ebb. The Estate remains the property of the Allgood family today.

A fine mansion once stood at White House, in the field behind the cottages, on the south side of the road leading to Ingram. Built for Lancelot Allgood, around the turn of the 18th century, it was the family home until estate interests of a later generation transferred to Simonburn and ultimately, in 1760, to a new family seat at Nunwick Hall, near Wark-on-Tyne.

Armstrong's illustrated map of 1769 shows the "White House" and, to the north, "High House" where the farmhouse stands today.

In 1855 a directory of the day described Brandon as a "township and hamlet near the southern extremity of the Cheviot Hills, the property of H. L. Allgood Esq." It listed the principal residents, the most important of whom was John Davidson Esq. The term "esquire" set him apart from the rank and file, denoting a gentleman of some status. Indeed, the directory tells us that he resided in the mansion at Brandon White House.

It burnt down sometime between 1855 and 1886, the year in which E.J. Wilson's delightful little book "Eglingham and its Vicinity" was published. He was able to say that Hedgeley Cottages, built on leases of 45 years, were partly erected out of its ruins.

Returning to the principle residents: just three others were listed - William Davidson, blacksmith, Andrew Dodds, joiner and Thomas James, farmer. Coupled with White House the population in 1851 was 173 "souls".

Just thirty years later the census of 1881 recorded only 78 people living in sixteen houses. The decline in population coincided, in part, with the rise of Newcastle-upon-Tyne as an industrial and manufacturing centre. Many people left the countryside, drawn to jobs in the new factories and processing plants which sprang up along the banks of the river.

An early postcard of Hedgeley Cottages franked 1906.

In May 1891 a farm sale was held at Brandon following the death of the farmer Mr. R. H. Robertson. Two adverts appeared in the Alnwick County Gazette.

One drew attention to "a quantity of valuable household furniture belonging to the deceased", the other to his livestock: 600 half bred ewes, 25 Shorthorn steers, 60 head of poultry and several horses - 15 for the draught, 2 fillies unbroken, 1 and 2 years old and 1 harness cob.
In addition: "All the implements of husbandry. A waggonette, gig, harness, riding saddles and bridles and a set of breaking tackle, nearly new."

A subsequent report of the sale mentioned no prices, but commented: **"Not a few were surprised at the high figures offered for some of the lots. Horses, four smart looking animals, were sold to the incoming tenant Mr. J. Davison, who also became a large purchaser of sheep and implements.**
"The farm is beautifully situated and is considered to be one of the finest turnip and sheep raising farms in the beautiful vale of Breamish."

By 1910, the 11th edition of "Kelly's Directory of Northumberland" listed Robert Lancelot Allgood Esq. of Titlington Hall as the principle landowner. We read that Brandon covered 1057 acres with 30 acres of water. The population in 1901 was 61. "Letters through Powburn arrive at 11.30a.m. Powburn is the nearest money order office and Glanton the nearest telegraph office. Children attend school at Branton."

During the Great War, and through the 1920s, Mr. J. K. Annandale, a businessman, farmed Brandon. It was quite usual then for the local paper to carry details of the festivities and presents that some local farmers accorded their workers at Christmas time.

So we read of the annual dance on Christmas night in 1914 that Mr. Annandale gave for his "workpeople and some of their friends".

"At 8.30p.m. upwards of fifty couples assembled in the large granary, which was beautifully decorated, and transformed into a ball room. The dance was led off with a plain schottishe by Mr. Annandale and Miss Elliott, Mr. Loftus and Mrs Annandale to first class music, supplied by Messrs. Short and Dickinson.

"Dancing was kept up with great glee, and at 11p.m., a halt was called, when tea and refreshments were passed round, followed by various kinds of fruit. After all had partaken of the good things and were thoroughly satisfied, dancing was again resumed and kept up with the same keen and jovial spirit as before.

"Before the company dispersed, Mr. Chisholm, farm steward, proposed a vote of thanks to Mr. and Mrs Annandale for their kindness. He said it had been their custom to entertain their employees to a supper and dance at Christmas, but owing to the present national crisis, the workpeople had all desired to do without their supper, and hand the sum of £5, which went towards making their supper, over to the Belgian Relief Fund. This was received with great applause, and the singing of "He's a jolly good fellow."

"Mr. W. Straughan replied, and proposed a vote of thanks to the workpeople for the way they had so tastefully decorated the granary, and also to Miss Davidson and Miss Cockburn, for the way they had so kindly served out the refreshments. During the evening the company were entertained by songs given by Miss Lowrie, and A. Easton. The duties of M. C. were carried out by Messrs. J. Loftus and J. Chisholm.

"On the following day Mrs Annandale entertained the children and their mothers by giving them a splendid tea, and each child received a handsome present."

By 1915, as the War dragged on, dances, even though for "the benefit of wounded soldiers", drew some strongly worded letters to the newspaper. Such pleasure and enjoyment was described as "outrageous" at this time of conflict.

We read no more Christmas reports from Brandon until January 1919 when a retrospective little note appeared in the paper: "Mr. J. K. Annandale presented each household with a one pound note, also an allowance for the "Inner Man". Mrs Annandale never forgets the children. Each child received an Xmas parcel, a gift of clothing and a toy, sweets and nuts etc."

On Christmas Eve 1920, Mr. Annandale entertained his work people and friends to a Kirn Supper. Traditionally, going back to the days when the harvest was won with hook and sickle, and much hard labour, the farmer rewarded his workers with a supper, a night of merriment, once the harvest was home. Sometimes the supper was postponed to combine with Christmas or New Year festivities.

David Dippie Dixon, in his book "Whittingham Vale" describes the Kirn Supper as "an old world custom, a social gathering of the people which helped to foster that kindly feeling so desirable between master and men, as well as the occasion of much pleasant intercourse amongst friends and neighbours."

An account of the Brandon Kirn appeared in the paper. Held in the granary it was attended by forty people, the dancing going on until four o' clock in the morning with the house party kept busy 'attending to the wants of their guests'.

"A person who can go through a kirn supper dance programme must be much more accomplished than one who can only dance the fox trot, one-step and waltz."

Songs were by "Messrs Cowens, Bell and others", and a cap for the "blinded heroes" at St. Dunstan's collected almost £10.

In the same report we read about the Christmas tree at Brandon: **"After entertaining mothers and children to tea, the Christmas tree was "set alight" to the great delight of the children. Music was supplied by Mr. W. Givens** [Will Givens of Woodbine Cottage] **and the children indulged in musical games and dances. Mrs Annandale dismantled the tree, each child receiving a gift of clothing, a toy, chocolate, nuts, apples, oranges etc. Some had extreme difficulty in reaching home with their cargoes."**

During the 1930s, the time of the great agricultural depression, Mr. Taylor was tenant of Brandon. He was followed, in 1943, by the Shell family, John and Eleanor, their two sons Stephen and Jackson and daughters Sally, Janie, Daisy and May. Today, 61 years on, with the fourth generation in their teens, Stephen and his two sons, Stephen and James, run the 920-acre farm, combining arable cropping with suckler cows and a flock of half bred ewes. Much the same as in 1890, only without the horses.

Apart from census and directory statistics, little about Brandon appears in guidebooks. Indeed local historian, W. W. Tomlinson, noted for his attention to detail, appears to have passed through with hardly a glance. His "Comprehensive Guide to Northumberland" contains only two sentences: "There are the remains of an old chapel and disused graveyard. Three Celtic leaf-shaped bronze swords were found near the summit of a hill, east of Brandon Farm."

The site of the old chapel is quite hidden, in a little field, behind a wall. Today most people drive past, unaware of its existence.

The "History and Directory of Northumberland" (1887) observed: "Here is an ancient burial ground enclosed by a stone wall. It lies in a wild, neglected state, the tall rank grass obscuring from view the few tombstones that remain. Of the little chapel that once graced this God's acre only a few feet of the porch walls are left. It is now 67 years since the last interment took place here."

Styled as a Chapel of Ease, it was one of three associated with the mother church at Eglingham. Believed to date back to the 12th or 13th century, its history is chronicled in the pages of "A History of Northumberland" (Vol. XIV). 1935.

One of the earliest references is in 1467 when the vicar of Eglingham mentioned among his expenses "the maintenance of three curates at Lilburn, Bewick and Brandon and Branton". By 1663 the chapel was described as "totally ruined and destitute".

Reading on: **"In 1887 Maberley Phillips found no remains of the chapel. The north half of the graveyard became gardens for two cottagers and the west quarter a potato patch for Brandon farmhouse.**

"Thus it remained till 1903 when Mr. J.R. Carr-Ellison (Hedgeley Hall) and Mr. Algernon Gissing called the attention of the then proprietor the Rev. James Allgood [he had resigned as Rector of Ingram in 1887 on becoming head of the family] **to the impropriety of this arrangement.**

"On finding that both the tithe map at Eglingham church and a map dated 1832 in the estate office showed the churchyard undivided, Mr Allgood at once handed over the whole site to the churchwardens of Eglingham who excavated the ruined walls of the chapel, levelled them up

and protected them with a coating of cement, removed two or three feet of rubbish from the south part of the churchyard and repaired and extended the churchyard wall.

"As the road on the south side of the yard had been supplanted by the present main road on the north side, a new gateway was made to the north and the old south gate, the former principal approach, walled up."

There were three ways into Brandon: A track from the main turnpike road, now the A697, started beside the County Bridge and crossed the fields on the north side of the river. It passed close to the south wall of the churchyard, before coming out at Brandon. Today it is a footpath. Another route ran north-south, passing the east end of the hamlet, with a ford crossing through the Breamish; the last one linked White House to Brandon and passed Hill Head Cottage. Over time this became the preferred route. It provided a direct link to the turnpike and involved no river crossing.

The excavations of 1903-1904 revealed that the church had consisted of a nave and a choir, adjoined on the south side by a chapel or vestry. At that time it was hoped the churchyard would once again be used for interments.

In 1909, Brandon and Branton, then part of the ecclesiastical parish of Eglingham, were transferred to the parish and Rector of Ingram.

We jump apace now to the early 1980s when Canon Charles Hay, then team Rector of Ingram, received a letter from the Department of the Environment, with a map and schedule. It informed him that the site was to be protected as an ancient monument. According to the Church Commissioners, as incumbent of Ingram, he was the owner. Could he confirm this?

Canon Hay thought the answer to the question might be "Yes" but he had some doubts. Here he takes up the story that was later the subject of one his many talks to the Aln and Breamish Local History Society.

"Suspecting there might be a rival claimant to the field, I wrote to the owner of Brandon, Mr Lancelot Allgood of Nunwick Hall, asking for his views on the matter. His reply confirmed my suspicions! On the estate map in his estate office, the field appears as still included in the farm. This pointed to the fact that Mr Allgood owns the field.

"Neither the Diocesan Registry nor the Church Commissioners could throw any light on the matter. A third party could also have been brought into any possible litigation. This was one of the Ingram churchwardens who, for many years, without paying any kind of rent, had been using the field for rearing turkeys and for grazing a few sheep. Could he have established title through use?

"Lastly, there was a record - supported by a photograph of a service being conducted in the field by the late Archdeacon Pawson, with the priest in charge of Ingram.

"Clearly the question of ownership could have provided a field day for the men of law; and a case which could have dragged through the courts at immense cost in time and money for years to come.

"Fortunately, no one really was over-anxious to be named owner. Ingram Parochial Church Council agreed that we should relinquish all claim - for we could never see any future burials happening there - and Mr. Allgood and the Department of the Environment were informed accordingly."

The foundations of the chapel, whilst no longer clearly visible, can be partly traced underfoot. Some large table tombs, their inscriptions mostly worn away, can be seen amongst the grass. Of most interest though are the three standing headstones, all close together, and all over 200 years

old. Some have inscriptions on both the east and west sides. They were all recorded in the "History of Northumberland" 1935. Of the five legible then, only four are still readable today.

On one headstone, underneath the carving of a death mask resting on a ruff of wings (imagery allied to mortality and immortality, the wings representing the rise to eternal life) we read - **Here lies the Body of james jobson of Newton by the Sea, who departed this Life May 29th 1776, aged 76.**

A second stone records - **Here Lyes The Body of Alice Houey. Wife To John Houey. Gardener In The Whit House Who Departed This Life The 28 Day of May 1751. Aged 45 Years.**
The inscription on the west side is now illegible. It did say - Here lies the Body of John Houey husband of Alice Houey who departed this Life Dec. 19, 1765 (?)

A skull and cross bones, and another image, possibly an hour glass, are carved on the east side of the third headstone (the imagery again concerned with mortality and immortality). The inscription above reads - **Here lies The Body of Christopher Jobson of Brandon White House Who dyd May y. 13 1743. Agd 85. years.**

On the west side, the stonemason has misjudged the space; part of the inscription spills over onto the border and some letters are placed above one another. **Here Lyeth The Body of Ann Wif. Of Christopher (the 'p' is reversed with the 'h' above it) Jobson Who died The 26 of decembr 1748 Aged 79 Years.**

The south wall around the burial ground is now in a seriously dilapidated state, despite the site being a legally protected ancient monument. Sad to say the little churchyard still lies in a "wild, neglected state". At lambing time it becomes a nursery paddock for ewes and lambs. It is the only time of the year when the grass is grazed down.

In the late 1990s, with only limited space remaining in the churchyard at Ingram, the parochial church council hoped that the little field at Brandon could again be used for burials. The proposal, however, was totally unacceptable to English Heritage who feared that digging would disturb the archaeological remains.

Directory 2004

Brandon

Landowner: The Allgood Estates. Farmers: The Shells.
Residents - The Farmhouse: Stephen and Dorothy Shell; Stephen and Susan Shell and their children Philippa, Jonathon and Cameron.
Woodbine Cottage: Jimmy Givens, BEM, retired Northumberland National Park head warden, his wife Jean.
The Cottages: James and Yvonne Shell, their children Andrew, Edward and James Matthew. Terry Lowes, farm worker, his wife Linda. Alan Voutt, MBE, retired quarry foreman, his wife, Mary. Mick Ashworth, retired Reaveley shepherd, his wife Betty. Tony Lummis, seasonal warden, Northumberland National Park. Jack Hope, BEM, retired Northumberland National Park head warden.
Heddon Hill Cottage: Susan Cable and Anne Timlin.
Brandon Hill Head Cottage: Alan Williamson, retired civil servant, his wife Doreen.

White House

Landowner: The Allgood Estates. Farmers: The Dods.
Residents - the Farmhouse: Nigel Dods, his wife Janet and son, Roy.
The Cottages: Nicola Wearmouth; Andrew Foster, lorry driver, and Rosie Cowens; Pauline Dodds; Mrs Margaret Liddle, her son Keith; Peter Hedley, retired White House shepherd.

The population of Brandon and White House in 2004 is 36 people living in 16 homes.

I may add: no blacksmith, no joiner. No money order office at Powburn (The Post Office closed in 2004). The telegraph office at Glanton survives today as the Post Office. Closed in 2003, it re-opened in 2004 in the village shop. Today letters for Brandon arrive by post van from Alnwick at 10.30a.m. Stephen Tully, the postman, makes the 82-mile round trip every day, excepting Sunday. His round takes in the Lilburns, South Middleton, Ilderton, Roddam, Calder (for Threestoneburn), the Breamish Valley, Branton, Fawdon and Branton Middlesteads. The journey takes almost five hours.

Daily bottled milk deliveries are a thing of the past. Of the numerous vans that once called on a weekly basis, only one remains: John McCann, of Berwick, has travelled for eighteen years selling bread, fruit and vegetables and general groceries from his mobile shop. He calls at Brandon and Ingram on a Wednesday afternoon. Many other carriers, of course, deliver mail and internet-ordered goods to the valley.

Children still attend Branton School, now called a Community First School. Pupil numbers hover around 20. The children move on to middle school at Wooler, or elsewhere, at the age of nine. The future of both Branton and Wooler schools is currently in the melting pot following moves to re-structure education facilities in the county.

28
Brandon Ford

In October 2002, a once in a lifetime sight was captured on camera at Brandon Ford. Local resident Jean Givens watched as floodwaters ate away the banks, causing two big static caravans to drop quietly into the river. Carried downstream under the footbridge, they sailed for a few hundred yards before coming to rest on a gravel shoal.

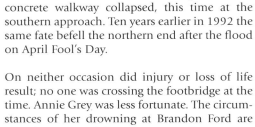

The unoccupied caravans were not the only casualties of the flood; yet again the bridge foundations were breached and part of the concrete walkway collapsed, this time at the southern approach. Ten years earlier in 1992 the same fate befell the northern end after the flood on April Fool's Day.

On neither occasion did injury or loss of life result; no one was crossing the footbridge at the time. Annie Grey was less fortunate. The circumstances of her drowning at Brandon Ford are now long passed from memory. Two reports that appeared in the "Alnwick and County Gazette" tell us what happened, over a century ago.

The first, in the newspaper of November 22nd 1890, was headed simply "Glanton".

"A girl missing - a servant girl in the employment of Mr Drysdale, Great Ryle, has been missing for over a week. It appears, that having been re-engaged, she had been allowed a few days holiday according to the usual custom, and had left Ryle with the intention of visiting her parents who reside at Brandon where her father is a farm steward with Mr. Robertson.

"As she failed to return at the stipulated time, Mr. Drysdale's groom was sent over to ascertain the cause, and found that she had never been home, and it was only then that the girl's parents became aware that she had left Ryle, or that anything was wrong, and as may be imagined, they were much distressed and alarmed.

Going....
Going....
Sailing.
(Photos: Jean Givens)

"Police Sergeant Hately having been communicated with, he and Police Constable Scott commenced a careful search and inquiry. It is feared that the girl has been drowned, as on the day she left, the waters were very much swollen, and the footbridge over the Breamish (which she would have to cross) was carried away.

"We are informed that, on returning, the groom made an examination of the river, about where the footbridge had been, and found a hat which he at once identified as that belonging to the missing girl."

Strange that Annie was not mentioned by name, the style of reporting differed then to today. There was no more news until Saturday, March 28th 1891 when the newspaper carried another report under the headline: "The Great Ryle Mystery Solved - Finding of the Body".

"On Monday afternoon, whilst Mrs Tweedie and Mrs Scott of Chillingham Barns, were walking by the river Till, Mrs Tweedie observed a body fastened to the willows. Raising the waterproof mantle which covered the head she found it to be the body of a female. James Allan, the Chillingham postman hastened to inform Constable Ritchie of the fact and accompanied him to the spot. Being unable together to get the body from its position, assistance was procured and the body conveyed to Chillingham Barns. The body was identified, and found to be that of the girl Grey who was drowned in the Breamish five months ago.

"On Wednesday Mr. Charles Percy, coroner for North Northumberland held an inquest at Chillingham Barns into the unfortunate circumstances attending the death of Ann Grey. John Grey, farm labourer, of Brandon, recognised the body as that of his daughter who lived at Great Ryle, near Whittingham, as a domestic servant, aged 27 years. She had been missing since the 7th November last. He learned eight days after that date that she had left Great Ryle to visit him, having got six days holiday, but she never arrived at his house. All possible enquiries and searches were made at the time to find her, but without success. Great Ryle was about two and a half miles from Brandon, and in coming home the deceased would have to cross the Breamish.

"On the Sunday following the 7th November last, he knew the Breamish was much flooded

The damaged walkway in 1992.

Annie Grey's broken headstone.

and the course of it near to Brandon was altered. He knew the handkerchief produced, well, it belonged to the deceased, but he could not identify the hat. "Sarah Clark, housekeeper at Great Ryle, gave evidence as to deceased leaving in a happy spirit between half past four and a quarter to five o' clock on her holiday. She had her hat box, a small paper parcel and a small hand bag carrying with her. It was getting dark when she left. It was not till the expiration of the six days that Mr. Beach rode over to Brandon to enquire after the girl, when he found she was missing. Witness identified the waterproof on the body and the hat (produced) as deceased's.

"William Pringle, farmer, Branton, proved that he found the hat, produced, on the 8th November last, about 50 yards below where a footbridge was, which persons would have to cross going from Ryle to Brandon. He noticed however that on that day the bridge was gone - evidently carried away by the flood.

"Mary Tweedie, widow, Chillingham Barns, deposed that on the 23rd March she found the body in the river Till in the Barns Haugh, near Chillingham. She observed a waterproof cloak hanging on a branch in the river. She came home and asked Mrs Scott. She went with her. She (witness) took up a stick and reached the waterproof, which she lifted up and then saw the face of the deceased. She sent directly for Police Constable Ritchie who came and got the body out. The Breamish and the Till were the same stream. It changed its name at Bewick Bridge.

"PC Ritchie deposed that in company with James Allan he took the body out of the water. He searched the pockets and found nothing but the handkerchief (produced). Dr. Dey of Wooler said he had carefully examined the body and found no marks of violence. It was not much decomposed. The scalp was mostly bare. The clothes were torn and branches were entwined with the clothes. He was of opinion deceased had met her death by drowning. A verdict of "Found Drowned" was returned."

Annie Grey was buried at St. Maurice's, Eglingham, which was then her parish church. Her headstone, a square plinth with a cross, is at the eastern end of the churchyard. The stone is now unstable, and the cross, broken. The inscription reads: "Erected by public subscription. In memory of Annie Grey, who was drowned in the Breamish near Brandon, Nov. 7 1890." For almost a century following Annie's death, a succession of timber footbridges, their life span largely dictated by floods, crossed the river at Brandon Ford.

The last wooden bridge stood until the early 1970s. Stephen Shell, junior, of Brandon, remembers how, as children, they swayed from side to side on the narrow walkway and made it 'rock' causing the rotten timber piers to lift out of the riverbed. Ian Davidson, of Branton, recollects it smelling of creosote, and 'bending' with the flow of water, rather like a jungle bridge. Crossing it could be a frightening experience because the handrails were rotten.

Former county bridges engineer, Robert Robson, recalls in his informative book "Bob's Bridges" that on one occasion the piers of the timber bridge were damaged by "debris and so forth" piled up against them.

"The timber footbridge was in poor condition and a complete reconstruction was required as the river works carried out by the Board had not benefited it. The ford was unpaved [it still is today] and as the gravel bed changes after every flood, the works improved the conditions to some extent, but the ford was still only safe for use by tractors when the water was at a very low level."

Over the years the former Northumberland and Tyneside River Board made several attempts to stabilise the river, to protect both the bridge foundations and the ford crossing on the route of an Unclassified County Road. The gravel bed was levelled, and gabeons (stone-filled wire cages) placed a short distance downstream from the ford. The work done in 1963 was estimated to cost about £1000 of which the county highways committee agreed to contribute £150.

Locals point to mechanisation of the former gravel workings, downstream near the County Bridge, as the root cause of the shifting riverbed. In the 1920s gravel was extracted with shovels in relatively small quantities. When machines took over, tons at a time were removed, upsetting the natural levels and speeding up the water flow.

Stephen Shell, senior, remembers that when his family moved to the farm in 1943, the river was just a 'big step down' from the fields. Then, when the river rose, water flooded over the fields, on several occasions threatening the village of Powburn. By the time a wall was built on the south bank, as a flood defence, the riverbed was lower and the wall never really tested.

Paddling in the river beside the old bridge. The year was 1966. Ian Davison, who now lives in Branton, is sporting a Stoke City shirt.

Today the appearance of the river is drastically changed, the riverbed in places some ten feet lower than the banks. Each year sees further encroachment into the north and south banks. The annual valley bonfire has been held at Brandon Ford for many years, the site diminishing annually as the river eats into the land.

The bridge we see today is the 1970s model, constructed with steel and reinforced concrete. The piles were sunk sixteen feet into the riverbed. When it was built the river ran between the two central piers, but now its bed has spread the entire width of the bridge. The damage wreaked to the south pier in the autumn floods of 2002 when the caravans sailed, is still only temporarily repaired. A timber walkway currently links the bridge and the bank, enabling pedestrians and cyclists using Route 68, (part of the Pennine Cycleway) to get across the river.

Annie Grey was immortalised in a ballad entitled "The Lost Maiden". It is to be found in James Thomson's book "Poems and Ballads", published in 1911, some twenty years after her death.

The Lost Maiden (A Ballad)

(Annie Gray who left Great Ryle on a visit to her parents at Brandon, on the night of Friday, November 7th 1890, and was found in the Till at the Barns Haugh, near Chillingham, March 23rd 1891.)

The Ryle hills, once so green and fair,
Their summer bloom had shed,
And Autumn sere upon their sides
Its russet mantle spread.

Dull and cheerless rose the morn,
That dark November day;
The drifting rain swept down the vale
Where Aln winds its way.

The mountain burns came rushing down
From all the hills around,
In every glen and dark ravine
You heard their eerie sound.

No fitful ray of sunshine broke
To light the cheerless morn;
Black as a pall across the sky
The leaden clouds were borne.

Up from her bed beneath yon roof
A maiden young arose,
Hope filled her heart, as joyfully
She donned her morning clothes.

That day would see her free to roam-
Free as the birds of air-
To spend her holidays at home,
Released from work and care.

What maiden loves not to appear
Clad in her best array,
When hope and joy fills her heart
And pleasure points the way?

In packing up in reverie sweet
She spent the morning hours;
Unheedingly she lingered on
Till dark the evening lowers.

Urged by all her household friends
Her visit to delay;
But their advice she heeded not,
And homeward took away.

And when at length she said "goodbye",
To her old master, kind-
For years she had liv'd neath the roof
That she had left behind.

Poor child! Of fate she little thought
As she left that friendly door,
That the friends she left behind
Her eyes would see no more.

With hope and joy she hurried on
Along the lonely road,
But ne'er before with lighter step
The well-known path she trod.

Her thoughts of home and parents dear
Lent swiftness to her feet;
She longed to see the homely hearth
Where child and parents meet.

Joy would fill each heart that night
Such joy is only given
To those who toil to win their bread,
And have for children striven.

She thought, within her yearning heart,
What words of kindly cheer
Would greet her in her lowly home,
From friends and parents dear.

Fierce blew the wind, with sleet and rain,
She passed the *Mile with speed;
Of wind and rain, that doleful night,
She took but little heed.

Like glimmering stars, through mist and rain,
The Brandon lights appear;
Hope and joy rose in her breast
To see her home so near.

By Branton, on she hurried fast,
Made neither stop, nor stay;
The home she longed to see so much
Was but a "little way".

Ah! Little did she think that night
That home she would never see;
The treacherous stream she had to cross-
Her death and grave would be.

The mighty flood in darkness rolled
In silence on its way;
It swept away from home and friends
The loving Annie Gray.

Poor Annie Gray, your fate we mourn,
And feel for your parents dear;
Time's gentle hand their wound will soothe,
And hope their hearts will cheer.

When summer decks the hills anew,
And lambs upon them play,
The loving friends around Great Ryle
Will think of Annie Gray.

Where God has laid you to your rest
His hand will deck your grave;
The scented thyme, and golden broom
O'er your low bed will wave.

*The farm of Mile Moor.
The ballad spells Annie's surname as Gray. On her headstone it is spelt Grey.

Glossary

Alderman -   an obsolete civic title.

Bow-le-hole -   a small door.

Bratted -   wearing a pinafore or apron, from 'brat'.

Cleading -   clothing, from clead or cloth.

Cleugh -   a ravine with steep sides through which a stream flows.

Glitters -   loose stones or scree. Often locally pronounced as 'glidders'.

Haugh -   grass land beside a river.

Hind -   a farm servant.

Knowe -   the rounded top or shoulder of a hill.

Kyloe -   a small breed of cattle with long horns traditionally reared in the Highlands and western isles of Scotland.

Separating -   the act of separating the milk from the cream.

Sike -   a small stream of water especially one flowing through flat or marshy ground, and often dry in summer.

Stint -   the number of cattle or sheep allotted to each person entitled to common pasturage.

Steading -   the farm buildings.

Stackyard -   an open walled yard where haystacks and cornstacks were stored.

Suckler cow -   rears a calf for beef production as opposed to a dairy cow that is kept for milking.

Tithe -   originally a tenth of the annual produce of the land devoted to supporting the clergy but later commuted to a rent charge.

Sheep Terms

Dinmont -   a castrated male sheep between first and second shearing.

Drove -   a group of sheep being driven.

Hirsel -   a group of sheep hefted to a particular area of hill ground.

Hogg -   a sheep before its first shearing.

Keb -   a ewe that has lambed a dead lamb, most usually prematurely. The word also describes the dead lamb.

Keb House -   a hut or building containing individual pens that are just big enough to hold a ewe and her lamb. A ewe that has 'kebbed' is housed in a pen to have another lamb 'set on'.

Speaning -   weaning lambs from ewes.

Tup -   a ram.

Wether -   a castrated male lamb.

Bibliography

Aln and Breamish Local History Society, 1967-1985,
Records and Recollections, the Journals of the Aln and Breamish Local History Society.
Alnwick and County Gazette and Guardian

Anderson, Valerie, Davidson, Sandra, Hannan, Louise, Harris, Linda, 1983,
Community Task Force Survey of St. Michael's Churchyard, Ingram. Unpublished.

Archaeological Services University of Durham,
The Ingram and Upper Breamish Landscape Project. Interim Reports 1994 & 1998

Bailey, Richard N, Eric Cambridge, H. Denis Briggs, 1988,
Dowsing and Church Archaeology, Intercept Ltd, Wimborne, Dorset.

Banks F. R., 1950, *A Guide to the Cheviot Hills,* Andrew Reid & Company,
Newcastle upon Tyne.

Beckensall, Stan, 1992, *Northumberland Place Names.* Butler Publishing.

Clark, Dr. C., 2004, *The Cloudburst of 2 July 1893 over the Cheviot Hills, England.*

Clark, Peter, 1995, *Where The Hills Meet The Sky, A Guide to Wartime air crashes in the
Cheviot Hills,* Glen Graphics, Wooler.

Collier, C., and Stewart, L.A, 1987, *Wooler & Glendale, A Brief History, Vol. II - Glendale.*
The Glendale Local History Society.

Countryside Commission, 1969, *Northumberland National Park,* H.M. Stationery, London.

Dickens, Tony, 1975, *The River Bridges of Northumberland, Vol. I*

Dixon, David Dippie, 1895, *Whittingham Vale,* Robert Redpath, Newcastle-upon-Tyne.

Dixon, David Dippie, 1903, *Upper Coquetdale,* Robert Redpath, Newcastle-upon-Tyne.

Donkin, Samuel, 1886, *Reminiscences of Samuel Donkin,* The "Daily Journal" Office,
Clayton Street.

Flatman, Brian, *Northumberland Railway Branch Lines, The Last Line, The Alnwick to Cornhill
Railway.* Brian Flatman. Printed Russell Studiocraft, Alnwick.

Frodsham, Paul, 2004, *Archaeology in Northumberland National Park,*
The Council for British Archaeology, York

Hall, Marshall, 1973, *The Artists of Northumbria*, Marshall Hall Associates, Newcastle.

Hall, James, 1889, *A Guide to Glendale (Wooler and Neighbourhood)* Second Edition.
M.Brand, "Atlas" Printing Works, Wooler.

Hall, P, 1908, *Breamish and other Poems,* The Gazette Co. Ltd., Alnwick.

Hay, A. C. de P., *St. Michael's Church, Ingram. The Story.* Russell Studiocraft Ltd, Alnwick.

Kelly & Co, 1858, *Post Office Directory of Northumberland,* Strand.
Kelly & Co, 1910.

Kempson, F.C., *The Trinity Foot Beagles 1862-1912.*

Knox, James, *The Trinity Foot Beagles.*

Macdonald, W. King H., 1932, *Glanton Meetin', The Story of the Presbyterian Church at
Glanton, Northumberland,* R. Aikman and Son, Manchester.

Northumberland County Council National Park and Countryside Department, 1990,
A Sense of Wilderness.

Northumberland, Alan Ian, Eighth Duke, 1990, *The Shadow on The Moor,* The Spredden Press, Stocksfield. First published 1931.

Northumberland County Council, 1964, *Northumberland National Park Handbook, Register of Accommodation,* First published 1959. Sole Distributors Harold Hill and Son Ltd, Newcastle upon Tyne.

Northumberland National Park Planning Committee, Minutes, Proceedings etc.

Northumberland County Records Office: Ingram School logbooks, Glendale Parishes Magazine.

Northumberland County History Society, 1935, *A History of Northumberland Vol. XIV,*

Northern Aggregates Limited, 1996, *Planning Application and Environmental Statement. Vol. 4,* Non-Technical Summary.

Robson, Robert, BEM, 1998, Bob's Bridges, *Jottings from a Northumbrian foreman's diaries,* Pentland Press.

Stobbs, Allan W., MS, BSc. 1996, *Memories of the LNER,* Published by author.

Symons, G.J. and Sowerby, W.H.,1893, *British Rainfall, The Distribution of Rain over the British Isles during the year 1893.* Edward Stanford, London.

Tate, G. 1863, *History of the Berwickshire Naturalists' Club (1856 - 1862)*

Thomson, James, 1911, *Poems and Ballads,* "Alnwick & County Gazette" Office.

Tomlinson, W.W. 1889, *Comprehensive Guide to the County of Northumberland,* Walter Scott, Paternoster Row, London.

*The Cheviot Sheep Society Flock Book,*1893, R. Deans & Co, Hawick.

*The Story of Ingram Church,*1962, How and Blackhall Printers, Berwick.

The Shorter Oxford English Dictionary on Historical Principles, Vols I and II. 1933, Clarendon Press, Oxford.

Watson, Godfrey, 1970, *Good Wife Hot,* Oriel Press.

Whellan and Co, William, 1855, *History, Topography and Directory of Northumberland.*

Wills, F.A., 1936, *The Rambles of Vagabond,* Reprinted by permission of Allied Newspapers Limited (Newcastle Chronicle Limited) J. & P. Bealls Limited, Stowell Street, Newcastle upon Tyne.

Wilson, E.J.,1886, *Eglingham and its vicinity, Chillingham and its wild cattle, Wooler, Chatton, etc,* The Alnwick and County Gazette.

"When I think back, I think how did we survive?
I think of young mothers now and wonder what they
would have done in those days."
Belle Armstrong, Reaveley Hill.

"You can hardly fathom
what has taken place in the last 100 years.
You just accepted life as it was and took things as
they came along.
I think I am still like that."
Betty Anderson, Linhope.

"Living out there you learn to adapt to life as it is,
not how you think it should be."
Margaret Robson, The Chesters